12 STEPS
— TO —
DESTRUCTION

*Codependency
Recovery Heresies*

D0027740

12 STEPS
—— TO ——
DESTRUCTION

Codependency Recovery Heresies

Martin and Deidre Bobgan

EastGate Publishers
Santa Barbara, CA 93110

All Scripture quotations in this book, unless noted otherwise, are from the Authorized King James Version of the Bible.

12 STEPS TO DESTRUCTION
CODEPENDENCY/RECOVERY HERESIES

Copyright © 1991 Martin and Deidre Bobgan
Published by EastGate Publishers
4137 Primavera Road
Santa Barbara, CA 93110

Library of Congress Catalog Card Number 91-72638
ISBN 0-941717-05-4

Printed in the United States of America.

This is our fourth volume on which Dr. Jay Adams has been kind enough to make theological and editorial comments. We appreciate his willingness to help and thank him for his encouragement over the years.

We are grateful to all our friends who have prayed for us, encouraged us, and sent us helpful research items. We also thank Rick Miesel for proof-reading our galleys.

God created man in his own image, in the image of God created He him: male and female created He them.

Man refers to all humans in Genesis 1:27. The word *man* has been used to refer to humanity and *he* has been the pronoun used to refer to a person (male or female) in the generic sense. Therefore, we use the pronoun *he* throughout this book, even though the people referred to in many places are mainly women.

Table of Contents

1

AND CODEPENDENCY
FOR ALL. . . .

Thousands of people are flocking to the bookstores to read about "codependency." Most of them are women. They read books that describe the symptoms, join self-help groups, and seek therapy to find out if they are "codependent." They enter an endless cycle in hopes of curing their newly discovered "disease," and they find they are not alone. In fact, there seems to be an epidemic of self-diagnosed, group-diagnosed, and therapist-diagnosed "codependents." The list of symptoms is so long and the possibilities so wide that everyone in any kind of unsatisfactory relationship may conceivably be labeled "codependent."

The codependency/recovery movement is one of the newest and largest offshoots of the addiction treatment industry and the Alcoholics Anonymous Twelve-Step program. Every week 500,000 self-help meetings are held in this country. The fastest growing of these "free, confessional meetings" is Co-dependents Anonymous.[1] There are over 1800 Co-dependents Anonymous groups in this country, as well as other self-help groups, such as Adult Children of Alcoholics (ACOA) and Al-Anon.[2] There are also numerous workshops, conferences, treatment centers and therapists. And it must be admitted that the professionals are glad to have the business. One writer who contends that "the vicious cycle of co-dependency can only be stopped through intervention and professional care," declared in 1984: "Happily, our profession is on the cutting edge of making co-dependency a national issue, both on the social level and on the health level."[3] Indeed, the awareness level has reached new heights of popularity and expanded revenues. And as the world goes, so goes the church in this newest rage of psychoheresy. Not to be outdone, many psychologists, psychiatrists, and treatment centers offer the same theories and therapies under the guise of being biblical. And churches are joining ranks with Twelve-Step addiction and codependency/recovery programs.

The estimated numbers of supposedly afflicted codependents range from tens of thousands[4] to 40 million[5] to 100 million[6] and upwards to 96% of the population.[7] That last estimate is a bit high when one considers that most of the people who are labeled "codependent" are women. But such numerical inconsistencies do not seem to bother the experts in the field. John Bradshaw, a leading recovery guru, claims that "Codependency is a plague upon the land." He dramatically adds, "The Black Plague doesn't even compare to the ravages of our compulsions caused by codependency."[8]

Considering how many people are attempting to cope with unsatisfactory relationships and difficult situations, the potential market for self-help books and codependency/recovery treatment is astronomical. The list of books on codependency/recovery swells along with those dealing with addictions. They are popular best-sellers in Christian bookstores as well as in general bookstores. Evidently something is there. Something is wrong. People are looking for answers. Suggested remedies and supposed cures lie hidden in the books. But are those remedies the kind that Jesus offers? Are the so-called cures consistent with the Word of God?

Serious Problems with Problem Solutions.

People are attempting to address serious problems. Some are suffering in relationships that have little or no resemblance to the kind of love demonstrated and taught in the Bible. Numerous people are entangled in their own destructive sinful habits and in the life-dominating sins of those around them. Relationships that are supposed to reflect the love relationship of Christ and His church may indeed more resemble a macabre dance of death.

Yes, there are serious problems. However, we question the diagnoses, answers, formulas and systems that are being offered in the name of help, in the name of love, and even in the name of Christ. Beneath many programs that purport to be Christian lurk ideas, philosophies, psychologies, and religious notions that are antithetical to biblical Christianity. Codependency/recovery books, groups, programs, and therapists attempt to rescue people from what they believe to be unhealthy relationships. They give so-called codependents strategies to empower the self, build self-esteem, emotionally separate from others, and focus on their own feelings, ideas and desires.

Most systems of codependency and addiction recovery are based upon various psychological counseling theories and therapies and upon the religious and philosophical teachings of Alcoholics Anonymous (AA). In short, such programs are based upon the wisdom of man and the worship of false gods. While the Bible may be used, it is not used in its fullness nor as solely sufficient for all matters of life and conduct. Instead, the Bible is placed in a subservient role to support popular psychological theories, therapies, and techniques. Furthermore, God is repeatedly redefined according to the limited understanding of human beings.

Besides serious theological problems inherent in the codependency and addiction recovery movement, there are many questions about the effectiveness of such programs and about the high rate of recidivism. We will be citing research which shows that faith in recovery programs is misplaced because of their lack of proven effectiveness. There is no scientific reason to add the philosophies and psychologies of the recovery movement to the principles and promises in the Bible. And there are strong theological reasons not to.

In voicing our concerns we are not minimizing the problems being addressed. Instead, we believe the problems are even more serious than any of the propagators of popular programs and systems of help realize. While such programs

aim at helping a person solve certain problems and unsatisfactory patterns of living, we must remember that there are
eternal consequences.

In this book we will look at relationships in dire need of
repair, at habitual attitudes and behaviors that characterize
those who are now calling themselves "codependent," and at
the remedies and religious ideas offered through Twelve-Step
recovery programs, therapy, and self-help books. And we will
contrast them with what the Bible says. The purpose of this
book is to point out the dangers of popular codependency and
addiction recovery programs in order to encourage both
Christians and nonChristians to turn to the Word of God and
the work of the Holy Spirit in the midst of problems. Our
hope is that those caught in the riptide of habitual, life-dominating sin might find Jesus Himself sufficient for overcoming
the power of sin. Jesus said, "I am come that they might have
life, and that they might have it more abundantly" (John
10:10).

Our Concern

As in our previous books, our concern is with the opinions
of men which take precedence over the Word of God in explaining why people are the way they are and how they
change. Authors of books on codependency/recovery base their
ideas on unproven psychological theories and subjective
observations which are based on neither the rigors of scientific investigation nor the rigors of exegetical Bible study. The
field of addiction and codependency treatment is filled with
human opinions on the nature of man, how he is to live, and
how he changes. Christian treatment centers, recovery
programs, and books on addiction and codependency are also
based upon the same flimsy foundation of psychological opinion rather than on science or the Bible.

Jesus came to give life and liberty to all who are in bondage. He said:

> The Spirit of the Lord is upon me, because he hath
> anointed me to preach the gospel to the poor; he
> hath sent me to heal the brokenhearted, to preach
> deliverance to the captives, and recovering of sight

> to the blind, to set at liberty them that are bruised,
> to preach the acceptable year of the Lord (Luke
> 4:18).

Jesus preached the gospel to those who were poor in spirit,
who were cast down, who were discouraged, who had ex-
hausted their means of coping with life, and who realized
they were destitute. He came "to heal the brokenhearted,"
those whose dreams have turned to despair and whose love
has been fused with pain and disappointment. Jesus came to
preach deliverance to those in bondage to sin, to themselves,
to other people, and to life-crippling habits. He came to give
sight to those blinded by the wisdom of men and the enemy of
their souls. Jesus came to set at liberty those who have been
bruised by the world, the flesh and the devil.

Who is not included among those who are in desperate
need of the Savior? Indeed, all who find themselves caught in
the wreckage of their lives and who are now turning to
addiction and codependency/recovery programs need Jesus
more than anything or anyone else. Therefore the question
must be asked: If Jesus is truly the answer to life's problems
and indeed the very source of life, why are both nonChristians and Christians looking for answers elsewhere?

If Jesus Is the Answer, Why Look Elsewhere?

NonChristians turn to the vast recovery movement because the programs offer hope, help, and promises of recovery. And there is no encouragement to believe in the God of
the Bible, whom they have never understood or known. They
don't turn to Christ because they have accumulated plenty of
reasons not to. They remind themselves of Christians who
have failed. Some have heard pastors say what they didn't
want to hear. Furthermore, they cannot understand a God
who might condemn anyone or offer such a narrow way. However, beyond all of the human excuses, the actual reason non-
Christians do not turn to Christ is because their eyes and
ears are closed to the merciful grace of God.

But why do Christians look for answers outside the Bible
and their relationship with Jesus Christ? Paul wrestled with

this problem in his letter to the Galatians. The Galatians had started out well in the Christian walk, but then, under the influence of the Judaizers, they lost confidence in the sufficiency of the gospel. In his salutation Paul reminds them of what Jesus had already accomplished for them:

> Grace be to you and peace from God the Father, and from our Lord Jesus Christ, who gave himself for our sins, that he might deliver us from this present evil world, according to the will of God and our Father: to whom be glory for ever and ever. Amen. (Galatians 1:3-5.)

Then Paul presents his concern:

> I marvel that ye are so soon removed from him that called you into the grace of Christ unto another gospel: Which is not another; but there be some that trouble you, and would pervert the gospel of Christ (Galatians 1:6-7).

The Galatians were attempting to be justified by the works of the law rather than by faith in what Jesus had accomplished for them by dying in their place and giving them new life through His resurrection. And this is true today.

Paul admonishes them and all who fall into this error:

> O foolish Galatians, who hath bewitched you, that ye should not obey the truth, before whose eyes Jesus Christ hath been evidently set forth, crucified among you? This only would I learn of you, received ye the Spirit by the works of the law, or by the hearing of faith? Are ye so foolish? Having begun in the Spirit, are ye now made perfect by the flesh? (Galatians 3:1-3.)

In adding requirements, they entered into bondage. They evidently did not understand that just as they were saved through faith in the finished work of Christ, they were to live by faith in the finished and ongoing work of Christ in them. Therefore Paul reminds them and us: "But that no man is justified by the law in the sight of God, it is evident: for, the just shall live by faith" (Galatians 3:11).

People confuse the works of the law with the works of

faith. Works of the law undermine a person's ability to please God, because they are limited to self-effort. Works of faith, however, are the fruit of faith that grow from the Holy Spirit who indwells and empowers believers to obey and please God. Trying to keep the law by way of the flesh leads to bondage and death, because no one can keep the law. The way of the Spirit is freedom to please God and leads to life eternal.

Just as the Galatians, some Christians start out well and then shift into works. They lose confidence in the efficacy of the gospel and the Holy Spirit. When they sin, they may admonish themselves and try to change through trying harder, rather than responding through faith (1 John 1:9). Or, when they sin, they may not think it really matters that much since they already have the righteousness of Christ. One slips off course by trying to do it on his own, and another doesn't bother to obey. Both responses lead to disaster and bondage; both are bondage to the world, the flesh, and the devil. Therefore Paul presents the solution to both errors:

> Stand fast therefore in the liberty wherewith Christ hath made us free, and be not entangled again with the yoke of bondage. . . . For, brethren, ye have been called unto liberty; only use not liberty for an occasion to the flesh, but by love serve one another. . . This I say then, walk in the Spirit, and ye shall not fulfil the lust of the flesh. (Galatians 5:1, 13, 16.)

Just as Christians are saved by grace through faith, they are to walk by grace through faith. The very source of walking in the Spirit comes through the profound relationship of the believer to the Lord Jesus Christ.

Another reason why some who call themselves Christians may be looking for some program in place of (or in addition to) Christ is that they have misunderstood the gospel and what it entails. The gospel might not have been presented clearly. Rather than recognizing their need for a savior to save them from their own sins, they may have been looking for a savior who would save them from their circumstances and/or who would make life easy and pleasant. They may have misunderstood the need to die to self and thought that

Jesus was there to make them feel better about themselves, build their self-esteem, and cater to their desires. While Jesus meets every true need for the believer, and while life in Him holds a marvelous new dimension of peace with God and the hope of eternal life, all problems do not simply vanish. Jesus being the answer to problems of living does not mean that He necessarily takes them away. He gives strength and purpose, and He even uses problems to make a believer more like Himself. Three well-known sections of Scripture speak to this issue: Romans 5:1-5; Romans 8:28-29; and 1 Corinthians 10:13.

Christians who expect God to take away problems and change circumstances may begin to think poorly of God and even begin to blame Him for allowing bad things to happen. They may resent God for letting them down. Those feelings come from a misunderstanding of the character of God, the sinful condition of man, and the influence of "the prince of the power of the air" on the circumstances of this world. Rather than getting angry with God or forgiving Him, which some wrongfully teach, Christians who have an erroneous view of God need to have their vision restored by the Word of God and the work of the Holy Spirit. God is holy, pure, righteous, and full of compassion and mercy. He has provided salvation for the lost through the death of His only begotten Son. And He fulfills all His promises.

The Psychological Way or the Spiritual Way?

Another fundamental reason why Christians are turning to recovery programs is that they believe psychological theories about the nature of man. The encroachment of the psychological way into Christianity has been a subtle, gradual movement which began in the world and moved into seminaries and pastoral counseling classes. Liberal denominations became psychologized much earlier than conservative ones. Pastors were concerned about their parishioners seeking help outside the fold and turned to the wisdom of men to minister to souls.[9] Unfortunately many learned just enough to be intimidated and to think themselves incapable of ministering to people with "psychological" problems. Also, a number of evangelical Christians who had become psychologists worked to convince church leaders that psychological theories and therapies are necessary for helping Christians.

It is disheartening to see conservative churches, denominations, and fellowships running after psychological theories and therapies and acting as if Jesus Christ is not enough, as if the Holy Spirit indwelling a believer is impotent, or nearly so, and treating the Word of God as only useful for minor problems or theological questions. Instead of searching the Scriptures and warning their sheep, too many pastors believe two lies: (1) that they can only deal with spiritual matters (with a very limited definition) and (2) that only those who are psychologically trained are equipped to deal with psychological matters (which virtually includes everything about understanding the nature of man and how to help him change).

The church increasingly reflects a society which is saturated with the kind of psychology that seeks to understand why people are the way they are and how they change. Psychological language is part of everyday language and psychological solutions are accepted as life's solutions. Concerning the codependency/recovery movement, Dr. Robert Coles says, "You don't know whether to laugh or cry over some of this stuff." He says this movement is a "typical example of how anything packaged as psychology in this culture seems to have an all too gullible audience."[10]

Dr. John MacArthur, in his book *Our Sufficiency In Christ*, warns:

> Human therapies are embraced most eagerly by the spiritually weak—those who are shallow or ignorant of biblical truth and who are unwilling to accept the path of suffering that leads to spiritual maturity and deeper communion with God. The unfortunate effect is that these people remain immature, held back by a self-imposed dependence on some pseudo-Christian method or psychoquackery that actually stifles real growth.[11]

Many Christians do not realize that the psychological theories, therapies, and techniques used by Christians were

created by nonChristians, many of whom repudiated and
opposed Christianity. MacArthur says that even though the
word *psychology* means "the study of the soul," psychology
"cannot really study the soul." He says:

> Outside the Word and the Spirit there are no solu-
> tions to any of the problems of the human soul. Only
> God knows the soul and only God can change it. Yet
> the widely accepted ideas of modern psychology are
> theories originally developed by atheists on the
> assumption that there is no God and the individual
> alone has the power to change himself into a better
> person through certain techniques.[12]

Christians use the same theories, therapies, and techniques as secular psychological counselors and psychotherapists. Many Christians mistakenly believe that such theories
are science, when in fact they are simply unproven, unscientific notions of men. The part of psychology which deals with
the nature of man, how he should live, and how he should
change is filled with contradictions and deceptions. Moreover,
because those theories deal with the nonphysical aspects of
the person, they intrude upon the very essence of biblical
doctrines of man, including his fallen condition, salvation,
sanctification, and relationship of love and obedience to God.
Christians who embrace the psychological opinions of the
world have moved from absolute confidence in the Word of
God for all matters of life and conduct to faith in the unproven, unscientific psychological opinions of men. And this
move in faith has led many into the popular recovery movement with its numerous psychologically-based treatment programs.

The Gospel or Twelve Steps?

What is the answer to the vast problems that are being
addressed by the addiction and codependency recovery movement? Is it the good news of Jesus Christ or is it some version
of Twelve-Step recovery and/or psychological treatment programs? The biblical answer is Jesus Christ and Him crucified:

> For I am not ashamed of the gospel of Christ: for it

is the power of God unto salvation to every one that believeth; to the Jew first, and also to the Greek. For therein is the righteousness of God revealed from faith to faith: as it is written, the just shall live by faith. (Romans 1:16-17.)

Jesus Christ enables people to be free to please and serve God. Jesus said: "I am the way, the truth, and the life: no man cometh unto the Father, but by me" (John 14:6). Twelve-Step recovery programs and psychological treatment programs are based upon the wisdom of men. Most promise the ability to please and serve self and others. But they cannot please God, because they are not of Him (Romans 8:8). While they may free a person from one kind of bondage, they lead into another: bondage to self and even bondage to the "prince of this world."

This book is written for those who are suffering from the trials of life and for those who want to help. This book is for all who are thinking about joining a recovery group or entering a treatment center for addiction or codependency. It is for those who have tried Twelve-Step programs and recovery treatment centers and found them lacking. It is also for those who are currently in such programs. And, finally, it is to encourage those professing Christians who offer such programs to return to the faith once delivered to the saints.

A New Religion?

Through the language of addiction and recovery, Christians are being enticed into a totally different belief system based on psychological foundations. MacArthur warns:

> There may be no more serious threat to the life of the church today than the stampede to embrace the doctrines of secular psychology. They are a mass of human ideas that Satan has placed in the church as if they were powerful, life-changing truths from God.[13]

Instead of following the Great Commission to "teach all nations. . . to observe all things whatsoever I [Jesus] have commanded you" (Matthew 28:19-20), Christians are teaching

and embracing a psychological religion of recovery. The shift
is subtle but swift. Throughout this book we attempt to shed
light on the differences between the popular teachings of the
recovery movement and "the faith which was once delivered
unto the saints" (Jude 3). Because these faith systems are
antithetical to each other, the attempt to merge the
psychological, codependency/recovery teachings with the
Bible and Christianity results in one big psychoheresy.

2

AND HER NAME IS CODEPENDENCE

What Is Codependency?

What is this thing called "codependency"? Who is codependent? Definitions vary. Melody Beattie, the shining star of the "codependent-no-more" movement, confesses that definitions of the terms *codependent* and *codependency* "remain vague."[1] Definitions vary from one person to the next, depending upon one's theoretical orientation.

The word *codependent* was first used in the late 1970s to describe those people "whose lives had become unmanageable as a result of living in a committed relationship with an alcoholic."[2] In looking at the early usage of the term *codependent*, Robert Subby and John Friel say:

> Originally, it was used to describe the person or persons whose lives were affected as a result of their being involved with someone who was chemically dependent. The co-dependent spouse or child or lover of someone who was chemically dependent was seen as having developed a pattern of coping with life that was not healthy, as a reaction to someone else's drug or alcohol abuse.[3]

Elizabeth Kristol, an associate editor at the Ethics and Public Policy Center in Washington, D.C., says:

. . . the term codependent has shifted from its original limited meanings: one who was married or related to an addict and therefore was affected by his behavior and in unintended ways was complicit in the addiction. **In contrast, the latest definitions of codependency are so broad as to be all-encompassing.**[4] (Emphasis added.)

Anne Wilson Schaef, in her book *Co-Dependence Misunderstood-Mistreated*, says that:

. . . *everyone* who works with, lives with, or is around an alcoholic (or a person actively in an addictive process) is by *definition* a co-dependent and a practicing co-dependent. This includes therapists, counselors, ministers, colleagues, *and* the family.[5] (Emphasis hers.)

Expanded definitions range from including those in the environment of a substance abuser to vague definitions that include everyone. Subby defines *codependency* as:

An emotional, psychological, and behavioral condition that develops as a result of an individual's prolonged exposure to, and practice of, a set of oppressive rules—rules which prevent the open expression of feeling as well as the direct discussion of personal and interpersonal problems.[6]

Those who follow the teachings of Virginia Satir's Family Systems would identify a codependent as being any member of a so-called dysfunctional family. This would therefore include all children of less-than-perfect parents. David Treadway says:

Until relatively recently, codependency was simply a term used in the substance abuse field to describe the enabling behavior of the typical spouse of an alcoholic. But all of a sudden, being codependent is fashionable. . . . Currently, codependency is loosely used to describe the caretaking member of any complementary couple relationship. Sometimes it seems as if anyone who subordinates his or her own needs to take care of others might be labeled codependent.[7]

Dr. Thomas Szasz reveals the ridiculous implications of the term *codependence*. He says:

> Suppose the daughter of a man with angina or cancer colludes with her father in denying his illness and avoiding treatment for it: Does that make her "co-anginal" or "co-cancerous"?[8]

Certain characteristics or behaviors enter into the definitions. For instance, one definition of *codependency* is: "a psychological condition characterized by a preoccupation with another person and his problems, hindering one's ability to develop healthy relationships with people."[9]

Another definition centers on control. The life-dominating sin of one person can also dominate a close family member. However it is the codependent who is accused of controlling. Beattie says:

> A codependent person is one who has let another person's behavior affect him or her, and who is obsessed with controlling that person's behavior.[10]

The Christian authors of *Love Is a Choice* echo Beattie. They say:

> Codependency is the fallacy of trying to control interior feelings by controlling people, things, and events on the outside.[11]

This is not only a definition; it is also an assumption about what's going on inside.

The idea of compulsive behavior also enters into the definition of *codependency*. The working definition at the first national conference on codependency (1989) used this definition:

> Codependency is a pattern of painful dependence on **compulsive** behaviors and on approval from others in an attempt to find safety, self-worth, and identity.[12] (Emphasis added.)

Pat Springle, another Christian author, says in his book *Codependency*:

> Most psychologists define *codependency* as an inordinate and unhealthy **compulsion** to rescue and take care of people. . . . Rescuing, caretaking, and controlling are the central characteristics of the problem, but it usually has other contributing characteristics as well, such as hurt, anger, guilt, and loneliness.[13] (Emphasis added.)

Here *codependency* is defined as compulsion. The psychological definition of *compulsion* is "a psychological state in which an individual acts against his own will or conscious inclinations."[14] Therefore these definers must be saying that people rescue and take care of others against their own will or "conscious inclinations." The implication is that this compulsion arises from a motivating unconscious, which is a Freudian invention.

Another psychological definition of the word *compulsion* is "an irresistible, repeated, irrational impulse to perform some act."[15] Codependency or any other so-called addiction may feel like that, but such a description takes it out of the realm of personal responsibility and morality. Even if you choose to use the word in its generic form, a compulsion is a "driving force," something that compels or coerces. It is easy to see how this fits Freudian theories about so-called unconscious drives that compel a person to act. Thus even the nontechnical use of the word in reference to sinful habits carries the baggage of a Freudian diagnosis. Also, the term *compulsive* implies that a person cannot resist and that the behavior is outside moral restraint or judgment.

Beattie's most passionate definition of *codependency* includes a list of attitudes and behaviors that she attaches to the label "codependent." She says:

> But, the heart of the definition and recovery lies not in the *other person*—no matter how much we believe it does. It lies in ourselves, in the ways we have let other people's behavior affect us and in the ways we try to affect them: the obsessing, the controlling, the obsessive "helping," caretaking, low self-worth bordering on self-hatred, self-repression, abundance of anger and guilt, peculiar dependency on peculiar

people, attraction to and tolerance for the bizarre, other-centeredness that results in abandonment of self, communication problems, intimacy problems, and an ongoing whirlwind trip through the five-stage grief process.[16] (Emphasis hers.)

We will look at those attitudes and behaviors a bit later on, but there are some definite problems with Beattie's appraisal.

It is also interesting that this very definition encourages the so-called codependent (usually female) to conclude, "The problem is me." But whoever thinks that way could once again be labeled "codependent" because that is one of the so-called symptoms—taking on more of the problem and blame than should be owned. So it's like a merry-go-round. Once a person hops onto the codependence carousel she will go round and round. The road to recovery is a circle, never to be escaped. Once buying into the label, the person may be forever doomed to say, "I'm a codependent" in the same way members of AA forever repeat, "I'm an alcoholic."

Does Femininity Equal Codependency?

In the early days of Alcoholics Anonymous the great majority of drunks were men. Therefore the behaviors ascribed to codependency are quite often traditionally feminine, such as nurturing and caretaking. And the focus of the movement is definitely feminine, even though men are joining the ranks of codependency through ACOA (Adult Children of Alcoholics). While everyone in the movement denies blaming anyone, a heavy load of blame is squarely laid on the shoulders of women, who are the prime participants in codependency/recovery, and their mothers. Women are not only blamed for their own inadequate attempts to make relationships work; they are also blamed for their husband's addictions. The authors of the popular codependency/recovery book *Love is a Choice* declare: "At the unconscious level, Mom needs Dad's dependence just as much as Dad needs his booze."[17] This not only reveals their ignorance of the research, but it demonstrates their Freudian faith.

Blaming the wife for the husband's sinful behavior is common in our culture. When a man commits adultery, how many people hold his wife at least partly responsible? Likewise, when a man drinks, his wife has evidently either driven him to drink or enabled him to do it. And because of her particularly feminine trait of accepting responsibility for relationship, she bears the blame and tries harder.

The prime target is women and they are eager participants. One person estimates that "85 percent of the codependency market is female."[18] In her article on codependency, Marianne Walters asks, "Are we addicted to codependency?"[19] Walters refers to "the rapid development and popularity of the codependency/recovery movement and the concurrent proliferation of books and articles **directed at women** and their problematic relationships."[20] (Emphasis added.) Walters says: "The self-help books for women are basically about the ways that women bring about their own destruction." Walters makes a very perceptive and sweeping statement. She says:

> . . . the codependent movement and the self-help literature, while clearly intended to empower, in fact **pathologize behaviors and personal characteristics that are associated with the feminine**.[21] (Emphasis added.)

Traditional feminine traits and behaviors are thus being viewed as symptoms of codependency. This degrades women in general and traditional female roles and values in particular.

A powerful feminine characteristic is that of nurturing. Another powerful characteristic is the tendency to form and sustain relationships and to develop intimacy. A third one is mothering. These characteristics are all interrelated and definitely feminine. They are the very characteristics that are being pathologized. Characteristics of nurturing, relating, and mothering are the ones that are made culpable for either originating the problem or sustaining it.

While each person is accountable to God for his/her own sins, wives of alcoholics have been held responsible for more than their share of the burden. That is because most of the early work in this area was for the benefit of the alcoholic rather than to benefit or help the spouse. This has carried over to the present. Ironically, one of the characteristic criticisms of so-called codependents is that they take on more of the responsibility than they should. And why not? That responsibility has been laid at their feet, first by their heavy-drinking spouses and families, then by the helping and professional community, and finally by society at large. Even Al-Anon in the early years was to help women help their alcoholic husbands.

Wives of alcoholics were labeled "enablers" as though they shared in the responsibility for the perpetuation of the so-called disease of alcoholism. Thus the drunk was alleviated from his responsibility to be sober through the label "disease" and the wives were burdened with the guilt of *enabling*, which implied causing. Thus the blame was shifted from the drunk to his wife. He was absolved at both ends and she was blamed for helping him continue in his "disease." No wonder, the women felt guilty! They weren't just failures at helping their husbands stop drinking. Now it was at least partly their fault! Because of this early assumption of enablement, the two labels, "codependent" and "enabler" are often used interchangeably.[22]

A typical scenario is that of an alcoholic husband with a wife who is nurturing him along. She is expending her energy trying her best to keep her husband working and the family intact. These activities become the focus of her efforts, and because of the heavy demands, she has precious little time for herself. Then, because this becomes an endless task replete with failures along the way, she becomes frustrated, angry, depressed—and yet she keeps on trying.

Besides not being appreciated at home for all her efforts, she is singled out by "recovering alcoholics" and psychological professionals as the enabler of her husband's drinking and perhaps even the cause of it. For years it was even thought that wives of alcoholics were actually neurotics who chose alcoholics to satisfy their own needs. It was even said that "they secretly wanted their husbands to drink."[23] The University of California Berkeley *Wellness Letter* points out that:

In the 1950s the wives of heavy-drinking men were

> singled out by researchers as being active collabora-
> tors in their husbands' addiction or actually the
> cause of it. Women who were married to heavy
> drinkers, according to the theory, had personality
> disorders: they were "Suffering Susans," "Control-
> ling Catherines," "Wavering Winifreds," and "Puni-
> tive Pollys," who chose alcoholics to satisfy their
> own neurotic needs. . . . In short, their misery was
> their own fault.[24]

However, that theory has been completely debunked by follow-up research which revealed that wives of alcoholics "had
personalities of all types" and "were no more likely to be dysfunctional than other wives."[25]

The personality disorder theory claimed that wives of
heavy-drinkers deteriorated when their husbands stopped
drinking, but later research revealed just the opposite. The
research showed that women actually felt better when their
husbands stopped drinking.[26] In spite of such research evidence, there are still many who hold on to the personality disorder theory.

While we believe that one must confess one's own sins,
there is a serious danger in blaming the so-called codependent for perpetuating the sins of the other parties in the
relationships. Contradictions abound which put mainly
women in a position of being blamed for doing what seems
right (altruistic, caretaking activities) and for not doing what
seems wrong (putting one's own feelings and desires above
those of others). But all follow Freud's example. Blame it on
the woman and send her to a psychologist or treatment
program.

Christian virtues are also being equated with codependent behavior. For instance, Beattie says, "Sometimes, codependent behavior becomes inextricably entangled with being
a good wife, mother, husband, brother, or Christian."[27] She
also says, "By their nature, codependents are benevolent—
concerned about and responsive to the needs of the world." [28]
She also quotes Thomas Wright as saying:

> I suspect codependents have historically attacked
> social injustice and fought for the rights of the

underdog. Codependents want to help. I suspect they have helped. But they probably died thinking they didn't do enough and were feeling guilty.[29]

However, the virtues of many people labeled "codependent," are clouded by sin and their good intentions have turned sour. One woman is thus described this way:

> She devoted her life to making them happy, but she didn't succeed. Usually, she feels angry and unappreciated for her efforts, and her family feels angry at her.[30]

People wonder why women tolerate bad relationships for so long—why they stay married to men who drink excessively and beat them. Remaining in a miserable relationship and hoping against hope that it will improve is now considered a symptom of codependency. However, that scenario has existed since the curse Eve brought upon herself and all of her daughters. The explanation is found in Genesis 3:16:

> Unto the woman He said, I will greatly multiply thy sorrow and thy conception; in sorrow thou shalt bring forth children: **and thy desire shall be to thy husband**, and he shall rule over thee.

While feminism and the wisdom of men have tried to deny or get rid of this curse, only Jesus can turn the curse into a blessing.

Another reason women stay in abusive relationships is fear of putting themselves in even greater danger if they attempt to leave. This is not an ill-founded concern.

> A recent study had shown that women in physically or emotionally abusive relationships are in the most danger when they try to leave. Statistics show that women are most apt to be severely hurt or killed after they have fled to a shelter, sought police or legal help or filed for divorce.[31]

Thus women stay and try to improve what they can.

Is Codependency a Disease?

Many people who believe that chemical addictions are

diseases also believe that codependency is a disease, "a chronic, progressive illness," because of its habitual, self-destructive nature.[32] Sharon Wegscheider-Cruse declares: "Co-dependency is a primary disease and a disease within every member of an alcoholic family."[33] Instead of being addicted to alcohol and drugs, the *codependent* is seen as one who is addicted to another person or to unhealthy relationships and behaviors. Thus it is placed in the same so-called disease category as other addictions.

Anne Wilson Schaef reveals her faith in the disease myth in the dedication of her book *Co-Dependence: Misunderstood Mistreated*:

> To all those persons who are suffering from this previously unnamed **disease** and who have not known that they have a **disease** that can be treated and from which they can recover.
>
> To those courageous enough to acknowledge having this **disease** and be willing to teach us about it.
>
> To those professionals who have stretched their conceptual boundaries to name and begin to treat this insidious and pervasive **disease**.[34] (Emphasis added.)

She has even invented the origin of the "disease," which she calls the "addictive process." She says:

> I would like to suggest that what we are calling co-dependence is, indeed a *disease* that has many forms and expressions and that grows out of a disease process that is inherent in the system in which we live. I call this disease process the *addictive process*.[35] (Emphasis hers.)

She continues, "In some treatment circles, we have been saying that the disease of alcoholism and the disease of co-dependence (or co-alcoholism or para-alcoholism) is, in essence, the same disease."[36]

In contrast, the Bible says that everyone is a sinner, but people don't like that word. They would rather be called sick than sinful. The sinfulness of man is changed to sickness and all need therapy for recovery rather than the Lord for regeneration and repentance. Even the use of the word *recovery* implies disease. One recovers from disease; but one repents from sin. Is a moral condition a disease? Although sinful behavior and sin-filled relationships may cause or contribute to bodily disease, they are not diseases in themselves.

Codependency has been put into the mental illness category and is thus considered a disease in the same manner as many other so-called mental illnesses.[37] But *mental illness* is in itself a misnomer. Such an expression puts behavior and relationships into the medical realm and indicates the necessity of treatment. Psychiatry professor Thomas Szasz says:

> If we now classify certain forms of personal conduct as illness, it is because most people believe that the best way to deal with them is by responding to them as if they were medical diseases.[38]

Since the mind is not a physical organ, it cannot have a disease. While one can have a diseased brain, one cannot have a diseased mind, although he may have a sinful or unredeemed mind. Research psychiatrist E. Fuller Torrey aptly says:

> The mind cannot *really* become diseased any more than the intellect can become abscessed. Furthermore, the idea that mental "diseases" are actually brain diseases creates a strange category of "diseases" which are, by definition, without known cause. Body and behavior become intertwined in this confusion until they are no longer distinguishable. It is necessary to return to first principles: a disease is something you *have*, behavior is something you *do*.[39] (Emphasis his.)

One can understand what a diseased body is, but what is a diseased mind? And if one cannot have a diseased mind it is obvious that one cannot have a diseased emotion, a diseased behavior, or a diseased relationship. Nevertheless, therapists and authors continually refer to mental, emotional, behavioral, and now relational problems as illnesses. Szasz says that such people support "a common, culturally shared desire to equate and confuse brain and mind, nerves and nervousness."[40]

Szasz contends that:

> . . . the notion of a person "having a mental illness" is scientifically crippling. It provides professional assent to a popular rationalization—namely, that problems in living experienced and expressed in terms of so-called psychiatric symptoms are basically similar to bodily diseases.[41]

The notion that codependency is an illness is even more crippling. At least some therapists in the business believe that it is counterproductive to label codependency as "disease." Dr. Harriet Lerner says:

> I don't think it is useful or accurate for women to see themselves as sick and diseased instead of taking a larger view of the situation and seeing their symptoms as part of a complex system in which they are embedded.[42]

On the other hand, calling codependency a disease is lucrative for the treatment industry. According to Elizabeth Kristol there may be a monetary connection between Sharon Wegscheider-Cruse's theory that codependency is a disease having to do with the neurotransmitter dopamine and the fact that she and her husband "happen to run a residential center especially designed to aid the dopamine-driven" codependents. She quotes Wegscheider-Cruse as saying that "if you don't pathologize it then you can't have a treatment plan."[43]

Melinda Blau reports:

> Between 1978 and 1984, the number of private residential treatment centers in the country increased 350%, and case loads quadrupled. Thanks to the marketing genius of the recovery industry, these rehabs, with their promises of "renewal" and "hope," are becoming the spas of the '90s.[44]

Not only is the disease idea useful for getting people into treatment. It is useful for getting third-party insurance payments.

Codependency/recovery books feed prospective patients right into the system. In fact, the Hazelden Foundation (addiction treatment center) has joined together with Harper & Row to publish codependency and addiction recovery books.[45] However, the most blatant connection between books and treatment centers can be seen in the Christian market. Books such as *Toxic Faith*, *Love Is a Choice*, and Pat Springle's *Codependence* are examples of the crass commercialism involved in the psychology, codependency/recovery movement. Under the guise of the main message, which is "we have the answers," is the blatant message: "come to our facility." Underneath it all is a commercial business that, according to *Forbes* magazine, can be a tremendous money maker for investors.[46] At the end of each book are enticing advertisements and phone numbers to call for treatment. In spite of the research, which fails to support the effectiveness of such programs and the potential for harm, each of these books abounds in glowing testimonials and implied promises.

Calling codependent behavior disease undermines God's explanation of the problems and His provision for change. People who are under the domination of sinful habits of living got there through moral choices they have repeatedly made. They need a living Savior who can cleanse them from their sin and guide them into holy living. Those who claim to have that Savior need to walk according to their new life, not their old sinful ways. By faith, they can daily put off the old habits and put on the new by the power and grace of the one true God who has revealed Himself in the Bible.

By calling behavior disease, those who are in rebellion to Almighty God avoid the truth of their condition and encourage others to join them. Paul explains it this way:

> Because that, when they knew God, they glorified him not as God, neither were thankful; but became vain in their imaginations, and their foolish heart was darkened. Professing themselves to be wise, they became fools. . . . Who changed the truth of God into a lie, and worshipped and served the creature more than the Creator, who is blessed for ever. Amen. . . . . And even as they did not like to retain

> God in their knowledge, God gave them over to a
> reprobate mind, to do those things which are not
> convenient . . . . Backbiters, haters of God, despite-
> ful, proud, boasters, inventors of evil things, disobe-
> dient to parents, without understanding, cove-
> nantbreakers, without natural affection, implacable,
> unmerciful: Who knowing the judgment of God, that
> they which commit such things are worthy of death,
> not only do the same, but have pleasure in them
> that do them. (Romans 1:21-22, 25, 28, 30-32.)

The way some Christians parrot the codependency/recov-
ery teachings makes them appear to be "ashamed of the gospel of Christ," which Paul declares "is the power of God unto
salvation to every one that believeth" (Romans 1:16). Salvation through Jesus Christ is both initial regeneration **and**
power for living according to the ways of the Lord.

Indeed this desire to call codependency "disease" is related to rebellion against God. Underlying the codependency/re-
covery movement is a real hatred of God, His Word, and those
who believe that Jesus' death and resurrection provide the
only means of salvation. That is why they continually encourage "spirituality" and criticize religion. For instance
Schaef points out that one of the worst things the church has
done has been to cause people to have an "external referent"
for determining what is good and right. Of course that "external referent" is the Bible and the Lord Himself as He has
revealed Himself in His Word. Instead, she believes that
people must relate to the world from their own internal perspective without such an "external referent." In fact, she
blames Christianity for creating codependents. She says: "The
prototype for the 'good' co-dependent is the 'good Christian'
martyr." Schaef declares, "The 'good Christian woman' is syn-
onymous with co-dependence."[47]

Schaef disdains suffering for others and says, "Co-dependents believe that they are suffering for a holy cause, such as
keeping the family together or hiding a spouse's drinking."
She does not differentiate between legitimate sacrificial suffering and sinful activities, such as being deceptive. In fact,
she probably does not even believe there is such a thing as

legitimate sacrificial suffering unless it is for some self-referented purpose. Thus, according to Schaef, anyone who endures suffering for the sake of "keeping the family together" is exhibiting signs of codependency. She denies the authority of the Bible and the authority of the God of the Bible, who exists outside the individual as the Creator of mankind and who is entitled to be the "external referent." This reveals the anti-Bible, anti-Christ basis for much of what passes as "recovery" and "true spirituality."

Many in the codependency/recovery industry who oppose biblical Christianity also support the extremes of feminism. The one-flesh principle of the Bible is equivalent to codependency and is therefore pathological. There is often no distinction made between a biblical relationship of one flesh with mutual concern and a sinful relationship, where family members allow a member under the domination of habitual sin to rule their feelings, thoughts, and actions. In her enthusiasm to define close relationships as addictions, Schaef literally destroys the framework of the family as created by the Lord. That is because she is opposed to any kind of external standard. Self must be the source and standard of truth, and self must be responsible for one's own good, even if it is at the expense of another.

Schaef looks at codependency/recovery as disease from her vantage point as an active feminist.[48] From her feminist bias and her subjectivity as a "recovering codependent," she contends that the characteristics of a codependent person are identical with those of a nonliberated woman. That inadvertently puts all women she would label as "nonliberated" into the codependent disease category. Does this mean that if a woman is not a feminist she is diseased? Schaef thinks so. She says: "The nonliberated woman and the co-dependent are the same person." It appears that the woman who devotes her life to her husband and her children ends up with a horrible description and a horrible disease according to Schaef. This is typical in the codependency/recovery literature and makes a mockery of a biblical marriage of devotion and commitment. Biblical mutual dependency is presented as an addiction.[49]

Adult Children.

A large sub-group in the codependency/recovery movement is Adult Children of Alcoholics (ACOA). The number is
estimated between 28 and 34 million.[50] Lists of so-called common characteristics of adult children abound in books and on
questionnaires. Elizabeth Kristol says:

> The original Adult Children of Alcoholics movement
> focused on creating a paradigm of the alcoholic
> home, in which every family member was entwined
> in a web of addiction, conspiracy, and silence.[51]

The purpose was to indicate what destructive ways of thinking and behaving they learned in their family. Now people
mistakenly assume that there is a predictable pattern of feelings and behavior among Adult Children of Alcoholics. But
while most therapists assume that ACOAs have similar problem characteristics, more thorough and recent research has
disproven that myth.

A study conducted at the University of Wisconsin indicates that the personality adjustment of ACOAs is generally
the same as that of children of nonalcoholics. After researchers measured the subjects on 12 general traits thought to be
related to ACOAs, they found no positive correlation, even
among those ACOAs who identified with being ACOAs. In
comparing the test results with the highly popularized ACOA
characteristics introduced by Janet Woititz in her best-selling
book *Adult Children of Alcoholics*, they found no correlation.
In other words those "common characteristics" were **not** fun-
damentally tied to ACOAs any more than to the general population.[52] Therefore if you see a list of "common characteristics," don't assume it's valid.

Mark Lyon, coauthor of the research study along with
Richard Seefeldt, reports:

> Our results have led us to argue that the label—
> ACOA—is superfluous. . . . We feel that Woititz's
> conclusions were premature, based more on hypoth-
> eses than empirical research. Yet her guidelines had
> gotten past the point of questioning—and very pos-
> sibly to where well people began believing they

must be sick.[53]

One problem with such labels (Adult Children of Alcoholics) and lists ("common characteristics") is that people are assigned to boxes and categories. Lyon and Seefeldt are concerned about people believing inaccurate information about themselves based upon information found in popular self-help books for ACOAs. They say:

> . . . many ACOAs might be persuaded that they possess certain characteristics simply because the information is presented in what they perceive to be an authoritative source by a person with "expert" status. Similarly, the characteristics presented are nebulous, facilitating ease of application to any person, in much the same way as reading and believing a horoscope. The result may be that many individuals are misled into perceiving that they have special problems which require treatment, (or at least another self-help book or two), when in fact they may do just as well never having stumbled upon the information.[54]

Besides being a simplistic and ineffective way of dealing with problems of living, diagnosing oneself as an ACOA may be a convenient way of blaming the present on the past. Furthermore, after identifying with "common characteristics" of ACOAs, people may conclude they are sick, need to recover, and therefore need treatment. While such a conclusion may line the pockets of publishers, therapists, and owners of treatment centers, it may very well harm the ones who are attempting to deal with problems of living. The ACOA lists of characteristics have also drifted into the general codependency area so that all people have the "benefit" of diagnosing themselves as sick, seeking treatment, and joining the ranks of recovery.

Unfortunately, Christians pick up such lists and make irresponsible statements. For instance, the authors of *The Twelve Steps for Christians* erroneously assert:

> Research involving chemically dependent or emotionally repressed individuals and their families

has determined that certain behavior characteristics are common in adult children from these
homes.[55]

As usual, no reference source is given to substantiate the
statement. Instead, it is followed by a list of behaviors that
could apply to any number of people, ACOA or nonACOA.
Like most of the codependency/recovery books written for
Christians, *The Twelve Steps for Christians* is a mixture of
erroneous psychological notions and misapplied Bible verses.
In their eagerness to make the Twelve Steps "Christian," the
authors give the following commentary-meditation for John
3:16-17:

> Seen in the light of God's love, the Twelve Steps are
> a pathway to our salvation.[56]

They thus equate God's gift of salvation through His Son with
"the Twelve Steps are a pathway to our salvation." Besides
contradicting the meaning of John 3:16-17, they also contradict Ephesians 2:8-9:

> For by grace are ye saved through faith; and that
> not of yourselves: it is the gift of God: Not of works,
> lest any man should boast.

That is just one example from "Christian" books that have
been written especially for ACOAs and other codependents,
who supposedly have "common characteristics" and need a
Twelve-Step program as a "pathway to salvation."

Is Anyone and Everyone Codependent?

Because of the broad scope of definitions and the great
variety of characteristics and behaviors associated with codependency, some therapists contend that "Codependency is
anything and *everything*, and *everyone* is codependent." One
psychiatrist declares: "Just about everyone has some of it."[57]
And if everyone is codependent, and therefore sick, everyone
needs some kind of treatment to get well.

In spite of all the pages Beattie has devoted to defining
and describing *codependency*, she finally comes to the excessively generalized conclusion that codependency "is about the

ways we have been affected by other people and our pasts." In fact, she moves beyond the limits of even defining the word and declares: "Whatever codependency is, it's a problem, and recovering from it feels better than not."[58] But what kind of illness is it that has such a broad range of definitions and descriptions and that everyone has it, and **whatever it is**, "it's a problem, and recovering from it feels better than not"? By such logic one could easily conclude that poverty is a disease.

Obviously there is a wide range of opinion as far as codependency is concerned. And that's all it is—**opinion**. A Special Report on "Codependency" in the University of California, Berkeley, *Wellness Letter* says:

> **The literature of codependency is based on assertions, generalizations, and anecdotes.** . . . To start **without the slightest shred of scientific evidence** and casually label large groups as diseased may be helpful to a few, but it is **potentially harmful and exploitative** as well. If as the best sellers claim, "all society is an addict" and 96% of us are codependents, that leaves precious few of us outside the rehab centers—but at that point the claims become ludicrous at best.[59] (Emphasis added.)

Unfortunately, the label "codependent" easily affixes itself to all kinds of persons and behaviors. One look at the vast list of "codependent characteristics" in Beattie's book should cause a person to wonder how anyone can escape the indictment: **codependent**. And once a person is labeled "codependent" because of a few characteristics, the rest come along as further indictment. As soon as the label is attached, everything the "codependent" does can be seen as "codependent behavior." The label itself is both harmful and self-perpetuating. It also ends up providing a simplistic answer—"I'm a codependent"—to a complex set of problems. Worse than that, it embraces a vast amount of self-focus and bad advice.

The Power of a Label.

The power of a label was demonstrated quite graphically

through a courageous experiment conducted by Dr. David Rosenhan from Stanford University. He and seven other valiant participants entered mental hospitals. Using pseudonyms, fictitious occupational backgrounds, and a limited number of fake symptoms (including hearing voices), they were diagnosed as mentally ill and admitted as patients. From the point of admission they discontinued the fake symptoms, acted normally, and presented themselves as they normally were. When appropriate, they talked about their own family, work relationships, and positive and negative feelings. In fact, part of the experiment was that each participant had to be discharged from the hospital through his own efforts of convincing the hospital staff of his sanity. Naturally each volunteer was motivated to be released as soon as possible.[60]

None of the hospital psychiatrists, nurses or attendants suspected the pseudopatients were fakes. Even though staff reports included such descriptions as "friendly," "cooperative," and "exhibited no abnormal indication," the staff members did not notice that these people were sane even though they acted and spoke normally. Instead, the staff viewed the pseudopatients through the labels of the initial diagnosis. Therefore everything the pseudopatients did was seen in the light of the label. For instance, when the pseudopatients wrote notes on what was going on, note-taking was seen as a symptom of delusions or compulsive behavior. When one of them paced the hall out of boredom, the nurse asked if he was nervous. Even when they were discharged they retained the same label. All who were initially diagnosed as schizophrenic were discharged with the label "schizophrenia in remission." One pseudopatient had been admitted with the label "manic-depressive" and was discharged with the same label.[61]

The label "codependent" is also a label that will have a powerful affect on a person. And worse than professionals seeing that person through the label "codependent" is the person seeing himself through that label. Pretty soon everything is seen in reference to codependence. And it may stick for life—a perpetual "recovering codependent."

No More Codependent.

While the words *codependence*, *codependency*, and *codependent* are conveniently (though vaguely) used to identify a group of behaviors and people, they stand in the way of a person confronting problems biblically. In fact, such labels are actually harmful to a person's spiritual well-being. The treatment for codependency is often tied together with the definitions, descriptions, and the assumptions of those labels. Furthermore, the treatment offered is generally a mix of psychological opinions and false religious sentiments.

Codependent literature abounds with such psychological concepts as a so-called unconscious need for self-worth, unconscious repression and denial, obsessions, compulsions, and dysfunctional families. *Love Is A Choice*, one of the most popular books in Christian bookstores, was written by three professing Christians who argue that the causes of codependency are unmet emotional needs, which they graphically illustrate and describe as unfilled "love tanks." Their simplistic explanation says that all problems related to codependency can be traced to not having been loved enough or in the right way as children. But, the person doesn't really know that's the reason because he has repressed the hurt and denied that he didn't get enough love. The whole idea matches the Freudian invention of an unconscious which drives behavior, with its ego-defense mechanisms (including repression and denial), and the Adlerian unconscious need for self-worth.[62]

Like Robin Norwood, author of *Women Who Love Too Much*,[63] the authors of *Love Is a Choice* contend that codependents have a compulsive need to recreate the original family situation. They say:

> If the original family was painful (even if the child doesn't specifically remember it as being painful), that pain must be replicated, for several reasons.

> Reason number one: *If the original situation can be drummed back into existence, this time around I can fix it. I can cure the pain.* . . . The codependent possesses a powerful need to go back and fix what was wrong. . . .

> Reason number two: *Because I was responsible for that rotten original family, I must be punished. I deserve pain* . . . the codependent may actually be hooked on misery. . . .
>
> Reason number three: Finally, then, *there's that yearning for the familiar, the secure* . . . the codependent seeks the refuge of the familiar. (Emphasis theirs.)[64]

They conclude that this is the reason "why adult children of dysfunctional families almost always end up in dysfunctional relationships."[65] But, all of this is postdictive, not predictive. It is pure unmitigated supposition without support. They are finding out about the past and connecting it to present behavior. But causation is only a guess—an assumption. Otherwise they would be able to predict behavior by now. But, psychologists are not able to predict behavior. They cannot look at a child and predict what he will be like as an adult. Therefore, how can they be so certain the other way around? In fact those who have researched the area of addictions clearly state: "There's no way to predict who'll become an addict."[66] Therefore, how can one predict who will become a codependent?

The Christian authors of *Love Is a Choice* depend upon the unproven opinions of Sigmund Freud, Alfred Adler, and other psychological theorists. They believe that the present is determined by the past and that there is a powerful motivating unconscious that drives people to do what they do against their conscious will. That is why they say to their patients: "You're asking for these problems! You're deliberately putting yourself in situations that will bring nothing but pain."[67] Rather than addressing the problems found in sinful relationships from a solely biblical perspective, the authors view everything through the colored glasses of psychological theories, which are simply opinions of men. The part of psychology they use is not science, but rather the wisdom of unredeemed men.[68]

The Bible addresses the issue of using such worldly wisdom rather than the Bible in matters of understanding who man is, why he does what he does, and how he changes.

> And my speech and my preaching was not with enticing words of man's wisdom, but in demonstration of the Spirit and of power: That your faith should not stand in the wisdom of men, but in the power of God (1 Corinthians 2:4-5).

> As ye have therefore received Christ Jesus the Lord, so walk ye in him: Rooted and built up in him, and stablished in the faith, as ye have been taught, abounding therein with thanksgiving. Beware lest any man spoil you through philosophy and vain deceit, after the tradition of men, after the rudiments of the world, and not after Christ. (Colossians 2:6-8).

Such wisdom of men is often in conflict with the Bible and some is downright antagonistic. Popular T.V. codependency guru John Bradshaw goes a step farther. He believes that the need for love and lack of self-acceptance plays a part, but he declares: "It is my belief that internalized shame *is the essence of co-dependency.*"[69] (Emphasis his.) He contends that a "shame-based identity" is one that says, "I am flawed and defective as a human being."[70] **Bradshaw's gospel is the goodness of man, rather than the goodness of God.** He is particularly critical of the biblical teaching that everyone is born in the condition of sin. He contends that such teaching produces a "shame-based" personality destined to become an addict.

Bradshaw tells the story of Max and says:

> Max's religious upbringing was rigid and authoritarian. He was taught at any [*sic*] early age that he was born with the stain of sin on his soul, and that he was a miserable sinner. He was also taught that God knew his innermost thoughts and was watching everything he did. . . .

> Many religious denominations teach a concept of man as wretched and stained with original sin. . . . With original sin you're beat before you start. . . . [71]

Bradshaw thus blames codependency and other addictions on

those Christians who teach doctrines of original sin, total depravity, and eternal punishment. He ought to know. He studied for the priesthood while being an habitual drunkard. He also taught philosophy, psychology, and theology "at the university level."[72]

Bradshaw argues that codependents are "shame-based" with "toxic shame" being the "inner core" of all their "wrongdoing." He further declares, "I think shame-based people are premoral because of the disabled will."[73] The implication is that no addict or codependent need feel guilty because he couldn't help it. After all, it's everybody else's fault he's shame-based. The answer then is to replace toxic shame with feeling "good enough about ourselves to believe that God will remove these defects of character."[74] According to Bradshaw, Adam's problem was not sin in the Garden of Eden. It was his toxic shame. Bradshaw says:

> Genesis suggests that four relationships were broken by Adam's toxic shame: the relationship with God; the relationship with self; the relationship with brother and neighbor (Cain kills Abel); and the relationship with the world (nature).[75]

Not a word about sin here. And guess what the solution is. Bradshaw declares: "The 12 Steps restore those relationships."[76] He avoids sin by completely misunderstanding Genesis 3. Bradshaw rejects the biblical doctrine of original sin—that people are born sinners and have sinful natures. He has rejected what the Bible says about mankind. Moreover, he has replaced Jesus Christ with the Twelve Steps. And yet Christians eagerly embrace John Bradshaw and his teachings.

Either through ignorance or gullibility one Christian women's magazine writer says:

> Co-dependency hinders a healthy conscious marriage relationship, however, because it blocks real communication and inhibits growth, affecting the entire family structure and passing on what Bradshaw calls "poisonous pedagogy" from one generation to the next.[77]

Does she realize that Bradshaw's "poisonous pedagogy" includes such biblical doctrines as original sin?

In spite of such antibiblical teachings, the support between Christians and nonChristians in this popular fad of codependency/recovery is mutual. For instance, Bradshaw "heartily" recommends *Love Is a Choice*, written by its Christian authors, who are also recommended by Moody Bible Institute, Dallas Theological Seminary, and various Christian notables.[78]

Stories and Tales.

Besides relying upon the ungodly wisdom of men, most authors of codependency and other addiction books depend heavily upon detailed stories to prove their points. However, such stories do not prove their theories, but rather reveal them. Generally when a person is counseled according to certain theoretical concepts, even the counselee learns to define his problems according to the language and expectations of the counselor. Psychologists will generally find what they are looking for because they create the atmosphere and gain the cooperation of the client. If the therapist is looking for childhood pain, the person is sure to remember something painful. If the therapist is looking for dream symbols the person is sure to come up with them. If the therapist is looking for repressed memories, he may inadvertently or purposefully help the client create new memories or alter old memories through a heightened state of suggestion.

Such stories and case histories should be regarded as biased and contrived. While the events may indeed have occurred, the descriptions of feelings and responses may actually have been learned during therapy, from books, or from members of a support group. For instance, one woman is quoted as saying: "My doctor sent me to a counselor who opened my eyes. I know now that I was addicted to Nick as surely as if he were a drug."[79] In other words, she learned from the counselor that she was "addicted." Such stories and testimonials give a reality to the psychological theories promoted by the authors of the various books.

Just because psychological systems and personality theo-

ries **seem** to explain the person and his behavior, that does
not mean that the explanations are accurate. When we consider that there are numerous competing systems, each of
which pretends to explain personhood, something must be
amiss. World-renowned scholar and philosopher of science Sir
Karl Popper examined these psychological theories. He says:

> These theories appeared to be able to explain practi-
> cally everything that happened within the fields to
> which they referred. The study of any of them
> seemed to have the effect of an intellectual conver-
> sion or revelation, opening your eyes to a new truth
> hidden from those not yet initiated. Once your eyes
> were thus opened you saw confirming instances ev-
> erywhere: the world was full of *verifications* of the
> theory. Whatever happened always confirmed it.[80]
> (Emphasis his.)

At first glance this looks like promising evidence. However,
Popper insists that constant confirmations and the seeming
ability to explain everything do not indicate scientific validity. What looks like a strength is actually a weakness. He
says:

> It is easy to obtain confirmations or verifications, for
> nearly every theory—if we look for confirmations . . .
> Confirming evidence should not count *except when it
> is the result of a genuine test of the theory.*[81]
> (Emphasis his.)

And he indicates that psychological theories, such as those of
Freud and others, do not meet scientific requirements: "A
theory which is not refutable by any conceivable event is non-
scientific. Irrefutability is not a virtue of a theory (as people
often think) but a vice."[82] He concludes that "though posing
as sciences," such theories "had in fact more in common with
primitive myths than with science; that they resembled
astrology rather than astronomy."[83]

Besides stories being used to verify the theories and diagnoses, they are used to give the reader the idea that the concepts presented in the books are true. They also serve as testimonials of healing. Statements declaring healing and imply-

ing promises are laced throughout the books to assure the reader that cures are available through therapy and Twelve-Step programs. Here is an example. After describing the case of "Beryl" for whom "without intervention and help life would never get better," the authors declare:

> We pieced together her sorry childhood, every bit of it, and her disastrous relationships. We examined the whats and whys. Over the weeks she dealt with each item. She hurt terribly during the process, **but she emerged whole.**[84] (Emphasis added.)

Of course this was only possible through hospitalization. Two authors of the book, Paul Meier and Frank Minirth, own psychiatric clinics. The suggestion is there and so is the implied promise—with a large price tag (barely noticeable because of third-party insurance payments).

Unfortunately, most books on codependency and other addictions written by Christians rehash the same psychological definitions, diagnoses, explanations, and treatments that the pop psychology books offer. However, those written by professing Christians have enough Christian-sounding language and references to God and the Bible that unsuspecting readers assume they are getting sound Christian, biblical understanding and advice. Such books, while appearing to be helpful to Christians, are often more dangerous than the purely secular books. A Christian might at least exercise a little more discernment when reading a secular book than one written by a Christian. Dr. John MacArthur, Jr. speaks about those "who wish to mix psychology with the divine resources and sell the mixture as a spiritual elixir." He says:

> Their methodology amounts to a tacit admission that what God has given us in Christ is not really adequate to meet our deepest needs and salve our troubled lives.[85]

3

LOVE MISUNDERSTOOD AND MISAPPLIED

The central issue being dealt with in the numerous code-pendency/recovery books and programs is love. Book titles, such as *Women Who Love Too Much*,[1] give the impression that problems in relationships come from too much love, indeed too much sacrificial love and giving of self to others. The beauty of love enduring through difficulties and disaster has been the theme of great literature and music throughout the ages. Moreover, it has been the theme of agapé love in the Bible. But now sacrificial love, faithful to the uttermost, is branded "addictive," "codependent," and "compulsive." In fact, the only love which seems acceptable and healthy in the ever-expanding recovery movement is self-love.

In her book *Codependent No More*, Beattie suggests that God's commandment to "Love thy neighbor as thyself" is the problem,[2] and her solution is blatantly the title of her Chapter 11: "Have a Love Affair with Yourself." She believes that in order to have healthy relationships with other people, one must deliberately and actively love oneself. Rather than devoting one's life to serving others and bringing happiness into their lives, Beattie's plan is to help women serve themselves and make themselves feel good. The codependency/recovery movement has set up a standard of righteousness taken directly out of secular psychological theories and therapies. The

43

golden rule, "Do unto others as you would have them do unto you" has been reversed to "Do unto **yourself** what you would have others do unto you." After all, the goal of recovery is to feel better.[3]

Foundational philosophical premises of the codependent movement are both unbiblical and antibiblical. First of all, there is a total lack of understanding of biblical love and particularly agapé love (sacrificial, giving love). This lack of understanding about the very nature of love and of the God of love reveals that the primary source is **not** the Bible. In fact, most of the teachings originated in darkened minds that do not know Almighty God, who has revealed Himself in the Bible.

Proponents of self-love have their foundation in secularism and paganism. Self-love, self-acceptance, and self-esteem are popularized teachings of humanistic psychology, which is based on the belief that all are born good, that society is the culprit, and that man is the measure of all things. The emphasis on self is exactly what began in the Garden of Eden and it is being intensified through humanistic teachings on self-love, self-esteem, self-fulfillment, self-realization, and self et cetera. Even though the Bible does **not** teach self-love, self-acceptance, and self-esteem as needs or virtues, both Christians and nonChristians have come to assume that self-love, self-acceptance, and self-esteem are essential for personal well-being.

Self-Love and Self-Esteem Teachings for Codependency/Recovery.

Self-esteem, self-worth, self-love, and self-acceptance comprise a major theme in codependency/recovery books, groups, and therapies. One of the unbiblical tenets of recovery programs is the mistaken notion that people do not love themselves and that they need to raise their self-esteem. This assumption comes from faith in the secular psychological notion that every person has a compelling need for self-worth that motivates all that he does.

A characteristic commonly assigned to codependents and other addicts is "low self-esteem." However, as far as substance abusers are concerned, they most assuredly put their own lusts before anything else. They may indeed be filled with self-pity and self-deprecation at the end of a binge, but self is still central because rather than repenting, they do something to make themselves feel good—go back to their sinful indulgence. And while those labeled "codependent" may center much of their attention on others, pride, rather than low self-esteem, may lurk beneath their good works.

Indeed, many relationships identified as "codependent" do involve pride, not low self-worth or a deficiency of self-love. An underlying lie of people married to drunks and other "losers" may be their own sense of mastery and self-confidence in being able to change others through their own wonderful goodness and love. They may have excessive belief in their own ability to help another person, or they may think that others will change just because of being married to them. They may also have high expectations of the spouse being forever grateful for being rescued by such an excellent partner. Then when their heroic efforts fail, they may cast blame onto themselves as well as their spouses, parents, or whomever else might be in the picture. They may then experience feelings of hopelessness about themselves and their circumstances. They may be filled with self-pity and be dissatisfied with themselves. But that is not true self-hatred. That is self-love that does not want to suffer.

And what about low self-esteem? Do such people not esteem themselves? Or are they angry with the discrepancy between what they desire and their lack of fulfillment? Are they angry with themselves for not having done better? Thinking that one could have changed the circumstances or accomplished more than one did can be a form of pride.

The notion that problems can be traced to unmet psychological "needs" permeates the codependency/recovery movement. Melodie Beattie lists low self-worth as one of the major characteristics of codependency.[4] She says, "We need to value ourselves and make decisions and choices that enhance our self-esteem."[5] She quotes Nathaniel Brandon from his book *Honoring the Self*, which she refers to as "an excellent book on self-esteem." These are some of Brandon's words which

Beattie chose to give as an answer to those suffering from codependency:

> To honor the self is to preserve an attitude of self-acceptance—which means to accept what we are, without self-oppression or self-castigation, without any pretense about the truth of our own being. . . .
>
> To honor the self is to be in love with our own life, in love with our possibilities for growth and for experiencing joy, in love with the process of discovery and exploring our distinctively human potentialities.
>
> Thus we can begin to see that to honor the self is to practice *selfishness* in the highest, noblest, and least understood sense of that word. And this, I shall argue, requires enormous independence, courage, and integrity.[6]

Beattie declares:

> We need to love ourselves and make a commitment to ourselves. . . . Out of high self-esteem will come true acts of kindness and charity, not selfishness.
>
> The love we give and receive will be enhanced by the love we give ourselves.[7]

Even Christians join the ranks of faith in need psychology when they contend that unmet "needs" for self-worth and self-esteem are the major reasons for sinning. The Christian authors of *Love Is a Choice* declare that codependents carry distorted messages about their own sense of worth and that such messages originated in "dysfunctional" families. They include these phrases among their lists of those messages: " 'I am unloved.' 'I am unlovable. . . .' 'I'm not worthy.' 'I do not deserve this success I'm having.' "[8] And of course those messages must be erased through regressive therapy and replaced with positive, self-enhancing messages.

Another Christian writer, Pat Springle, says, "All codependents, when they are honest with themselves, feel that they are unworthy of love and acceptance."[9] The foreword to his book *Codependency* is written by Robert McGee, founder and president of Rapha Ministries and Rapha Hospital Treatment Centers. The brochure for the twenty Rapha Hospital Treatment Centers advertises:

> . . . clinical programs administered in a Christian environment which help the individual overcome emotional or substance abuse problems. Part of Rapha's success is found in their unique ability to target and resolve problems of low self-esteem. . . .
>
> **At the core of *all* emotional problems and addictive disorders is low self-worth**. It is never the only problem; but it is so major an issue that, if not dealt with adequately, one is kept from experiencing lasting, positive results. . . . (Italics in original; bold emphasis added.)
>
> All our programs are led by caring professionals (M.D., Ph.D., M.S.W. [i.e., psychiatrists, psychologists, and social workers]).[10]

Springle echoes the psychological theories presented in McGee's book *Search for Significance*, which is an amalgamation of Adlerian-Maslowian need psychology and the Bible. Springle declares:

> Codependency is not just a set of isolated feelings or behaviors. It is not a surface problem. Consequently, superficial solutions don't help.[11]

The implication here is that a psychological understanding of the problem and a psychological process of cure must supplement the Bible. The further implication is that the application of the Bible alone to such problems would be a superficial solution.

Springle continues:

> A deep hurt; an unmet need for love and acceptance either numbs the codependent or drives him to accomplish goals so he can please people and win their approval. Codependent emotions and actions are designed to blunt pain and gain a desperately needed sense of worth.[12]

He thus believes that codependents attempt to fill their needs for self-esteem and self-worth by pleasing others:

> The codependent gets his worth—his identity—from what he does for other people. He rescues, he helps, he enables, but no matter how much he does for others, it's never enough.[13]

Springle also contends that codependents suffer a unique kind of guilt and shame. He says:

> It [the guilt] lacks objectivity. It is devoid of forgiveness. It is without love and acceptance. It is the painful, gnawing perception that you are worthless, unacceptable, and can never do enough to be acceptable, no matter how hard you try.[14]

He says, "The crushing effects of guilt, shame, worthlessness, self-hatred, and self-condemnation take a heavy toll."[15] Therefore he declares:

> We need a bold new plan to expose and attack the root of our need: our identity and sense of worth.[16]

Thus, in attempting to help a so-called codependent woman who was concerned about all of the things she had to do, he said:

> You're asking the wrong questions. The question is not, "how can I get more done?" The question is, "how do I get my worth?" As long as you try to get your worth from being productive and incessantly serving others, you will feel pressured, condemned, and confused for having any desires and dreams of your own. But you already have worth! You already have value! You can be yourself. Everything you do doesn't have to be productive. You don't have to serve others all the time. As you express yourself and gain a sense of confidence, you'll feel the freedom to be yourself more often. And you'll do things that are productive and helpful for others, but you'll do them because you *want* to, not because you think you *have* to.[17] (Emphasis his.)

You may wonder where God is in all of this. What might be His will? It is not even asked, because the erroneous assumption of such teachers is that God's will is for everyone to realize how much he is really worth and that God is his source for self-worth, self-esteem, and self-acceptance. In spite of the fact that neither the Bible nor research lend adequate support for promoting self-love, self-acceptance, and self-esteem, codependency/recovery programs emphasize loving self, accepting self, and esteeming self.

Psychological Foundations of Self-Love.

The self-love, self-acceptance, self-esteem teachings embraced by the codependency/recovery movement are built upon the shaky foundations of psychological theories that attempt to understand and change the human condition. This kind of psychology has more to do with personal opinion than with science and resembles religion more than research.[18] Theories of William James, Sigmund Freud, Erich Fromm, Alfred Adler, Abraham Maslow, Carl Rogers, and others have heavily influenced the codependency/recovery movement concerning emotional needs.

Humanistic psychology has provided the justification for emphasizing the self through its hierarchy of needs for self-acceptance, self-worth, self-love, and self-actualization. Self, rather than God or others, is the central focus. Lest this sound selfish and self-centered, the proponents of the self assure us that only through meeting the needs of the self can people become socially aware and responsive. Their erroneous thinking follows this pattern: only when a person loves himself can he love others; only when a person accepts himself can he accept others; and only when his needs are met can he meet the needs of others. This logic is the underlying justification for most of what goes on in humanistic psychology, and it spills over into almost every other issue of life.

Two major assumptions follow this logic: One assumption is that lack of self-love, self-acceptance, and self-esteem causes just about everything that might be wrong with society: crime, violence, substance abuse, teenage pregnancy, child and spousal abuse, school failures, "dysfunctional families," codependency and even wars. The matching assumption is that positive self-love, unconditional self-acceptance, and high self-esteem will prevent such personal and social disasters and even correct them. Those two assumptions are basic tenets of codependency/recovery programs. Almost any list of symptoms of codependency will include such words as *bad self-image, negative self-worth, low self-esteem,* and *low self-worth.* And of course at least part of the solution to codependency, as well as other addictions, is to learn to love, accept, and esteem oneself. However, neither scientific research nor the Bible supports such assumptions for cause or help.

Research Perspective on Self-Esteem/Self-Love Assumptions.

Faith in the assumption that self-love, self-acceptance, and self-esteem are necessary for preventing crime, violence, substance abuse, teenage pregnancy, child and spousal abuse, school failures, and other social ills led the California legislature to create the California Task Force to Promote Self-Esteem and Personal and Social Responsibility. As part of their preliminary work, the Task Force funded research with the expectation that it would support self-esteem programs throughout the state. The Task Force spent $735,000 during a three-year period in an unsuccessful attempt to prove the relationship of self-esteem to social problems. The Task Force hired eight professors from the University of California to look at the research on self-esteem as it relates to the six following areas:

1. Crime, violence and recidivism.
2. Alcohol and drug abuse.
3. Welfare dependency.
4. Teenage pregnancy.
5. Child and spousal abuse.
6. Children failing to learn in school.

Seven of the professors researched the above areas and the eighth professor summarized the results. The results were then published in a book titled *The Social Importance of Self-Esteem.*[19]

In the Preface to the book, John Vasconcellos (the legislator behind the bill to create the Task Force) makes it appear as if the research supports a relationship between self-esteem and social problems. However, Dr. Neil Smelser, the professor who summarized the research, does **not** agree. He says: "One of the disappointing aspects of every chapter in this volume. . . is how **low** the associations between self-esteem and its consequences are in research to date."[20] (Emphasis added.) Smelser also says:

> The authors who have assessed the state-of-the-art knowledge of factors important in the genesis of many social problems have been unable to uncover many causally valid findings relating to that genesis—and they have therefore been correspondingly unable to come up with systematic statements relating to cure or prevention.[21]

After reading the research results in *The Social Importance of Self-Esteem*, David L. Kirk, syndicated writer for the *San Francisco Examiner*, says it more bluntly: "There is precious little evidence that self-esteem is the cause of our social ills." Kirk continues: "Those social scientists looked hard . . . but they could detect essentially **no cause-and-effect link between self-esteem and problematic behavior**, whether it's teen pregnancy, drug use or child abuse."[22] (Emphasis added.)

The research presented in *The Social Importance of Self-Esteem* is full of statistical and methodological problems. Anyone who uses the book and its findings to support self-esteem as the cause or cure for the so-called "epidemic level of social problems" listed above is grossly distorting the research.

In spite of the lack of evidence, Vasconcellos still contends that self-esteem "most likely appears to be the social vaccine that inoculates us to lead lives apart from drugs and violence." However, Smelser, the professor who summarized the research, says in response to Vasconcellos:

> . . . self-esteem and social problems are too complicated to result in any simple conclusions. . . . When you get to looking for clear relationships as to cause and effect, particularly in areas so unclear as this one, you're not going to find them.[23]

Also, Dr. Thomas Scheff, one of the University of California

professors who did the research, said that "thousands of studies have been done on self-esteem since World War II, but the
results have been inconclusive."[24]

One member of the Task Force was candid enough and
perceptive enough to say: "The Task Force's interpretation of
the UC professors' academic findings understates the
**absence of a significant linkage of self-esteem and the
six social problems.**"[25] (Emphasis added.)

One research study supported by the National Institute
of Mental Health attempted to find a relationship between
self-esteem and delinquent children. The researchers concluded that "the effect of self-esteem on delinquent behavior is
negligible." The researchers say, "Given the extensive specu-
lation and debate about self-esteem and delinquency, we find
these results something of an embarrassment."[26]

Concerning drug abuse, one researcher says:

> . . . there is a paucity of good research, especially
> studies that could link the abuse of alcohol and
> drugs with self-esteem. What evidence there is
> remains inconsistent.[27]

He continues: "Empirical studies concerning the relationship
between alcohol and drug abuse and self-esteem show mixed
results."[28] A report on Diana Baumrind's study which com-
pared both discipline and self-esteem with drug use reveals:

> Children of "democratic" parents, who were support-
> ed but not highly controlled, also **scored high on
> all self-esteem and competence measures but
> were likelier to become heavily involved with
> drugs**.[29] (Emphasis Added.)

Abraham Maslow, one of the most well-known psychological theorists promoting self-esteem and self-actualization,
found in his later research that his theories had been wrong.
He tried to curb the enthusiasm for his earlier theories and
wrote in the second edition of *Motivation and Personality*:

> . . . the high scorers in my test of dominance-feeling
> or self-esteem were more apt to come late to ap-
> pointments with the experimenter, to be less re-
> spectful, more casual, more forward, more conde-

scending, less tense, anxious, and worried, more apt to accept an offered cigarette, much more apt to make themselves comfortable without bidding or invitation.

The stronger [high self-esteem] woman is much more apt to be pagan, permissive, and accepting in all sexual realms. She is less apt to be a virgin. . . more apt to have had sexual relations with more than one man. . . . [30] (Emphasis added.)

In other words, Maslow found that satisfying the so-called self-esteem needs did **not** produce the desired results. And that is the problem with so many of the self theories. They begin with fallen flesh and simply end up with another face of fallen flesh. Nevertheless, few people pay attention to research that does not support their faith in self-love, self-acceptance, and self-esteem.

Do People Actually Suffer from Low Self-Esteem and Self-Hatred?

What about people who claim to hate themselves? Do they actually hate themselves or are they trying to gain sympathy and support? If they tell someone they hate themselves, the common response is to rescue them from that idea. In the process they receive sympathy and support not normally given. It is a predictable transaction that once begun can become a habitual way of relating to others and receiving support. There are also those who are unhappy about themselves and their circumstances and generalize them into some kind of self-revulsion, all the while loving themselves.

On the other hand, there are some who do experience personal revulsion because of their sin. In fact, unconfessed known sin, such as resentment, bitterness, hatred, and self-pity, may make the person feel guilty and therefore uncomfortable. The actual guilt may then be transformed into feelings of self-hatred and worthlessness. In that case, the person does not need more self-love, self-acceptance, or self-esteem. The person needs to repent and confess and be cleansed.

We are not saying that there are no individuals who genuinely think they hate themselves. But, what they generally hate is something about themselves or their circumstances. They exhibit actual love for themselves in that they continue to spend most of their time concerned about themselves, even if it is with unhappy thoughts. They generally get to the point where they are unhappy about themselves because a discrepancy exists between their aspirations or desires and their performance or condition. This intensive hatred is evidence of high self-interest.

Thus a woman who aspires to be thin and beautiful rather than fat and ugly by cultural standards could end up hating her **condition** and thereby think that she hates her**self**, because her desire for a perfect figure is discrepant from the reality of being fat and "ugly." She is reacting to the discrepancy, but the root of the problem is self-love and even pride. She does not actually hate herself. She hates the discrepancy. If she truly hated herself she would be happy, or at least satisfied, to be fat and ugly. But, her self-love in tandem with the discrepancy makes her miserable.

Dr. David Myers, in his book *The Inflated Self*, discusses research having to do with how people view themselves and others. The research demonstrates that there is definitely a self-serving bias at work in individuals. Myers says:

> Time and again, experiments have revealed that people tend to attribute positive behaviors to themselves and negative behaviors to external factors, enabling them to take credit for their good acts and to deny responsibility for their bad acts.[31]

Numerous research studies contradict the common notion having to do with self-image. In his book, Myers presents research to support his statement that:

> Preachers who deliver ego-boosting pep talks to audiences who are supposedly plagued with miserable self-images are preaching to a problem that seldom exists.[32]

Another book, coauthored by Myers and Malcolm Jeeves, states that "the most common error in people's self images is not unrealistically low self-esteem, but rather self-serving pride; not an inferiority complex, but a superiority complex."[33]

A recent study conducted by Scott Allison *et al* indicates that people give themselves reasons to think positively about themselves. For instance, they regard themselves more highly than others by remembering unfair actions against themselves instead of their own unfairness to others.[34]

There is a definite self-serving bias in all of us. Self-esteem and self-love do not need to be encouraged; they are part of the fallen, sinful nature. In Jeremiah 17:9 we are told, "The heart is deceitful above all things and desperately wicked." Man is self-serving, self-affirming, self-loving, and self-esteeming because he is self-deceiving. Many of the ways that man serves, affirms, loves, esteems, and deceives himself are found in the research as well as the Bible.

Biblical Perspective on Self-Love Assumptions.

The Bible does not present self-esteem, self-worth, self-love, self-confidence, or self-fulfillment as needs that must be met to create capable, loving, well-adjusted people. Instead, the direction of Scripture is away from self and toward God and others. Self is not to be enhanced or catered to. Self-esteem is not even mentioned. On the other hand, Paul warned that a Christian is "not to think of himself more highly than he ought to think" (Romans 12:3). And when it comes to esteem, Paul says, ". . . let each esteem other better than themselves" (Philippians 2:3). From the context of Scripture, the fallen nature is already biased in the direction of self. Self-love is already there or Jesus would not have commanded us to love others as we (already) love ourselves (Matthew 22:39).

There are those who try to use the Great Commandment to justify self-love. However, the Great Commandment teaches just the opposite: to love God and others.

> Thou shalt love the Lord thy God with all thy heart, and with all thy soul, and with all thy mind. This is

the first and great commandment. And the second is like unto it, Thou shalt love thy neighbour as thyself. On these two commandments hang all the law and the prophets (Matthew 22:37-40).

Is the commandment to love self a commandment of God or is it a commandment of men? We found no Bible commentary that said that Matthew 22:39 (or parallel verses in Mark and Luke) commands us to love ourselves.

However, many people have distorted the meaning of Matthew 22:39 to give credence to their self-love teachings. For instance, humanistic psychologist Erich Fromm says:

> If it is a virtue to love my neighbor as a human being, it must be a virtue—and not a vice—to love myself, since I am a human being too. There is no concept of man in which I myself am not included. A doctrine which proclaims such an exclusion proves itself to be intrinsically contradictory. The idea expressed in the Biblical "Love thy neighbor as thyself!" implies that respect for one's own integrity and uniqueness, love for and understanding of one's own self, can not be separated from respect for and love and understanding of another individual. The love for my own self is inseparably connected with the love for any other self.[35]

> If an individual is able to love productively, he loves himself too; if he can love *only* others, he can not love at all.[36] (Emphasis his.)

Fromm was an atheist who argued against the fundamentals of the Christian faith. It is even more disturbing when Christians parrot such misunderstandings of Jesus' words about loving neighbor as one loves himself. Rather than properly exegeting the passage, they use Scripture to support a pet theory.

The notion of self-love is not the subject of the Great Commandment. It is only a qualifier. When Jesus commands people to love God with "all thy heart, and with all thy soul, and with all thy mind, and with all thy strength" (Mark 12:30), He is emphasizing the all-encompassing nature of this love (beyond the possibility of the natural man and only possible through divine grace). If He had used the same words for loving neighbor, He would have encouraged idolatry. However, for the next degree of intensity he used the words *as thyself.*

Jesus does **not** command people to love themselves. He does **not** say there are three commandments (love God, love neighbor, **and** love self). Instead, he says, "On these **two** commandments hang all the law and the prophets" (Matthew 22:40). **Love of self is a fact, not a command**. In fact, Jesus would not command people to love others as themselves if they do not already love themselves. It would be a pointless statement. To fit self-love theology, the first commandment would have to read: "Love yourself first so that you will be able to love God and others."

Scripture teaches that people **do** love themselves. Paul says, "For no man ever yet hated his own flesh; but nourisheth and cherisheth it, even as the Lord the church" (Ephesians 5:29). Some biblical references to people loathing themselves have to do with knowing that their deeds are evil (i. e., Ezekiel 36:31). In those instances they are still committed to themselves and retain biases that are favorable to themselves until they turn to the Lord and confess their sin. Often those who complain about not loving themselves are dissatisfied with their lives—their feelings, abilities, circumstances, and behavior. People love themselves even when they are not **feeling fond** of themselves.

From the "whole counsel of God," the love one naturally has toward self is commanded to be directed upward to God and outward to others. We are not commanded to love self. We already do. We are commanded to love others as much as we already love ourselves. The story of the Good Samaritan, which follows the commandment to love one's neighbor, illustrates not only who is our neighbor, but what is meant by the word *love.* Here love means to extend oneself beyond the point of convenience to accomplish what is deemed best for the neighbor. The idea is that we should seek the good of others just as fully as we seek good (or what we may want or even mistakenly think is good) for ourselves—just as naturally as we tend to care for our own personal well-being.

Another Scripture that parallels this same idea of loving others as we already do ourselves is Luke 6:31-35, which begins with: "And as ye would that men should do to you, do ye also to them likewise." Evidently Jesus assumed that His listeners wanted to be treated justly, kindly, and mercifully. In other words, they wanted to be treated according to expressions of love rather than expressions of indifference or animosity. They already loved themselves.

Biblical love for others comes **first** from God's love and then by responding in wholehearted love for Him (with all of one's heart, soul, mind and strength). And, one cannot do that unless he knows Him and is infused with His love and life. The Scripture says, "We love Him because He first loved us" (1 John 4:19). A person cannot truly love (*agapao*) God without first knowing His love by grace; and one cannot truly love neighbor as self without first loving God. The proper biblical position for a Christian is not to encourage, justify, or establish self-love, but rather to devote one's life to loving God and loving neighbor as self.

Jesus tells this story:

> Two men went up into the temple to pray; the one a Pharisee, and the other a publican. The Pharisee stood and prayed thus with himself, God, I thank thee, that I am not as other men are, extortioners, unjust, adulterers, or even as this publican. I fast twice in the week, I give tithes of all that I possess. And the publican, standing afar off, would not lift up so much as his eyes unto heaven, but smote upon his breast saying, God be merciful to me a sinner.

> I tell you, this man went down to his house justified rather than the other: for every one that exalteth himself shall be abased; and he that humbleth himself shall be exalted (Luke:18:10-14).

Which man exhibited high self-esteem? If Jesus had wanted to teach the importance of self-esteem He would have ended this parable differently. He would have justified the Pharisee and sent the poor publican to a local psychologist to build his self-esteem.

While popular Christian teachers encourage self-esteem,

self-worth, self-acceptance and thereby self-love, the Bible warns about the danger of having a fondness for oneself, of cherishing the self. Paul says:

> This know, also, that in the last days perilous times shall come. For men shall be lovers of their own selves, covetous, boasters, proud, blasphemers, disobedient to parents, unthankful, unholy, without natural affection, trucebreakers, false accusers, incontinent, fierce, despisers of those that are good, traitors, heady, high-minded, lovers of pleasures more than lovers of God, having a form of godliness, but denying the power thereof; from such turn away (2 Timothy 3:1-5).

Everything that follows "lovers of their own selves" originates from that self-love. Every adjective has to do with pleasing self and having one's own way rather than pleasing God and doing His will. The blatant marketing of self-love over the past thirty years has certainly contributed to the matching increase in illicit entertainment, materialism, teenage rebellion, fornication, rape, adultery, divorce, drunkenness, hatred of God, and other forms of pleasure-seeking self-centeredness (including so-called addictions).

The escalation in self-centered, self-pleasing crimes should be an obvious indictment on the increasing emphasis on self-love, self-esteem, self-acceptance, and self-seeking. Nevertheless, psychologists and educators continue to present self-esteem and self-love as the remedy for illegal drugs and illicit sex. They seem to ignore the fact that those social problems have increased proportionately to the increase in self-esteem and self-love teachings. And, at least one study links high self-esteem with heavy involvement in drugs.[37]

Paul says that lovers of themselves are covetous, not satisfied with what they have. And is this not at the root of sinful habits and sinful attitudes? Covetousness can include wanting more abilities, more significance, more love, more attention, more material possessions, and more pleasure. Covetousness does not disappear by acquiring more. The more a person's covetousness and lust are gratified, the more he wants until he becomes so covetous and lustful that normal means of finding pleasure no longer satisfy.

Boasting, another description of self-love, has also increased during the past few decades. And while pride always seems to hide in the depths of the soul, its outward expression is much more acceptable now than just a few decades ago. Richard Baxter of the seventeenth century wrote: "A proud mind is high in conceit, self-esteem, and carnal aspiring; a humble mind is high indeed in God's esteem, and in holy aspiring."[38] While psychologists would not want to be accused of encouraging blatant pride, their teachings on self-esteem and self-love make personal pride more acceptable and comfortable.

Often pride is difficult to detect because it hides behind hurts and false humility. Pride leads to unforgiveness, resentment, bitterness, revenge, and many other outward expressions of sin. Pride is one of the most insidious, self-deceptive forms of sin which lurks in the flesh, always ready to defend, justify, exonerate, and glorify the self. That is why the thrust of the Bible is upward to God and outward to each other, rather than inward to the self. In contrast, feelings of self-worth and self-esteem make fertile soil for the inborn roots of pride to flourish.

Paul describes "lovers of their own selves" as "unthankful, unholy," and "without natural affection." One of the prime teachings of the codependency/recovery movement is to disconnect from other people, especially parents and spouses. Rather than teaching the commandment to honor parents, those in "recovery" are encouraged to see their parents as the source of their present problems. And while some programs include forgiving the parents, few encourage gratitude to parents. Instead parents are being emotionally bashed and abandoned by their adult children. And, of course, separation and divorce are often modeled and recommended as part of the "recovery."

Perhaps one of the most devastating descriptions of "lovers of their own selves" and "lovers of pleasures more than lovers of God" is their "having a form of godliness but denying the power thereof." And this is exactly what happens in the codependency/recovery movement. They have turned to psychology to understand the human condition and to remedy the problems of living. Instead of having confidence in the sufficiency of the Word of God and the work of the Holy Spirit, they are "denying the power" of Christ working in and through believers.

In looking to such men as Freud, Skinner, Adler, Maslow, and Rogers, they have become "heady, highminded" in their knowledge of psychology. But worse than that, they are encouraging others to drink from the cistern of men's minds rather than from the pure water of the Word. There is something distinctly "unholy" about adding self-esteem and self-love to the teachings of Jesus. That is why Paul warns: "From such turn away."

Meekness and humility, not self-esteem or self-worth, were the credentials of those whom God used mightily. God chose a man devoid of self-esteem and self-confidence to deliver His people from bondage in Egypt. Moses was "very meek, above all the men which were upon the face of the earth" (Numbers 12:3). When God called Gideon to save Israel from the Midianites, Gideon protested, "Oh my Lord, wherewith shall I save Israel? Behold my family is poor in Manasseh, and I am the least in my father's house" (Judges 6:15). God called Job "a perfect and upright man" (Job 1:8). But when Job saw God face to face he cried out:

> I have heard of thee by the hearing of the ear: but now mine eye seeth thee. Wherefore I abhor myself, and repent in dust and ashes (Job 42:5-6).

There is no record of Jesus encouraging self-esteem or self-love. He commended the Canaanite woman, who referred to herself as a dog under the table eating the master's crumbs, and granted her request to heal her daughter (Matthew 15:27-28). Paul repudiated his past successes and called himself "less than the least of all saints" (Ephesians 3:8) and the chief of all sinners (1 Timothy 1:15). He was not preoccupied with himself, but with the Lord Jesus Christ. He counted it a privilege to suffer for Jesus' sake.

Throughout the ages, saints and Bible commentators have regarded self-esteem anathema. Jesus said, "Blessed are

the poor in spirit: for theirs is the kingdom of heaven"
(Matthew 5:3). Charles Spurgeon says that Jesus "is speaking
of a poverty of spirit, a lowliness of heart, an absence of self-
esteem."[39] Matthew Henry says that to be "poor in spirit" is:

> To be humble and lowly in our own eyes. To be *poor
> in spirit*, is to think meanly of ourselves, of what we
> are, and have, and do. . . . It is to acknowledge that
> God is great, and we are mean [lowly]; that he is
> holy and we are sinful; that he is all and we are
> nothing. . . . To come off from all confidence in our
> own righteousness and strength, that we may de-
> pend only upon the merit of Christ and the spirit
> and grace of Christ. That *broken and contrite spirit*
> with which the publican cried for mercy to a poor
> sinner, is the poverty of spirit. We must call our-
> selves poor, because we are always in want of God's
> grace. . . .[40] (Emphasis his.)

A. W. Tozer says:

> To be specific, the self-sins are these: self-righteous-
> ness, self-pity, self-confidence, self-sufficiency, self-
> admiration, self-love and a host of others like them.
> They dwell too deep within us and are too much a
> part of our natures to come to our attention till the
> light of God is focused upon them. The grosser
> manifestations of these sins, egotism, exhibitionism,
> self-promotion, are strangely tolerated in Christian
> leaders even in circles of impeccable orthodoxy. . . .
>
> One should suppose that proper instruction in the
> doctrine of man's depravity and the necessity for
> justification through the righteousness of Christ
> alone would deliver us from the power of the self-sins;
> but it does not work out that way. Self can live
> unrebuked at the very altar. . . .
>
> Self is the opaque veil that hides the Face of God
> from us. . . . . We must bring our self-sins to the cross
> for judgment.[41]

Does Anyone Love Too Much?

Clinical psychologist Dr. Margaret Rinck asks in her

book title, *Can Christians Love Too Much?* She believes they can. But it all depends on what one means by *love*. Rinck confuses quantity (too much) with quality by saying:

> When "love" turns into control and is used to man-
> age and manipulate others, then we are "loving too
> much." The children, spouses, relatives, and friends
> that we "love" in this way can easily get along with
> a bit less of our love.[42]

Is that truly love for others or is it the desire to have one's own way? We agree that people can and do mis-love both in how and what they love.

If the word *love* means desire, one can desire another person too much. In that case people may want more from a relationship than they are getting. That kind of love is an extension of self-love. Another extension of self-love is loving the world. The apostle John says:

> Love not the world, neither the things that are in
> the world. If any man love the world, the love of the
> Father is not in him. For all that is in the world, the
> lust of the flesh, and the lust of the eyes, and the
> pride of life, is not of the Father, but is of the world.
> (1 John 2:15-16.)

Rinck contends that Christians can love others too much in quantity as well. She says:

> Even when our love and affection is of a more au-
> thentic, self-sacrificing nature, it can still be a code-
> pendent excessive love. How is that possible?, you
> may ask. We love others "too much" when loving
> others causes us to chronically and severely neglect
> our own needs. This kind of love is out of balance. It
> is one thing for me to sacrifice *some* of my needs for
> an hour, a day, a week, or even for a lifetime. But
> when I neglect myself "for others" to the point that
> this becomes an unhealthy pattern of behavior, I
> begin to love too much.[43] (Emphasis hers.)

This describes the apostle Paul, who did **not** limit his active loving sacrifice to *some* of his needs. He was beaten many times, left for dead, shipwrecked, and went without food when necessary to take the gospel to the Gentiles. He rejoiced in the midst of suffering. He did not carefully "balance" his love by looking after his own needs. He obeyed the Lord, and he trusted God to take care of him either directly or through other Christians. But then, he wasn't into the late twentieth century self-love and self-esteem teachings.

Where is Rinck's biblical support for saying that Christians can love too much? She uses the example of Jesus withdrawing from the multitude for solitude and time with a "few close friends." Then she says that Jesus "understood that there is a necessary balance between loving others and loving oneself."[44] Where did Jesus teach this? We must ask, did Jesus love too much (codependently) when He went to the cross to rescue us? If He had wanted to teach the codependency/recovery message through example, He would have heeded his taunters and gotten down from the cross.

The key to ministry and even to love is obedience to the Lord. Jesus did not obey "needs." He obeyed the Father. Through His obedience, he met many needs, but the needs did not rule Him. The mistake of Christians is not that they love too much, but that they may not love God above all else. If our love and service are not for the Lord, we may indeed over-extend ourselves and excessively exhaust ourselves because we are not listening when He calls us aside to rest and to be nourished by His Word. If we are walking closely with the Lord we will not wantonly neglect His dwelling place, which we are. On the other hand, if we follow codependency/recovery teachings, we will tend to take care of ourselves for ourselves' sake rather than for the Lord.

Agapé Love.

While suffering may be involved as one loves biblically and self-sacrificially, biblical, self-sacrificing love is not a fault to be corrected. People suffer because of their own sin, sins of others, and general circumstances of living in a fallen world. They may also suffer for the cause of Christ. Whoever is in a difficult relationship needs to pray:

Search me, O God, and know my heart: try me, and

> know my thoughts: And see if there be any wicked
> way in me, and lead me in the way everlasting
> (Psalms 139).

Then if one's heart is clean concerning the problem, then he can look to Christ and follow His example. Furthermore, if the relationship is not bound by biblical law, as it is in marriage, it may either be mended biblically, as with another believer, according to Matthew 18, or it may be broken, especially if the other person is not a believer (2 Corinthians 6:14ff). If the relationship is binding, it may be that the Lord is calling a person to deny self and live sacrificially according to Jesus' example (Hebrews 12:1-4). Women have suffered through the ages, but rather than label them codependent and give them Twelve Steps, the Apostle Peter advised them to look to Christ (1 Peter 2-3).

There are also biblical parameters for suffering for Christ's sake. "For Christ's sake" would only include attitudes, words and actions that would be in obedience to the Word of God. Those who are under obedience to Christ will not be coerced into participating in known sin. The Word of God is a safeguard as a standard of judgment. Because it clarifies right from wrong, it wards off wrongful condemnation. And when sin is detected and confessed, Jesus forgives and cleanses.

God has an eternal goal in mind for each one of His children. While the purpose of mankind is to love God and enjoy Him forever, the goal is not personal happiness gained through loving self and working on feeling good. God's goal is to conform us to the image of Christ so that we may live in His presence forever "that He might show forth the exceeding riches of His grace in His kindness to us through Christ Jesus" (Ephesians 2:7). Christianity is relationship with God. It is true spiritual intimacy.

While we may endure suffering here, even in extremely difficult relationships, God's Word has promised this:

> And we know that all things work together for good
> to them that love God, to them who are the called
> according to his purpose. For whom he did fore-

> know, he also did predestinate to be conformed to
> the image of his Son, that he might be the firstborn
> among many brethren (Romans 8:28-29).

During suffering, spiritual agapé love grows in the life of the
believer.

> Therefore being justified by faith, we have peace
> with God through our Lord Jesus Christ: By whom
> also we have access by faith into this grace wherein
> we stand, and rejoice in hope of the glory of God.
> And not only so, but we glory in tribulations also:
> knowing that tribulation worketh patience; And
> patience, experience; and experience, hope: And
> hope maketh not ashamed; because the love of God
> is shed abroad in our hearts by the Holy Ghost
> which is given unto us (Romans 5:1-5).

Even in the midst of suffering, the believer can count on the
very presence of God, the enabling of the Holy Spirit, the
experience of love, and the fruit of God's life flowing through
him.

Sins Against Love.

But what about those people who call themselves Christians who are absolutely miserable in relationships that seem
to do them no good? What about those who have endured for
years and are sick and tired of trying so hard and doing all of
the work and putting up with other people's sins? And what
about those who are so preoccupied with the sins of their
spouses that their own lives are swallowed up by them? If the
problem which the codependence movement is attempting to
address is **not** loving the other person too much, what is it?
Problems in relationship have to do with sin.

What people in the midst of difficult relationships and
problems need is a fresh look at Jesus, a new relationship
with Him through salvation or a renewal in their love for Him
as believers. They need specific application of biblical principles in their lives. They need the change that only the Word
of God can bring:

> For the word of God is quick, and powerful, and

> sharper than any two-edged sword, piercing even to the dividing asunder of soul and spirit, and of the joints and marrow, and is a discerner of the thoughts and intents of the heart. Neither is there any creature that is not manifest in his sight: but all things are naked and opened unto the eyes of him with whom we have to do. (Hebrews 4:12-13.)

As the Word of God points out their own sin, they need not feel condemned. Jesus has come both to save and to forgive sinners.

Jesus is willing and ready to be our advocate before the Father:

> Seeing then that we have a great high priest, that is passed into the heavens, Jesus the Son of God, let us hold fast our profession. For we have not an high priest which cannot be touched with the feeling of our infirmities; but was in all points tempted like as we are, yet without sin. Let us therefore come boldly unto the throne of grace, that we may obtain mercy, and find grace to help in time of need. (Hebrews 4:14-16.)

Our own sins are the ones that separate us from the Father. Sins of bitterness, wrath, and unforgiveness eat away at our very souls. Our own sins make us far more miserable than the sins of others.

In addition, the Lord has given the means of seeking justice through church discipline. Jesus gives the guidelines for dealing with sins of others in Matthew 18. In following the progression of confronting sins committed against oneself, it may be necessary to institute church discipline against those who refuse to change. An excellent resource is Dr. Jay E. Adams' book *Handbook of Church Discipline*.[45]

Choose You This Day. . . .

There is a distinct difference between what the world offers (self enhanced) and what Jesus Christ gives and commands (self crucified). John Vasconcellos, the Assemblyman who authored the self-esteem legislation in California, sees the difference clearly. He says that there are two competing

visions in America today. One he describes as the old vision, a
theological one of man as sinner. He says it's the one he grew
up with. He says, "I had been conditioned to know myself
basically as a sinner, guilt-ridden and ashamed, constantly
beating my breast and professing my unworthiness."[46] Vasconcellos distorts Christianity and totally leaves out the Savior and the love of God. He rejects the doctrine of man as sinner and in need of a Savior and promotes the new psychological vision of man as perfectible on his own. To support this
new vision, he quotes humanistic psychologist Carl Rogers,
who says:

> You know, I've been practicing psychology for more
> than sixty years, and I have really come to believe
> that we human beings are innately inclined toward
> becoming constructive and life-affirming and respon-
> sible and trustworthy.[47]

Vasconcellos praises the goodness-and-trustworthiness-
of-man vision over the traditional sinfulness-of-man vision.
One is a humanistic, man-centered view, while the other is a
biblical, God-centered view. The humanistic, man-centered
view is the very foundation for the self-esteem movement.
Vasconcellos says:

> It is the latter vision—that human beings are in-
> nately inclined toward good and that free, healthy
> people become constructive and responsible—which
> underlies the philosophy and work of what has been
> called the "self-esteem movement." There is within
> this movement an implicit (and increasingly ex-
> plicit) intuition, an assumption—a faith, if you
> will—that an essential and operational relationship
> exists between self-esteem and responsible human
> behavior, both personal and social.[48]

Vasconcellos's words are enticing. On the surface they sound
very moral and even religious. Indeed, they are an expression
of the religion of secular humanism. But, his underlying philosophy and faith system oppose the gospel of Jesus Christ.

More clearly than the numerous Christian promoters of
self-esteem and codependency/recovery teachings, Vasconcel-

los sees the difference between the self-esteem movement he espouses and the form of Christianity which he forsook. And indeed the self-esteem movement and the codependency/recovery movement are contradictory to true Christianity. The man-made movements race toward the self; the other moves toward God.

Those who are of the world will naturally choose the way of the world, but Christ has called His disciples to another way, the way of the cross and the way of eternal life. Because of the heavy influence of the world through psychology, self-esteem doctrines, and Twelve-Step programs, Christians face a choice. Will they love themselves and the world or will they love the Lord with all their heart, soul, mind and strength?

4

TWELVE-STEP PROGRAMS
SIN OR SICKNESS?

The first Twelve-Step program was devised by Bill Wilson. Alcoholics Anonymous began in 1935 when Wilson and Dr. Bob Smith invented a road to sobriety. Three years later Wilson began work on a manuscript that would become known as the "Big Book" of Alcoholics Anonymous. Until the publication of the book, most of what was done in AA was by word of mouth. In codifying the system for the book, Wilson divided general principles of AA into Twelve Steps.

Wilson originally wrote the Twelve Steps for alcoholics (a convenient euphemism for *drunks*), but eventually others adopted and adapted the Steps in an effort to overcome their own addictions (a convenient euphemism for *lusts* and *habitual sins*). Later the Twelve Steps were applied to all those who lived with or worked with people with such addictions (*life-dominating sins*). Thousands of groups across America use Wilson's Twelve Steps, and most codependency/recovery programs utilize the Twelve Steps in one way or another. Some groups hold strictly to the Steps. Others use eclectic combinations of psychological theories along with the Twelve Steps. And all seem to merge the philosophy, psychology, and religion of the Twelve Steps into whatever treatment program they happen to have devised.

Because of the central importance of the Twelve Steps

and the religious philosophy of Alcoholics Anonymous to code-
pendency/recovery programs, we will devote the next eight
chapters to examining the Twelve Steps. Each Step will be
described in reference to AA and to the codependency/recov-
ery movement. In addition, the philosophy, psychology, and
religion intrinsic to each step will be discussed in reference to
the Bible and to research when applicable.

Step One: "We admitted we were powerless over
alcohol—that our lives had become unmanageable."[1]

Each step of the original Twelve Step program was in-
tended for heavy drinkers who had developed the destructive
habit of drunkenness. These were people whose lives were
dominated by alcohol and who therefore felt powerless to
quit. As a result, they were not managing their lives responsi-
bly, but instead they were focusing their efforts on obtaining
liquor to satisfy their all-encompassing habit.

The primary idea behind Step One is that of being powerless over alcohol. Bill Wilson wrote this step from his own
experience. After years of struggling with the guilt and condemnation that came from thinking that his drinking was his
own fault and that it stemmed from a moral defect in his
character, Wilson was relieved to learn from a medical doctor
that his drinking was due to an "allergy." Dr. William D.
Silkworth had hypothesized that "the action of alcohol on . . .
chronic alcoholics is a manifestation of an allergy." Wilson's
biography relates his response this way:

> Bill listened, entranced, as Silkworth explained his
> theory. For the first time in his life, Bill was hearing
> about alcoholism **not as a lack of will power, not
> as a moral defect, but as a legitimate illness**. It
> was Dr. Silkworth's theory—unique at the time—
> that alcoholism was the combination of this mysteri-
> ous physical "allergy" and the compulsion to drink;
> that alcoholism could no more be "defeated" by
> willpower than could tuberculosis. **Bill's relief was
> immense**.[2] (Emphasis added.)

The alcoholism-as-disease concept is strongly promoted
in AA literature. In the book *Alcoholics Anonymous* Wilson

stresses the importance of teaching prospective members that alcoholism is a disease. He says:

> Continue to **speak of alcoholism as an illness, a fatal malady**. Talk about the conditions of body and mind which accompany it. Keep his [the prospective proselyte's] attention focussed mainly on your personal experience. Explain that many are doomed who never realize their predicament.[3] (Emphasis added.)

Whereas admission of being a sinner, who is totally depraved and under the domination of sin, is involved in conversion to Christianity, the Step One of AA is the admission that the problem is **not** sin, but rather disease—that one is not under the domination of sin, as clearly stated in the Bible, but under the domination of a destructive disease. In answering the question, "What is an alcoholic?" one AA publication says that "the active alcoholic is just as much a sick person as is an individual with diabetes, tuberculosis or a cardiac condition."[4]

Step One thoroughly contains within it the belief that addiction to alcohol is a disease. Wilson amplifies on this in *Twelve Steps and Twelve Traditions*.[5] He says:

> The tyrant alcohol wielded a double-edged sword over us: first we were smitten by an insane urge that condemned us to go on drinking, and then by an allergy of the body that insured we would ultimately destroy ourselves in the process.[6]

The idea of having a disease which prohibits one from taking even one drink was a relief to Wilson and to others who had reached a point of utter hopelessness. However, the doctrine of being "powerless over alcohol" was not palatable to those who had not yet hit bottom. Wilson claims that was the reason why AA was small in the beginning.

However, with the rise in popularity of AA and the increasing confidence in the disease model, numerous people have joined AA and followed the Twelve Steps. After bemoaning the early years when "less desperate alcoholics tried AA, but did not succeed because they could not make the admission of hopelessness," Wilson says:

> It is a tremendous satisfaction to record that in the
> following years this changed. Alcoholics who still
> had their health, their families, their jobs, and even
> two cars in the garage, began to recognize their alco-
> holism. As this trend grew, they were joined by
> young people who were scarcely more than potential
> alcoholics.[7]

How did AA accomplish this? According to Wilson, they did
this by raising "the bottom the rest of us had hit to the point
where it would hit them," by telling their own stories, sharing
their beliefs, and warning others of the misery to come.[8]
Thus, rather than fully experiencing the pit of hopelessness,
many new members believed they were powerless over
alcohol by a simple act of faith.

And, indeed, such an admission is a statement of faith.
Wilson truly believed in the disease explanation for heavy
drinking. His "discoveries" and the development of AA were
tied to his own experience and faith. In 1944, just five years
after the publication of *Alcoholics Anonymous*, the American
Medical Association embraced Wilson's faith in alcoholism-as-
disease. That same year Wilson was invited to speak about
that "serious medical problem" at a New York State Medical
Society meeting.[9]

Behavior or Disease?

The influence of AA has been tremendous in promoting
the belief that habitual heavy drinking is a "disease" of alcoholism. In spite of the fact that there is no clear etiology for
the disease, most people now assume alcoholism is indeed a
disease. And, even though the Bible clearly refers to drunkenness as sin, most Christians have hopped onto the AA band-
wagon of faith and believe that habitual drunkenness is due
to a disease called "alcoholism" or "addiction" rather than to
sin. In fact AA's influence has been so pervasive and widespread that Christians and nonChristians alike believe that
addictions of all sorts are serious diseases to be treated rather
than sinful habits to be changed.

Dr. Herbert Fingarette, a professor at the University of California and an internationally distinguished scholar, has written a book titled *Heavy Drinking: The Myth of Alcoholism as a Disease.*[10] The subtitle tells what the book is about. Fingarette contends that "the public has been profoundly misled, and is still being actively misled." He says:

> The public has been kept unaware of a mass of scientific evidence accumulated over the past couple of decades, evidence familiar to researchers in the field, which radically challenges each major belief generally associated with the phrase "alcoholism is a disease."[11]

He suggests one reason for this ignorance:

> It is not surprising that the disease concept of alcoholism is now vigorously promoted by a vast network of lobbies, national and local, professional and volunteer, ranging from the most prestigious medical associations to the most crassly commercial private providers of treatment. This is big politics and big business.[12]

But the disease concept of alcoholism is not good science. Fingarette says, "The disease concept of alcoholism not only has no basis in current science; it has *never* had a scientific justification."[13] (Emphasis his.)

When does behavior become disease? Certainly some behavior is sickening and may be called "sick" in a metaphorical sense. And there are certain neurological/brain diseases that affect behavior. But does that mean behavior itself can be diseased? Millions in America think so and the behavior-called-disease industry has mushroomed. In fact, according to the new definitions, everyone could be accused of having some form of this disease by at least one psychological counselor, psychiatric social worker, or addiction treatment group.

While the Bible clearly states that "all have sinned, and come short of the glory of God" (Romans 3:23), our psychological society has substituted the word *sin* with *sickness*, so that all are sick and come short of their highest potential. The disease idea has moved from physical disorders to so-called mental illness and to a broad spectrum of addictions, which include those labeled "codependent," who are supposedly addicted to those who are addicted.

Stanton Peele graphically illustrates the insanity of calling behavior "disease" in his book *Diseasing of America: Addiction Treatment Out of Control.* He lists estimates of so-called experts to demonstrate how many people in our country suffer from such "diseases." Here are some of his approximate figures:

20 million addicted to alcohol
80 million suffering from coalcoholism
     (family members of alcoholics)
20 million addicted to gambling
80 million food related addictions
75 million addicted to tobacco
25 million addicted to love and/or sex[14]

According to this list, the number of people with addictions-called-diseases adds up to a whopping 300 million (obviously some people are multiply addicted). While we are not discussing each of these "addictions," it is important to note the danger of turning sexual sins (including rape and sexual abuse) into illnesses. Calling sexual sins "diseases" not only excuses behavior; it leaves people irresponsible and powerless. In fact, calling any of those so-called addictions "diseases" denudes the dignity of man created in the image of God.

Treatment Programs.

Authors, therapists, treatment centers, and Twelve-Step programs fuel the industry with propaganda and with new definitions of disease. Many feed their pockets through expensive treatment programs that have not yet proved themselves to be any more effective than no treatment at all. After reviewing the research, Fingarette claims that "the elaborate treatments for alcoholism as a disease have no measurable impact at all."[15] He says that while many who have been in the expensive treatment programs "fervently believe that they could never have been cured without the treatment," the research shows that:

> . . . the rates of improvement in these disease-oriented treatment programs (which cost between $5,000 and $20,000) do not significantly differ from the natural rates of improvement for comparable but untreated demographic groups.[16]

The real benefactors of such programs are the owners, administrators and share holders of the treatment centers and hospitals.

Peele says that addiction treatment programs "are regularly forced upon people, supposedly for their own good" and that people are "then **persuaded that they have a disease, often through group-pressure techniques that closely resemble brainwashing**." (Emphasis added.) And while such psychological professionals claim to help people, the research indicates that far more people get over these "diseases" without psychological treatment. Peele even argues that treatment serves as "an impediment to the normal process of 'maturing out' of addiction," especially among teenagers and young adults.[17]

The *Harvard Medical School Mental Health Review* did a special publication titled "Alcohol Abuse and Dependence." The authors say:

> Most recovery from alcoholism is **not** the result of treatment. Probably no more than 10 percent of alcohol abusers are ever treated at all, but as many as 40 percent recover spontaneously.[18] (Emphasis added.)

The research contradicts Wilson's unfounded claim that it is "a statistical fact that alcoholics almost never recovered on their own resources."[19]

According to Peele:

> What works in fact for alcoholism and addiction is giving people the options and values that rule out addictive drug use. Investing more in futile but expensive treatment programs simply subtracts from the resources that are available to influence people's actual environments in ways that can

reduce their vulnerability to addiction. . . . The head of the NIDA [National Institute on Drug Abuse], Charles Schuster, indicates that in treating drug addicts, "the best predictor of success is whether the addict has a job."[20]

And while AA and other treatment programs testify of great victories, we shall show later that research does not support their claims.

Is Disease the Answer?

In an essay published by Harvard University, Fingarette asks, "Why do heavy drinkers persist in their behavior even when prudence, common sense, and moral duty call for restraint?" Then he says:

> That is the central question in debates about alcohol abuse. In the United States (but not in other countries such as Great Britain) the standard answer is to call the behavior a disease, "alcoholism," whose key symptom is a pattern of uncontrollable drinking. This myth, now widely advertised and widely accepted, is neither helpfully compassionate nor scientifically valid. It promotes false beliefs and inappropriate attitudes, as well as harmful, wasteful, and ineffective social policies.[21]

Elsewhere he says:

> When the facts are confronted, what seems to be compassion done in the name of "disease" turns out to subvert the drinker's autonomy and will to change, and to exacerbate a serious social problem.
> . . . Certainly our current disease-oriented policies have not reduced the scale of the problem; in fact, the number of chronic heavy drinkers reported keeps rising.[22]

Peele says:

> In the area of addiction, what is purveyed as fact is usually wrong and simply repackages popular myths as if they were the latest scientific deduction.[23]

An example of repackaging popular myths can be seen in

books written for the Christian audience. In their book *Dying for a Drink*, Dr. Anderson Spickard and Barbara Thompson attempt to distinguish between an "alcohol abuser" and an "alcoholic." They say:

> While the alcohol abuser chooses to get drunk, the alcoholic drinks involuntarily. His will power is in service to his addiction and he cannot resist his craving for alcohol.[24]

By such a distinction, they think that they can say that "alcoholic abuse, or drunkenness, is clearly immoral" and that "the Bible forbids drunkenness altogether" and still maintain the idea that the alcoholic has a disease which must be treated. This idea is echoed by Overcomers Outreach (a Christian copy of AA). In one of their pamphlets, the directors, Bob and Pauline Bartosch, say:

> Though there are references to "drunkenness" in the Bible, nothing is ever mentioned about "addiction" or "alcoholism." Neither are there references to "cancer," "diabetes," or "heart disease," yet these brutal killers must be dealt with vigorously or the victim will die.[25]

This makes as much sense as saying that taking poison is a disease since the ingestion of the substance may cause death.

In attempting to distinguish alcoholism from drunkenness, they also attempt to remove it from the category of sinful behavior and put it in the same category with cancer. Like Spickard and Thompson, the Bartosches do this by distinguishing between an "alcohol abuser" who "*chooses* to get drunk" and the "alcoholic" who "drinks involuntarily because his willpower is in service to his addiction and the craving is so overwhelming that he *can't not drink*."[26] (Emphasis theirs.)

Does this mean that anyone who is under the domination of repeated sin in his life has a disease? Neither the Bible nor the rigors of scientific investigation have indicated that there is a difference between the sin of drunkenness and alcoholism or that alcoholism is a disease or even that an alcoholic "can't not drink." It may feel that way to habitual alcohol abusers who are under the domination of their own sin, but the research evidence does not support those myths.

While the myths of alcoholism-as-disease continue to parade as facts, Dr. Herbert Fingarette reports:

> The United States Supreme Court, after reviewing detailed briefs pro and con, has consistently held in favor of those who say that alcoholics are responsible for their behavior, and has concluded that medical evidence does not demonstrate their drinking to be involuntary.[27]

In view of the research he says:

> Alcoholics do not "lack control" in the ordinary sense of those words. Studies show that they can limit their drinking in response to appeals and arguments or rules and regulations. In experiments they will reduce or eliminate drinking in return for such rewards as money, social privileges, or exemption from boring tasks. To object that these experiments are invalid because they occur in protected settings is to miss the point, which is precisely that the drinking patterns of alcoholics can vary dramatically in different settings.[28]

Nevertheless, strong proponents of AA firmly believe they are not responsible for their drinking because they have a disease and that their Twelve-Step program is essential to sobriety.

Is there an Addictive Personality?

Since no "allergy" or any other physical agent or other malady has been proved to cause habitual drunkenness, other theories have been developed. One of them is that there is an "addictive personality." There have been mixed results on research about the so-called addictive personality, but the bottom line is this: "there's no such thing as an addictive personality."[29]

The Harvard Medical School Mental Health Letter says:

> Now it has become clear that there is no single type of addictive or dependence-prone personality, and no personality traits that reliably indicate in ad-

vance who is likely to use or misuse drugs.[30]

The report continues:

> According to the most reliable studies, the great majority of alcoholics do not develop the disorder because they are anxious, depressed, victims of child abuse, or emotionally unstable. They tend to be active and self-confident as children and adolescents. Most alcoholics have no personality disorder or other psychiatric disorder before they become dependent. . . . Depressed people in general do not have a high rate of alcoholism..[31]

On the other hand, a study of Swedish children examined at age 11 and again at age 27 indicated that "the children most likely to become alcohol abusers are relatively fearless, constantly in search of novelty, and relatively indifferent to other people's opinions of them."[32] This seems to fly in the face of the prevalent myth that people become addicts because they have low self-esteem.

Is Alcoholism in the Genes?

Even though there is no "addictive personality," could alcoholism be inherited? Peele says:

> In the case of alcoholism, the inability to control one's drinking is today described as an inherited trait. This is wrong. In fact, even biologically-oriented research has shown that loss of control is not an inheritable trait, as A.A. originally claimed. Rather. . . researchers see alcoholism as the cumulative result of a long history of drinking.[33]

Many believe that it's all in the genes. Because research was being conducted, people assumed there was a link. Unfortunately too many people stated the possibility as a fact. For instance in her book *Can Christians Love Too Much*, Dr. Margaret Rinck states decisively (but erroneously):

> In the case of alcoholism, there is a clear genetic predisposition which sets people up for this problem.[34]

As with many authoritative-sounding statements she makes, Rinck gives no research evidence, **because there is none**.

While there has been research into the possibility of genetic involvement in alcoholism, nothing had been conclusive until recently. But now the research results are in and they do **not** reveal any genetic involvement in alcoholism! An article in *Psychiatric News* sums up the research conducted by the National Institute of Alcohol Abuse and Alcoholism:

> Contrary to data reported last April, the new study revealed no significant difference in the number of alcoholics or nonalcoholic control subjects who carried the A1 allele, the form of the dopamine receptor gene touted as the genetic link to alcoholism in the earlier study.[35]

The researchers concluded: "This study does not support a widespread or consistent association between the D_2 receptor gene and alcoholism."[36]

In spite of those clear results, many people will continue to believe the gene theory. Whenever research is being done to support an already held belief, many jump to conclusions too fast. And that is what happened in the early genetic research having to do with alcoholism. Later follow-up research simply does not support the earlier claims.

Dr. Richard J. Frances, member of the American Psychiatric Association Council on Addiction Psychiatry, urges researchers to exercise caution in even talking about their research before the results are established. He says that "we are in danger of losing our credibility when findings are rushed into print without sufficient review."[37] But, he may have little to worry about since news coverage is usually minor when such widely believed myths are exploded by follow-up research. Only his colleagues who read the professional journals might notice the scandal. By now nearly everyone erroneously believes there is some genetic link to alcoholism vulnerability. To refute that belief will take more than extensive scientific research. It will require a giant shift in faith.

Dangers of Calling Behavior a Disease.

Calling alcoholism a disease when it is not a disease is not simply a matter of semantics. There is a very serious possibility that those who treat such "diseases" are doing more harm than good by calling addictions and other related behaviors diseases. Peele says:

> By revising notions of personal responsibility, our disease conceptions undercut moral and legal standards exactly at a time when we suffer most from a general loss of social morality. While we desperately protest the growth of criminal and antisocial behavior, disease definitions undermine the individual's obligations to control behavior and to answer for misconduct. . . . **Disease notions actually increase the incidence of the behaviors of concern.** They legitimize, reinforce, and excuse the behaviors in question—convincing people, contrary to all evidence, that their behavior is not their own. Meanwhile, the number of addicts and those who believe they cannot control themselves grows steadily.[38] (Emphasis added.)

Fingarette says:

> It is not compassionate to encourage drinkers to deny their power to change, to excuse them legally and give them special government benefits that foster a refusal to confront the need to change. Alcoholics are not helpless; they can take control of their lives. In the last analysis, alcoholics must *want* to change and *choose* to change.[39] (Emphasis his.)

Besides the problems cited by Fingarette and Peele, calling behavior "disease" has a number of problems and consequences from a biblical perspective. The Bible identifies behavior as sinful or not sinful. Sinful behavior is also called the "works of the flesh." Drunkenness is listed among the works of the flesh along with a number of other behaviors. Paul lists them in Galatians 5:19-21:

> Adultery, fornication, uncleanness, lasciviousness, idolatry, witchcraft, hatred, variance, emulations, wrath, strife, seditions, heresies, envyings, murders, drunkenness, revellings, and such like.

Is drunkenness a "disease"? Is adultery a "disease"? Or idolatry or wrath or murder? If Christians relabel those behaviors as diseases, they are saying that the Bible is not true, that it is antiquated and does not adequately address drunkenness and other problems of living. They are, in effect, calling God a liar.

In past centuries addictions were looked upon as sinful habits. Jesus came to save people from their sin and to enable them to overcome sinful behavior. Nevertheless, Christians are turning away from biblical words (*drunkenness* and *sin*) and embracing worldly words (*alcoholism* and *addictions*) and the disease mentality. In doing so they are following the ways of the world pointed out by Dr. Thomas Szasz in his book *The Myth of Psychotherapy*:

> . . . with the decline of religion and the growth of science in the eighteenth century, the cure of (sinful) souls, which had been an integral part of the Christian religions, was recast as the cure of (sick) minds, and became an integral part of medical science.[40]

The words *sinful* and *sick* are in the original quote and show the shocking shift from the cure of souls (ministering the gospel of Jesus Christ) to the cure of minds (using psychological notions of men).

Because most Christian leaders already believe the myths of psychotherapy, there are few who have not bought into the Alcoholics Anonymous mentality and a Twelve-Step world view. Christian books on alcoholism (not called "drunkenness") and other addictions (not called "sinful habits") copy the world in both diagnosis and treatment, except that they engage God in their worldly explanations and admonitions.

Peele warns:

> Disease conceptions of misbehavior are bad science and are morally and intellectually sloppy. Biology is not behavior, even in those areas where a drug or alcohol is taken into the body. Alcoholism involves a host of personal and environmental considerations

aside from how alcohol affects the bodies of drinkers. Furthermore, once we treat alcoholism and addiction as disease, we cannot rule out that anything
people do but shouldn't is a disease, from crime to
excessive sexual activity to procrastination.[41]

With "anything people do but shouldn't" labeled
"disease," those who oppose Christianity may very well call
prayer, worship, reading the Bible, faith in Jesus Christ, and
obeying the Lord "diseases" or symptoms of a religious "disease." The organization Fundamentalists Anonymous is
based upon the idea that conservative Christianity (believing
that Jesus is the only way and that the Bible is the inerrant
Word of God) is a serious, debilitating addiction. Unfortunately, the three Christian authors of *Love Is a Choice* have listed
this anti-Christian organization at the end of their book with
this recommendation: "Seek them out locally."[42]

The psychotherapeutic and addiction industries and
Twelve-Step groups are proliferating so rapidly that nearly
every citizen may someday join the ranks of patients and/or
addicts whether he wants to or not. George Orwell's *Nineteen
Eighty-Four* predictions of control through the Ministry of
Love may come true a decade later than he thought, but they
are on the horizon. In commenting on Orwell's book in 1983,
psychology professor Dr. Philip Zimbardo says:

> The current practitioners in our Ministry of Love
> come from the ranks of the mental health establish-
> ment (psychiatry and my own field, psychology),
> social welfare agencies, education and business.[43]

Addiction treatment centers and Twelve-Step groups must
now be added to that list.

By embracing worldly ideas, Christians have put aside
their armor. They have left themselves vulnerable, not only to
temptation, but also to deceptions and weakness. Many no
longer resist sin because they have relabeled it "disease."
They feel helpless and overwhelmed without the help of addiction priests and their recovery gospel. Moreover, they lay
themselves open to becoming captives of a world system that,
underneath all the fine rhetoric, hates Jesus Christ and all

who would follow Him to the cross.

Christians become friends with the world when they follow its psychological theories to understand themselves and others and to change behavior. They are friends of the world when they call sinful behavior "mental illness" and sinful habits "diseases." I John 2:15-16 says:

> Love not the world, neither the things that are in the world. If any man love the world, the love of the Father is not in him. For all that is in the world, the lust of the flesh, and the lust of the eyes, and the pride of life, is not of the Father, but is of the world.

James 4:4 says that whoever "will be a friend of the world is the enemy of God."

In an article in *The Journal of Biblical Ethics in Medicine*, Dr. Robert Maddox warns:

> When man defines disease, alcoholism becomes a disease. Then all manner of sin is labeled as disease, to be cured with chemical, electrical and mechanical treatments. Any sinful habit, from gluttony to fornication, from stealing to bestiality, can become a disease. Now even normal and good functions, such as conception and pregnancy, are seen as diseases. Fulfilling one's calling before God as a wife and homemaker has even been viewed as disease.[44]

One psychologist/critic adds, "When you look at the 'recovery movement,' you see a mass audience turning childhood into an illness you recover from."[45]

Fingarette says:

> I just don't understand why any churches would go for the disease idea, except insofar as they are taken by the notion that we have to be enlightened and that seems to be the enlightened view. The disease approach denies the spiritual dimension of the whole thing. People in the church may be afraid to take a different stand because it will be labeled antiscientific, antimodern, or old-fashioned. I think that's all misguided.[46]

Dr. John MacArthur is not afraid to take a different

stand. He objects to attempts to integrate psychological theories and therapies with the Bible and thereby treat sin as sickness. He says:

> The depth to which sanctified psychotherapy can sink is really quite profound. A local newspaper recently featured an article about a thirty-four-bed clinic that has opened up in Southern California to treat "Christian sex addicts." (The reason for the beds in this kind of clinic escapes me.) According to the article, the clinic is affiliated with a large well-known Protestant church in the area.[47]

He goes on to say that the center's director describes the staff as "real pioneers" and "all legitimate, licensed psychotherapists who happen to have a strong Christian orientation to therapy." MacArthur then poses this question: "Does their 'Christian' orientation happen to be solid enough to allow these psychotherapists to admit that lasciviousness is sin?" He responds to his own question by saying:

> Evidently not. Several were interviewed for the article. They consistently used the terms *illness*, *problem*, *conflict*, and *compulsive behavior*, *treatment*, and *therapy*. Words with moral overtones were carefully avoided. Sin and repentance were never mentioned.[48]

MacArthur continues:

> Worse, these so-called experts scoffed at the power of God's Word to transform a heart and break the bondage of sexual sin. The article quoted the center's program director, who explained why he believes his treatment center specifically for Christians is so crucial: "There are some groups of Christians who believe the Bible is all you need."[49]

MacArthur declares:

> That statement is the echo of neo-gnosticism. Belittling those who believe the Bible is sufficient, these latter-day "clouds without water" (Jude 12) insist they are privy to a higher, more sophisticated secret knowledge that holds the real answer to what

troubles the human soul. Don't be intimidated by their false claims. **No higher knowledge, no hidden truth, nothing besides the all-sufficient resources that we find in Christ exists that can change the human heart.**[50] (Emphasis added.)

The Codependent and Step One.

Step One is no longer limited to heavy drinkers. Step One is available to everyone. Just substitute the word *alcohol* with any other noun that might fit and *voila!* It's transformed into a disease. Along with AA and its Twelve-Step program comes a host of other "diseases," and "codependency" is one of the most popular. In this case, it is not a physical disease caused by a so-called "allergy." Instead, it falls into the ever-expanding category of mental illness with such so-called psychological symptoms as compulsions, repression, denial, and low self-esteem.[51] One writer quips, "So pervasive is the 'illness' of codependency that if you are not in recovery, are not a survivor, then you must still be in the throes of the disease, or in denial."[52]

If a person refuses to fall in line with Step One, the addiction priests and groupies would no doubt consider the reason to be denial and/or repression. And by this, they could very well be referring to unconscious denial, the Freudian ego-defense mechanism by which a person supposedly protects himself from pain by unconsciously refusing to see the truth about himself or his circumstances. And indeed, two of the so-called symptoms of codependency are repression and denial. This theory presupposes an unconscious that directs and motivates behavior unbeknownst to the person. Such an unconscious (Freudian) has never been proved by scientific research. Moreover, there is nothing in the Bible that supports a Freudian unconscious.

The very fact that the Bible speaks to conscious volition in matters of motivation and conduct refutes psychological theories of unconscious motivation. While a person may intentionally avoid facing the truth and while a person may be deceived because of his own sinfulness, he is held responsible for both his motivation and his behavior.

Once again sin is recast as illness, and as with other so-called mental illnesses, the professionals decide what is illness by majority opinion. Some professionals label codependency as disease, but others do not, even though they consistently refer to "healthy" and "unhealthy" relationships rather than God-honoring or sinful relationships. Some psychologists rank codependency among compulsive disorders and take such individuals through endless hours of therapy.[53]

Built on premises of Al-Anon and first applied to spouses of alcoholics who supposedly enter into an addictive relationship with the alcoholic, the diagnosis of codependency is now freely applied to thousands of people who may have a less-than-perfect relationship with parents, spouse, children, friends, or co-workers. However, there is some confusion over what exactly is the addictive agent. CoDA (Co-dependents Anonymous) replaces the word *alcohol* with *others*. They have reworded the AA Step One to say: "We admitted we were powerless over others—that our lives had become unmanageable."[54]

The authors of *Serenity: A Companion for Twelve Step Recovery* list descriptive phrases as the "addictive agents." Among their "catalog of addictive agents" they list: "Control addictions, especially if they surface in personal, sexual, family, and business relationships," "Approval dependency (the need to please people)," "Rescuing patterns toward other persons," and "Dependency on toxic relationships (relationships that are damaging and hurtful)."[55] They have taken behaviors that are popularly used to describe "codependents" and made them "addictive agents" equal to alcohol. A major target of their remarks in *Serenity* is the so-called "codependent." *Serenity* includes the New Testament laced with unbiblical codependency/recovery psychology and religion. This insidious implantation of psychological notions and Twelve-Step religious ideas into the Bible severely undermines the Scriptures.

Either way, whatever the substituted "addictive agent" is, Step One relieves the Twelve-Step believer from both responsibility and guilty feelings. While it is true that people in sinful relationships may be powerless to influence or change other people, Step One may actually give license to excuse oneself from certain genuine responsibilities and valid commitments. Believing oneself to be powerless over such so-called "addictive agents" as listed above may also serve to exonerate self from responsibility to others. Furthermore, certain sinful activities attributed to the so-called codependent are seen as symptoms of a condition requiring recovery rather than sin to be repented of.

In her sequel to *Women Who Love Too Much*, Robin Norwood contends that addiction "of all kinds" is "never immoral but simply amoral." Because she sees addiction as disease she believes that addiction "is not right or wrong any more than cancer is right or wrong."[56]

According to the Twelve-Step system, when the person admits being powerless over others or over responses to the actions of others, he is not guilty, but helpless. How can anything be a person's sin or fault if he is powerless to do anything constructive in the relationship? After all, it's an addiction! By coupling this with blaming another person, one can exonerate oneself from guilt. Saying the addiction made me do it is even more convenient and sophisticated than saying, "The devil made me do it."

By claiming to be powerless, one can wash one's own hands and walk away scot-free. Thus the admission of powerlessness over the so-called "addictive agent" empowers a person by relieving him from guilt and responsibility. Thus relieved of some guilt feelings—exonerated by it not being "my fault" but the addiction's fault—the person is supposedly free to do something about the so-called addiction. This is very similar to humanistic psychological theories that say that even though society has caused a person to be a certain way, he can change himself if he gets in touch with his real self. In fact, most of the material written on addiction and codependency repeats the humanistic lie that man is born good and that inside each person is a pure core, an innocent (yea, holy) child, which is a source of trustworthy wisdom and truth.

If a person's behavior is due to an addiction disease, it

needs healing. Thus the disease mentality takes over and recovery is the goal. Even though he has been a victim through codependency, he can extricate self by refusing to be responsible for others. Therefore recovery is all about taking care of self, loving self, and being good to self. And it's available to everyone. Beattie says: "You don't have to be in a lot of trouble to recognize unmanageability and begin recovering from codependency."[57]

A Dangerous Counterfeit.

Step One is a dangerous counterfeit for both Christians and nonChristians. It serves as a substitute for acknowledging one's own depravity, sinful acts, and utter lostness apart from Jesus Christ, the only savior, and the only way to forgiveness (relief of true guilt). Step One is also a substitute for Christians to acknowledge that without the life of the Lord Jesus Christ in them, they are unable to live righteously. Apart from Christ in them, they are unable to please God.

Many Christians attempt to make Step One coincide with biblical confession. But they generally substitute powerlessness for sinfulness and admit a life that has become unmanageable without confessing disobedience. In fact, most of the popular codependency/recovery books indicate that feeling guilty is the last thing a codependent needs.

Step One is too broad a step and misses the mark. Instead of leading directly to Jesus as the way to salvation and eternal life, it leads anywhere that might please the self. Jesus said:

> Enter ye in at the strait gate: for wide is the gate, and broad is the way that leadeth to destruction, and many there be which go in thereat: Because strait is the gate, and narrow is the way, which leadeth unto life, and few there be that find it (Matthew 7:13-14).

When the Holy Spirit reveals a person's condition of total depravity to him and convicts him of sin, that person realizes he is undone and needs a Savior. When the Holy Spirit convicts a Christian of sin, the Christian realizes that he has been operating according to the flesh rather than living by faith in Christ and walking in the Spirit.

Instead of teaching people to admit powerlessness over an "addictive agent" that has produced an unmanageable life, the Bible indicates that all are powerless to please God. Paul is very clear about this in his letter to the Romans:

> For they that are after the flesh do mind the things of the flesh; but they that are after the Spirit the things of the Spirit. For to be carnally minded is death; but to be spiritually minded is life and peace. Because the carnal mind is enmity against God: for it is not subject to the law of God, neither indeed can be. So then they that are in the flesh cannot please God. (Romans 8:5-8.)

This is an indictment upon the entire human race, and it goes entirely against the popular humanistic notion that all are born good and that society spoils them.

By God's law, all are guilty. Before a person is converted to Jesus Christ, he is under the domination of sin, whether he acts it out in sinful habits of substance abuse or in other sinful ways. Nevertheless, such a pronouncement of guilt does not have to lead to hopelessness or helplessness. Instead it should lead to Christ. Paul explains in his letter to the Galatians:

> But the scripture hath concluded all under sin, that the promise by faith of Jesus Christ might be given to them that believe. But before faith came, we were kept under the law, shut up unto the faith which should afterwards be revealed. Wherefore the law was our schoolmaster to bring us unto Christ, that we might be justified by faith. But after that faith is come, we are no longer under a schoolmaster. For ye are all the children of God by faith in Christ Jesus. For as many of you as have been baptized into Christ have put on Christ. (Galatians 3:22-27.)

Therefore faith in Christ is the answer to all problems of sin, whether in relationships or substance abuse or whatever the complexity of sinning, being sinned against, and responding sinfully. Jesus Christ is the answer and faith in Him is the way out of hopelessness, helplessness, powerlessness, and sinfulness. Jesus empowers believers to overcome sin and to please God.

How grievous it is when hopeless and despairing people are sent to something or someone other than the One who is our only Hope! Is the Good News of Jesus Christ only for those who are suffering mild problems? While a person may gain temporary advantage through various programs that offer something else besides Jesus Christ and Him crucified, there will be dreadful loss in the long run. Jesus Himself declared: "I am the way, the truth, and the life; no man cometh unto the Father, but by me" (John 14:6).

5

TWELVE-STEP
RELIGIONS

Step Two: "Came to believe that a Power greater than ourselves could restore us to sanity."[1]

Step Two of Alcoholics Anonymous also came from Bill Wilson's personal experience and his own world view. Coming to Step One was actually a relief for him. His medical doctor, William D. Silkworth, had convinced him that his addiction was caused by an allergy. Wilson believed he could not help his drinking. It was a "disease" over which he was powerless. The same doctor had told him that his drinking would kill him within a couple of years.

When Wilson completed the drying out treatment at Towns Hospital in New York, he believed his problem was solved. He had been relieved of guilt for moral failure and he had been diagnosed as having an allergy. The cure was simple. Just don't take another drink. Nevertheless, his confidence in his newly found sobriety did not last long.[2]

When Wilson returned to Towns Hospital, Silkworth informed Mrs. Wilson:

> I though he might be one of the very few. But this habit of drinking has now turned into an obsession, one much too deep to be overcome, and the physical effect of it on him has also been very severe, for he's showing signs of brain damage. . . . Actually I'm

fearful for his sanity if he goes on drinking.

When Mrs. Wilson asked what that meant for his future, Silkworth is reported to have said: "It means that you will have to confine him, lock him up somewhere if he would remain sane or even alive. He can't go on this way another year, possibly."[3]

In describing his own plight, Wilson said:

> I thought over my past life. How and why could I have come to this? Save for my drinking, Lois and I had had a wonderful life together. My whole career had teemed with excitement and interest. And yet here I was, bedeviled with an obsession that **condemned me to drink against my will** and a bodily sensitivity that guaranteed early insanity at best.[4] (Emphasis added.)

Thus, in spite of his relief that his excessive drinking was not his fault, but rather due to an illness, Wilson felt doomed. The disease diagnosis was insufficient without a cure. He left the hospital "terror-stricken." He recalls, "By dint of the greatest vigilance, I stayed sober some weeks." Nevertheless he began drinking again and "settled hopelessly and without heart into a sort of bottomless bingeing."[5]

It was during this bleak time that Wilson received a phone call from an "old drinking buddy," Ebby Thatcher. They hadn't seen each other for five years and Thatcher seemed like a new man. When Wilson asked him why he wasn't drinking and why he seemed so different, Thatcher replied, "I've got religion."[6] Wilson describes it this way:

> He told me how he had got honest about himself and his defects, how he'd been making restitution where it was owed, how he'd tried to practice a brand of giving that demanded no return for himself. . . . Then, very dangerously, he touched upon the subject of prayer and God. He frankly said he expected me to balk at these notions.[7]

Then Thatcher told Wilson that when he had prayed God released him from the desire to drink and filled him with "peace of mind and happiness of a kind he had not known for years."[8] Thatcher had joined the Oxford Group, a popular religious movement of the day.[9]

Wilson was uncomfortable with Thatcher's testimony. Yet he desired Thatcher's freedom from alcohol. Thus he accompanied Thatcher to a rescue meeting and was moved by the testimonials. He says:

> There were hymns and prayers. Tex, the leader, exhorted us. Only Jesus could save, he said. Certain men got up and made testimonials. Numb as I was, I felt interest and excitement rising. Then came the call. Penitents started marching forward to the rail. Unaccountably impelled, I started, too. . . . Soon, I knelt among the sweating, stinking penitents.[10]

Wilson excitedly started speaking and giving some kind of testimony. Thatcher thought Wilson had given his life to God, but another person saw things quite differently—that others had tried to restrain Wilson, but that he had insisted on interrupting the meeting. Rather than giving his life to God, Wilson had told about Thatcher getting help at the mission. At the end of the meeting Wilson agreed to return to Towns Hospital. Several from the Oxford Group said they would meet with him there. But instead of going to the hospital right away, Wilson drank for several more days until he reached a point of great agony and hopelessness (the full intensity of Step One). He then returned to the hospital for detoxification.[11]

Religious Roots of AA.

Wilson's religious experience occurred at the hospital. He deeply desired the sobriety his friend from the Oxford Group had, but Wilson still "gagged badly on the notion of a Power greater than myself." Up to the last moment Wilson resisted the idea of God. Nevertheless, at this extreme point of agony, alone in his room, he cried out, "If there is a God, let Him show Himself! I am ready to do anything, anything!" [12] Because Wilson believed he was helplessly afflicted by a dread disease, he cried out to God as a helpless victim, not a sinner. He had already been absolved from guilt through

Silkworth's allergy theory. Therefore he approached God from the helpless but righteous stance of a victim, suffering the agony of his affliction, and commanded God to show Himself.

Here is Wilson's description of his experience:

> Suddenly, my room blazed with an indescribably white light. I was seized with an ecstasy beyond description. Every joy I had known was pale by comparison. The light, the ecstasy—I was conscious of nothing else for a time.[13]

He saw an internal vision of a mountain with a clean wind blowing through him. He sensed a great peace and was "acutely conscious of a Presence which seemed like a veritable sea of living spirit." He saw this as "shores of a new world" and concluded that "This must be the great reality. The God of the preachers."[14] He said:

> For the first time, I felt that I really belonged. I knew that I was loved and could love in return. I thanked my God, who had given me a glimpse of His absolute self. Even though a pilgrim upon an uncertain highway, I need be concerned no more, for I had glimpsed the great beyond.[15]

The experience had a profound effect on Wilson. From that point on he believed in the existence of God and he stopped drinking alcohol.

While this experience included God **as Bill Wilson understood Him**, there is no mention of faith in the substitutionary sacrifice of Jesus Christ and salvation from sin based upon Jesus' death on the cross. Rather than attempting to understand his experience in the light of the Bible, Wilson turned to William James's book *The Varieties of Religious Experience*, which had been recommended by a member of the Oxford Group.[16]

Philosopher-psychologist William James (1842-1910) was intrigued with mystical, existential experiences people reported to him. He contended that such experiences were superior to any religious doctrine.[17] James did not care about the religious persuasion of mystics as long as they achieved a personal experience. He was fascinated by what people experienced through mysticism. He says:

> In mystic states we both become one with the Absolute and we become aware of our oneness. This is the everlasting and triumphant mystical tradition, hardly altered by differences of clime or creed. In Hinduism, in Neoplatonism, in Sufism, in Christian mysticism, in Whitmanism, we find the same recurring note, so that **there is about mystical utterances an eternal unanimity**. . . .[18] (Emphasis added.)

It is easy to see how such a description fit Bill Wilson's experience. Besides the description itself being similar, Wilson found that he could relate to James' case histories. The mystical experiences reported by James also followed calamity, admission of defeat, and "an appeal to a Higher Power."[19] The official AA biography of Wilson says:

> James gave Bill the material he needed to understand what had just happened to him—and gave it to him in a way that was acceptable to Bill. Bill Wilson, the alcoholic, now had his spiritual experience ratified by a Harvard professor, called by some *the* father of American psychology![20] (Emphasis in original.)

Most people assume that the founders of Alcoholics' Anonymous were Christians. In fact, the Christian authors of *Love Is a Choice* make this naive assumption:

> Although the first AA workers themselves knew God intimately, they felt that in some way they had to sidestep this bitterness [of other alcoholics] toward God by using the phrase "God as I understand him" in their now-famous twelve steps.[21]

Unless they are speaking of some anonymous workers other than Wilson and Smith, they are wrong. Where is a confession of faith in Jesus Christ as exclusive Savior and Lord? One wonders how anyone who knows God intimately would not identify who He is. The apostle Paul declared:

> For I am not ashamed of the gospel of Christ: for it is the power of God unto salvation to every one that believeth; to the Jew first, and also to the Greek.

> For therein is the righteousness of God revealed
> from faith to faith: as it is written, the just shall live
> by faith. (Romans 1:16-17.)

Surely Paul spoke with many people who were antagonistic
toward God.

On one hand there is some basis for assuming that Wilson was a Christian because of his general references to God,
prayer, and morality, and because he and Bob Smith had
both attended meetings of the Oxford Group which claimed to
be like the early church. However, Jesus Christ as Lord and
Savior is absent from Wilson's spiritual experience. There is
no mention of Jesus Christ providing the only way of
salvation through paying the price for Bill Wilson's sin.
Wilson's faith system was not based on Jesus Christ and Him
crucified. Nor is there any mention of Jesus Christ being Lord
of his life.

Influence of the Oxford Group.

Both Wilson and Smith were members of the Oxford
Group and did their early work within that movement. Wilson's group, later called Alcoholics Anonymous, separated
from the Oxford Group because of disagreements over Wilson
holding his own meetings. However, one can see the influence
of the Oxford Group on the development of AA. Wilson
describes the Oxford Group this way:

> The Oxford Group was a nondenominational evan-
> gelical movement, **streamlined for the modern
> world** and then at the height of its very consider-
> able success. . . . They would deal in simple **com-
> mon denominators of all religions** which would
> be potent enough to change the lives of men and
> women.[22] (Emphasis added.)

Thus it was an ecumenical movement which used the "common denominators of all religions" rather than the exclusive
way of the cross of Christ.

In 1921 Frank Buchman, a Lutheran pastor, created the
Oxford Group, which he originally called the First Century
Christian Fellowship. Although it was called Christian, it was

based on experience rather than biblical doctrine. William Irvine, in his book *Heresies Exposed* reports:

> A Christian business man had a long talk on doctrine with Dr. Buchman, who professed to believe in every fundamental doctrine. However, he says, Dr. Buchman explained, *he never touched any doctrine in any of his meetings, as he did not want to upset or offend anyone.*[23] (Emphasis his.)

By keeping his doctrinal beliefs to himself, Buchman was able to appeal to people of all religious persuasions.

Rather than denying or denouncing biblical doctrines, the Oxford Group Movement cleverly avoided and evaded doctrinal issues. For instance, the group neither denied nor asserted such essential doctrines as the blood atonement of Jesus Christ. In his book *The Oxford Group Movement—Some Evaluations*, R. Wright Hay, Secretary of the Bible League in Great Britain, reports:

> I had a three hours' talk with Mr. Buchman, seeking to get at what he really believed himself. . . . Never once during those three hours did Dr. Buchman mention the blood of Christ. I have attended meetings in connection with the Movement in which men who imagined that they had received help through the Movement have given their testimony. Not one of them, in my hearing, made any mention of the blood of Christ.[24]

Hay declared, "The Movement is anti-Christian because it is non-Biblical."[25]

Instead of biblical doctrine, the Oxford Group Movement majored in personal experience, group sharing, channeled guidance, and testimonies. Rather than evaluating subjective experience with biblical doctrine, the Group developed its own subjective teachings. A group of clergy at Oxford (England) expressed their concern about the Oxford Group in a joint letter published in 1932. They said:

> . . . we find ourselves unable to approve some of their principal doctrines which have led to disastrous consequences in several cases known to us. . . .

In our opinion they dangerously over-emphasize the importance and authority of subjective experience in spiritual things; with the result that in their public meetings, as also in their private testimonies, little is heard about the objective facts of the Gospel or the work of Christ for us.[26]

Dr. Lewis Sperry Chafer wrote:

Doubtless the leaders of the so-called "Oxford Movement" or "the First Century Christian Fellowship" would be shocked to be told that their teaching is no nearer a comprehending of Christianity than is Christian Science . . . each system, behind its outward claims, offered the most violent contradictions to pure first century Christianity.[27]

A secular publication described the group this way:

The Oxford Group has no membership, no dues, no paid leaders. It has no new creed nor theological theories. It does not even have regular meetings. It is merely a fellowship of individuals who seek to follow a certain way of life. First-century Christian principles in 20th-century application. Identified with it are Roman Catholics, Episcopalians, Methodists, Presbyterians, Baptists—**members of all churches and none**.[28] (Emphasis added.)

Along with an emphasis on subjective experience was the group sharing at their meetings, which were also called "parties." One publication of the day said:

They urge the need of *"deep sharing,"* or open confession within the Group, as a means of release from sin and cementing the fellowship of the Group. This is especially dangerous when *the sharing of sexual sin is encouraged.*[29] (Emphasis in original.)

Under the guise of "confession," Oxford Group participants graphically shared their sexual exploits and received absolution and affirmation from the group. One can see the influence of the Oxford Group on the central place of "sharing" during AA and other Twelve-Step meetings today. Again there was concern among those who held to a biblical faith.

One person wrote:

> When I was in Boston, I found a good deal of
> scandal had been occasioned by mixed companies
> holding these parties and confessing their sins,
> many of which were of such a character that
> Scripture says, "It is a shame even to speak of those
> things which are done of them in secret" (Eph. 5:12).
> Yet they confessed these things openly, men before
> women, and women before men. You can under-
> stand that the result was anything but helpful.
> Where do you find anything in the Word of God that
> suggests this kind of confession of sin?[30]

In spite of the lurid confessions during the meetings, the
whole point of the Movement was to draw close to God
through "absolute purity, absolute unselfishness and absolute
love."[31] In other words, it was a works-oriented movement
rather than a Christ-centered faith. Wilson says that the
Oxford Group "felt that when people commenced to adhere to
these high moral standards, then God could enter and direct
their lives."[32] Notice that adherence to "high moral standards" was what allowed God to "enter and direct their lives."
In contrast Paul declared:

> For by grace are you saved through faith; and that
> not of yourselves: it is the gift of God: Not of works,
> lest any man should boast. For we are His
> workmanship, created in Christ Jesus unto good
> works, which God hath before ordained that we
> should walk in them. (Ephesians 2:8-10.)

The Oxford Group, which was later named Moral Re-Arma-
ment, did not offer salvation through faith, because there was
no creed. Instead members engaged in religious works so that
God could "enter and direct their lives."

Even with its goal of "absolute purity, absolute unselfishness and absolute love" the group was well-known for its
worldliness. *The Bible League Monthly* says:

> Worldliness is not only condoned among its ordinary
> members, but among those who have been sent
> forth as its missioners. Again, in our reading of its

literature, it appears that non-Christians may join a
group even though the non-Christian faith be not
abandoned.[33]

An editor of another Christian publication of the day noted
that the "Oxford Group Movement follows the fashions, the
foibles and follies of the world."[34] This included gambling and
provocative dress.[35]

Besides the emphasis on subjective sharing, the Oxford
Group's manner of prayer and guidance influenced Wilson.
Rather than using the Bible as a standard and guide for living, members of the Oxford Group practiced a "quiet time"
during which they would write down whatever came into
their minds.[36] Examples of such "guidance" are in the book
God Calling, edited by A. J. Russell of the Oxford Group.[37]
The book was written anonymously by two women who
thought they were hearing from God, but who passively
received messages in the same way spiritists obtain guidance
from demons.

Members of the Oxford Group primarily found their guidance from **within** rather than from a creed or the Bible.
Buchman, for instance, was known to spend "an hour or more
in complete silence of soul and body while he gets guidance
for that day."[38] J. C. Brown in his book *The Oxford Group
Movement* says of Buchman:

> He teaches his votaries to wait upon God with paper
> and pencil in hand each morning in this relaxed and
> inert condition, and to write down whatever
> guidance they get. This, however, is just *the very
> condition* required by *Spiritist mediums* to enable
> them to receive *impressions* from evil spirits. . . and
> it is a path which, by abandoning the Scripture-
> instructed judgment (which God always demands)
> for the purely occult and the psychic, has again and
> again led over the precipice. The soul that reduces
> itself to an automaton may at any moment be set
> spinning by a *Demon*.[39] (Emphasis his.)

Dr. Rowland V. Bingham, Editor of *The Evangelical
Christian* says:

> We do not object to their taking a pad and pencil to

write down any thoughts of guidance which come to them. But to take the thoughts especially *generated in a mental vacuum* as Divine guidance would throw open to all the suggestions of *another* who knows how to come as an angel of light and whose illumination would lead to *disaster*.[40] (Emphasis his.)

In a very real sense their personal journals became their personal scriptures.

Finally, the Oxford Group emphasized changed lives. But Irvine says: "The question is not: Are lives changed? but rather: What does this change signify? Is it Reformation or Regeneration? A work of man, or a work of God?"[41] We concur with Harold T. Commons, who repented after being involved in the group for three years. He wrote:

> The "changed lives" of the Group are nothing more than moral conversions, in no sense corresponding to the New Birth of the New Testament, which designates the passing of a soul from death to life by the acceptance of Christ's atoning work on the cross. Anything that omits God's one remedy for sin (1 John 1:7) leaves the human soul still guilty before God, regardless of how many moral conversions the person may have gone through.[42]

Changes were based on the works of men undergirded by so-called spiritual experiences and group involvement, but they were not based upon faith in the atoning work of Jesus Christ. While their lives may have been different and even exciting, they had no biblical confession. Their doctrine did not include this essential truth:

> That if thou shalt confess with thy mouth the Lord Jesus, and shalt believe in thine heart that God hath raised him from the dead, thou shalt be saved. For with the heart man believeth unto righteousness; and with the mouth confession is made unto salvation. (Romans 10:9-10.)

In 1933 the Sixteenth Annual Convention of the World's Christian Fundamentals Association issued the following

Resolution:

> The Convention recognizes with sorrow the increasing prevalence of false religious cults and movements, and especially that known as the Oxford Group Movement, or First Century Fellowship, or Buchmanism. The Convention believes that this Movement, while calling itself Christian, and while including in its adherents some who are undoubtedly Christians, nevertheless is a subtle and dangerous denial of the evangelical Christian faith, in which Modernists are as welcome as Fundamentalists, and varying shades of belief or unbelief unite on common and unscriptural ground. The Convention believes that the Movement substitutes human and natural psychological laws for the supernatural working of the Holy Spirit and the new birth, and that it puts experience ahead of doctrine, denying the necessity of true belief as essential to Christian life. **The Convention therefore urges all true believers to recognize the unscriptural character of this Group Movement, and to refrain from having fellowship with it.**[43] (Emphasis added.)

Wilson's group separated from the Oxford Group to become a religion of its own. However, many of the features of the Oxford Group live on today in Alcoholics Anonymous and cloned Twelve-Step programs.

The Jungian Connection.

Correspondence between Wilson and the well-known occult psychiatrist Carl Jung reveals that Wilson was looking for a religious experience as his only hope and that this experience was foundational to the AA movement. In his letter to Jung in 1961, Wilson says:

> This letter of great appreciation has been very long overdue. . . . Though you have surely heard of us [AA], I doubt if you are aware that a certain conversation you once had with one of your patients, a Mr. Roland H., back in the early 1930's did play a critical role in the founding of our fellowship.[44]

He then reminds Jung of what Jung had "frankly told him [Roland H.] of his hopelessness," that he was beyond medical or psychiatric help. Wilson says: "This candid and humble statement of yours was beyond doubt the first foundation stone upon which our Society has since been built." Moreover, when Roland H. had asked Jung if there was any hope for him, Jung "told him that there might be, provided he could become the subject of a spiritual or religious experience—in short, a genuine conversion." Wilson continues: "You recommended that he place himself in a religious atmosphere and hope for the best."[45] As far as Jung was concerned, there was no need for doctrine or creed, only an experience, which is true of AA to this day.

It is important to inject here that Jung could not have meant conversion to Christianity, because as far as Jung was concerned all religion is simply myth—a symbolic way of interpreting the life of the psyche. To Jung, conversion simply meant a totally dramatic experience which would profoundly alter a person's outlook on life. Jung himself had blatantly rejected Christianity and turned to idolatry. He replaced God with a myriad of mythological archetypes. He delved deeply into the occult, practiced necromancy, and had daily contact with disembodied spirits, which he called archetypes. In fact, much of what he wrote was inspired by such entities. Jung had his own familiar spirit whom he called Philemon. At first he thought Philemon was part of his own psyche. Later on, however, he found that Philemon was more than an expression of his own inner self.[46]

In his letter to Jung, Wilson describes his own critical point of hopelessness, as far as medical help was concerned, and his spiritual experience which followed. And, he shares his early vision for a society of alcoholics with similar realizations and experiences. His dream for AA was "to lay every newcomer wide open to a transforming spiritual experience." He declares: **"This has made conversion experiences—nearly every variety reported by James—available on almost wholesale basis."**[47] (Emphasis added.) Indeed Alcoholics Anonymous is a religious society, but it is not a biblically based Christian fellowship. It is a counterfeit with whatever god a person concocts, imagines and/or envisions.

Jung's response to Wilson's letter is confirming. In it he says the following about Roland H.:

> His craving for alcohol was the equivalent, on a low level, of the spiritual thirst of our being for wholeness; expressed in medieval language: the union with God.[48]

He notes that in Latin the same word is used for alcohol as for "the highest religious experience." Even in English, alcohol is referred to as *spirits*. But, knowing Jung's theology and privy counsel with a familiar spirit, one must conclude that the spirit he is referring to is not the Holy Spirit, and the god he is talking about is not the God of the Bible, but rather a counterfeit spirit posing as an angel of light and leading many to destruction. Could it be that through AA people are substituting one form of sorcery (*pharmakia*) with another (a false god and occult experiences)?

The Higher Power and the Occult.

Bill Wilson and Bob Smith, the cofounders of AA, attended Oxford Group meetings, which is why people think they were Christians. However, both were involved in other spiritual experiences as well. Wilson and Smith both practiced spiritualism and believed in the validity and importance of contacting and conversing with the dead (necromancy, which the Bible forbids).[49] Wilson described one particular encounter he had one morning in Nantucket with several entities, who supposedly told him their names. One, who called himself David Morrow, said he had been a sailor during the Civil War. Later that same day Wilson just happened to discover Morrow's name on a monument in the center of town.[50] The AA biography of Wilson says:

> It is not clear when he first became interested in extrasensory phenomena; the field was something that Dr. Bob and Anne Smith were also deeply involved with. Whether or not Bill initially became interested through them, there are references to

séances and other psychic events in the letters Bill wrote to Lois [Wilson's wife] during that first Akron summer with the Smiths, in 1935.[51]

The Wilsons were conducting regular séances in their own home as early as 1941. They were engaging in other psychic activities as well, such as using an Ouija board.[52] Also, as Wilson would lie on a couch he would "receive" messages (in a manner similar to that of the occultist Edgar Cayce) and another person would write them down. His wife described it this way:

> Bill would lie down on the couch. He would "get" these things. He kept doing it every week or so. Each time, certain people would "come in." Sometimes, it would be new ones and they'd carry on some story. There would be long sentences; word by word would come through.[53]

It is interesting to note that in 1938, between the séances at the Smiths' and Wilson receiving messages while in a prone position in the 40s, Wilson wrote the AA Twelve Steps. He was lying in bed thinking. The official AA biography of Wilson describes it this way:

> As he started to write, he asked for guidance. And he relaxed. The words began tumbling out with astonishing speed. He completed the first draft in about half an hour, then kept on writing until he felt he should stop and review what he had written. Numbering the new steps, he found that they added up to twelve—a symbolic number; he thought of the Twelve apostles, and soon became convinced that the Society should have twelve steps.[54]

Whether or not creating the Twelve Steps involved occultic activity, Wilson and Smith's commitment to spiritualism was intrinsically tied to their creation of and leadership in AA.

A regular participant in what they referred to as their "spook sessions" said:

> I was a problem to these people, because I was an atheist, and an atheist is, by definition, a material-ist. . . and a materialist is, by definition, someone

who does not believe in other worlds. Now these people, Bill and Dr. Bob, believed vigorously and aggressively. They were working away at the spiritualism; it was not just a hobby. And it related to A.A., because the big problem in A.A. is that for a materialist it's hard to buy the program.[55]

But Wasn't Wilson a Christian Anyway?

Wilson's interest in spiritual matters was all-inclusive, all except faith in Jesus as the only way. For a while Wilson seriously considered becoming a Catholic. He described his relation to the church this way:

> I'm more affected than ever by that sweet and powerful aura of the church; that marvelous spiritual essence flowing down by the centuries touches me as no other emanation does, but—when I look at the authoritative layout, despite all the arguments in its favor, I still can't warm up. No affirmative conviction comes.[56]

Wilson did not want to attach AA to any one faith. The official AA biography of Wilson declares:

> Bill felt it would be unwise for AA as a fellowship to have an allegiance to any one religious sect. He felt AA's usefulness was worldwide, and contained **spiritual principles that members of any and every religion could accept, including the Eastern religions**.[57] (Emphasis added.)

Wilson could not have believed in the "faith once delivered to the saints" because he did not believe Jesus' words when He said, "I am the way, the truth, and the life; no man cometh unto the Father, but by me" (John 14:6). Wilson complained, **"The thing that still irks me about all organized religions is their claim how confoundedly right all of them are. Each seems to think it has the right pipeline."**[58] (Emphasis added.) Obviously, according to Wilson, Jesus is not the only "pipeline" to God.

Alcoholics are often hypercritical of Christianity, especially organized churches and doctrines. They criticize Christians for being hypocrites. Condemned by the Bible, they resist the Word of God, but are happy to believe selected sections that only talk about love (separated from the whole counsel of God with God's righteous holiness and man's filthy wretchedness). Rather than worshiping the Holy God of the Bible they worship a god "understood" by them without any condemnation of sin.

On the other hand there are those who call themselves Christians but continue in habitual sin. They may expect God to do everything magically without their obedience to the Lordship of Christ. They are not daily engaged in putting off the old and putting on the new. While they may enjoy a season of relief from their besetting sin, they are not exercising their faith through the practice of obedience in every area of their life. They are not rooted and grounded in Christ. Therefore the religiosity of those who have not taken root is hollow and maintained superficially. Believing themselves to be saved, they may still be lost and under the domination of sin. Without the life of the Lord Jesus active in them, or the grace of God to enable them to obey, they are left to their own weaknesses. Thus, they may be enticed into a system of morality in which they will not feel guilty. And that is what a Twelve-Step program provides.

The Codependent and Step Two.

Codependency/recovery writers follow the same rationale as AA. Melody Beattie rehearses the same assertions. She says:

> The decision to refer to God as a "Power greater than ourselves" and to allow people to develop their own understanding of this power was intentional.

> This program is spiritual, not religious. The Steps were written to be compatible with all religious and denominational beliefs. They were also intended to be accessible to those without religious or denominational beliefs.[59]

She is also critical of any religion that might be "rigid" (with a definite standard for right and wrong behavior) and "shame-based" (that is, original sin). According to her, it is unhealthy to fear God.[60] She also wants to assure people that "Twelve Step programs have removed any gender reference to God."[61] But, in addition, she wants to appeal to Christians. Therefore she says, "Some of us are comfortable embracing a traditional concept of God. That's fine too."[62] What a condescension! As far as she's concerned, it's okay to believe in Jesus, as long as He's not the only way.

Wendy Kaminer says:

> Codependency literature combines pop psychology and pop feminism of these books with New Age spiritualism and some traditional evangelical ideals: addiction and recovery look a lot like sin and redemption.[63]

Maybe that's why so many Christians are fooled.

Even codependency/recovery programs that offer Christ as the answer tend to distort Christianity. For instance, Pat Springle, who firmly believes that everyone's basic need is that of self-worth through security and significance, says that the "Lordship of Christ can be frightening for a codependent."[64] He also says:

> Through the lenses of over-responsibility, perfectionism, repressed emotions, and guilt motivation, the beauty of an intimate relationship with Christ is distorted. Instead of a sense of belonging, trust, and affirmation, the codependent perceives the Christian message as one of more demands, more condemnation, and more guilt. Consequently, he feels driven and lonely.[65]

Springle's declaration that "the codependent perceives the Christian message as one of more demands, more condemnation, and more guilt" must mean that codependents have not heard the gospel of Jesus Christ, wherein one is saved from sin and condemnation and given new life. Then instead of taking this poor sinner to the cross to put self to death and to 1 John 1:9 for forgiveness and cleansing, Springle talks about how this poor codependent has been suffering from a lack of self-worth. In fact, he declares that the codependent's sin is the idolatry of trying to "get his security and value from someone or something other than the Lord."[66] Thus the answer is to get your self-worth from Jesus. This sounds more like the gospel of Adler, Maslow, and Rogers (with Jesus conveniently added to meet the hierarchy of needs) than the gospel Paul preached.

Paul had a few things to say about other gospels. He said:

> I marvel that ye are so soon removed from him that called you into the grace of Christ unto another gospel: Which is not another; but there be some that trouble you, and would pervert the gospel of Christ. But though we, or an angel from heaven, preach any other gospel unto you than that which we have preached unto you, let him be accursed. As we said before, so say I now again, if any man preach any other gospel unto you than that ye have received, let him be accursed. (Galatians 1:6-9.)

Another idea that is expressed by psychologically-based professing Christians is that God enables people to accept themselves. This, of course, is another facet of need psychology that permeates codependency/recovery literature. As an example, the Christian authors of *Serenity: A Companion for Twelve Step Recovery* give a Step Two meditation for John 12:46. The Bible passage says: "I am come a light into the world, that whosoever believeth on me should not abide in darkness." This is their meditation:

> . . . . those of us who have struggled with disabling conditions since childhood, may actually be totally unaware of the extent of our problems. Because of our traumatic childhood experiences, we may be defiant, resentful, self-deluded, or overcontrolling without ever realizing it.

> When we come to the light of God's Power and Love, we no longer have to abide in that crippling darkness. In the light of His Love we can accept ourselves as we truly are, and then in the light of His Power we can walk out of the darkness for eternity.[67]

This is another gospel of self. Where is the recognition of total depravity and the need for a Savior from the domination of sin? Instead, we have a picture of a person who really cannot help the way he is because of such horrible parents and a nice sentimental god who only loves in ways that will help make self accept self.

Amazingly, these same authors quote Wilson in their meditation on John 6:63. In the Bible passage Jesus says, "It is the spirit that quickeneth; the flesh profiteth nothing: the words that I speak unto you, they are spirit, and they are life." In spite of the fact that Wilson's spiritual experience was quite different from the biblical meaning of being born again, these authors (Robert Hemfelt and Richard Fowler) say:

> Our recovery literature describes this rebirth and infilling of the Holy Spirit in the following way: "As we felt new power flow in, as we enjoyed peace of mind, as we discovered we could face life successfully, as we became conscious of His presence, we began to lose our fear of today, tomorrow or the hereafter. We were reborn" (*Alcoholics Anonymous*, p. 63).[68]

That was Bill Wilson they quoted, as if he were speaking of the same thing as the Bible teaches. That is why Christians must "try the spirits [to see] whether they are of God" (1 John 4:1). The basic problems with the AA Step Two are repeated and even magnified in codependency/recovery programs and books.

The Wide Gateway of Step Two.

When Wilson first formulated the Twelve Steps, Step Two was: "Came to believe that God could restore us to sanity."[69] Wilson had had a religious experience he thought was God. Therefore, such a statement seemed natural. However, he met with opposition from those who were close to him in the AA movement. Thus he changed the wording of Step Two: "Came to believe that a Power greater than ourselves could restore us to sanity."[70] Wilson believed that those concessions regarding references to God were:

. . . **the great contribution of our atheists and**

> agnostics. **They had widened our gateway so that all who suffer might pass through, regardless of their belief or *lack of belief*.**[71]
> (Italics his; bold emphasis added.)

And indeed the gate is wide. The "Power greater than ourselves" can be anybody or anything that seems greater than the person who takes Step Two. It can be a familiar spirit, such as Carl Jung's Philemon. It could be any deity of Hinduism, Buddhism, Greek mythology, or New Age channeled entities. It could be one's own so-called higher self. It could even be the devil himself.

The extreme naivete of Christians comes through when they confidently assert that their higher Power is Jesus Christ. Since when did Jesus align Himself with false gods? Since when has He been willing to join the Pantheon or the array of Hindu deities? Jesus is not an option of one among many. He is the Only Son, the Only Savior, and the Only Way. All Twelve Step programs violate the declarations of the Reformation: Only Scripture; Only Christ; Only Grace; Only Faith; and Glory to God Only. Instead they offer another power, another gospel, another savior, another source, another fellowship, another tradition, another evangelism, and another god. Jesus' majesty and His very person are violated by joining Him with the gods of the wide gate and the broad way. Jesus emphatically stated that His gate is strait and His way is narrow. His is the only way to life, while all other ways lead to destruction (Matthew 7:13-14).

Twelve Steps into the New Age.

In an article in *The American Spectator,* Elizabeth Kristol says:

> God is being redefined each day by millions of individuals in thousands of Twelve Step meetings. As a result of this continual populist redefinition of God, the Twelve Steps of AA may have as profound an effect on the popular theology of our times as the 95 theses of Martin Luther did on his.[72]

Richard Rohr of the Center for Action and Contemplation

says he believes that "the 12 Steps will go down in history as the significant, authentic American contribution to the history of spirituality."[73] The atheist philosopher Aldous Huxley predicted that Bill Wilson "will go down as the social architect of the 20th century."[74]

Twelve-Step programs are in essence New Age religions and archetypical precursors of a one-world religion. They do not hold a common doctrine of God and His creation. Instead, each group holds a common goal, centered in saving self. In AA it's sobriety; in Co-dependents Anonymous it's feeling good through unshackled selfhood. The common goal of the one-world religion will be peace—for the sake of survival. Each goal is centered in self and in the now, not in God or eternity. The goal takes precedence over the One True God. Whatever god or goddess is chosen as the higher power is subservient to that goal. All of these fit into the New Age spirituality: no absolutes, many ways, self-enhancement.

When one configures his own image of god and places himself under that power, he is essentially his own god, because he finds that god within himself and within his own experience. Thus Self is truly the god of Twelve-Step groups and many other forms of New Age religions. Twelve-Step religions call on a nonjudgmental deity according to their own imaginations, rather than a God who is self-existent, holy, and external to the believer, but who has made Himself known through the Bible.

When self is god, one is left to a life-long religion of works, because one must be continually saving self. That is why one must continue to attend AA meetings, follow the Twelve Steps, and help other drunks. While sobriety itself is not one of the works listed among the Twelve, it is the goal of every step. Even the seeming self-giving to help other drunks (other addicts or other codependents) is for the sake of one's own sobriety. One's life is thus devoted to the goal of selfhood.

6

TWELVE-STEP
IDOLATRY

Step Three: "**Made a decision to turn our will and our lives over to the care of God** *as we understood Him*."[1] (Emphasis in original.)

Alcoholics Anonymous denies being a religion. The Foreword of the Second Edition of *Alcoholics Anonymous* emphatically states:

> Alcoholics Anonymous is not a religious organization. . . . by personal religious affiliation, we include Catholics, Protestants, Jews, Hindus, and a sprinkling of Moslems and Buddhists.[2]

Nevertheless, when the central activity of a society is to turn one's will and life over to God, that society is a religious society. Just because members belong to a variety of other religious organizations does not make AA a nonreligious organization. Instead, such a statement affirms the AA faith that it doesn't matter which god you turn your life over to. It can be Allah, Shiva, a dead ancestor, a god of one's own making, or some semblance of Jehovah or Jesus. The god of AA is whatever god you choose or create.

The *Beginner's Manual* published by the Greater Milwaukee Central Office of Alcoholics Anonymous declares:

> The core of technique by which ALCOHOLICS

117

ANONYMOUS has worked, what often seems like a miracle in the lives of men and women, is spiritual. Not religious . . . but SPIRITUAL.[3] (Emphasis and ellipsis in original.)

But it is merely doublespeak when AA claims to be **spiritual but not religious**. David Berenson explains:

AA early on made the distinction between religion and spirituality, a distinction that is only now becoming more widely understood. Religion often involves adopting a specific dogma about the attributes of what is called God, understood as being separate from the universe and from human beings. . . . With spirituality . . . direct experience and relationship with a Higher Power are primary, and belief systems are secondary, or may even be considered an impediment, to developing the relationship.[4]

With this distinction, AA freely abandons the Bible and all its revealed information about God and man. AA substitutes relationship with the only true God through Jesus Christ with an experiential relationship with idols. AA regards experience to be the basis of reality rather than revelation. That is because AA regards a radical shift in psychic experience essential to sobriety.

In addition to its mystical religious nature, the Twelve Steps and Twelve Traditions of AA are highly moralistic. When you are into spirituality and morality and when you are looking to a god for help, you're into religion, whether you admit it or not. Both the spirituality and the morality inherent in the Twelve Steps and Twelve Traditions make Alcoholics Anonymous a religious society. In contrast to most of AA's denials of being religious, a pamphlet published by AA of Akron, Ohio, clearly admits the religious nature of AA and even refers to the kitchen as being "the church of Alcoholics Anonymous" in its early days.[5]

A A books are filled with references to God. However, the god of AA is not a specific god with specific attributes. The use of the word *God* is so general that "God" could be anything, as long as he, she, or it is totally loving and nonjudgmental. Nevertheless, **the appeal to a Higher Power is central to the AA message**. In explaining "How It Works," the "Big Book," *Alcoholics Anonymous*, says:

> Without help it is too much for us. But there is One who has all power—that One is God. May you find Him now![6]

Also, consider this religious statement in Bill Wilson's essay on Step Three:

> Like all the remaining Steps, Step Three calls for affirmative action, for it is only by action that we can cut away the self-will which has always blocked the entry of God—or, if you like, a Higher Power—into our lives . . . . In fact, the effectiveness of the whole A.A. program will rest upon how well and earnestly we have tried to come to "a decision to turn our will and our lives over to the care of God *as we understood Him*."[7] (Emphasis his.)

This is religious, spiritual action. Moreover, how well a person will succeed through the Twelve Steps is largely dependent on conforming the will to a Higher Power.

In the Chapter titled "Working with Others" in *Alcoholics Anonymous*, Wilson tells AA members how to talk to an alcoholic. After telling the member how to stress that alcoholism is an illness, Wilson says:

> *Tell him exactly what happened to you.* Stress the spiritual feature freely. If the man be an agnostic or atheist, make it emphatic that *he does not have to agree with your conception of God.* He can choose any conception he likes, provided it makes sense to him. *The main thing is that he be willing to believe in a Power greater than himself and that he live by spiritual principles.*[8] (Emphasis in original.)

If indeed in AA "the main thing is that [the person] be willing to believe in a Power greater than himself and that he live by spiritual principles," AA is both a faith system and a religion.

According to Wilson, God's will for the individual is consistent with the Twelve Steps.[9] And since Wilson wrote the Twelve Steps, Wilson's god's will is identical to that of his own. In addition to the various gods' wills being expressed through peer group pressure and the moral admonitions of AA (which gives AA groups lots of power), the gods' wills may be found by looking inside self. Since those gods are individually defined and have revealed no authoritative external definition, moral standard, or creed, those gods' wills turn out to be exactly what various people make theirs to be. "I define my Higher Power as I understand him/her/it and I (or my therapist or group) decide its will and purpose for me—which can only be what is pleasing to me (or my therapist or my group) at the time."

AA and Christianity.

The numerous references to God and spiritual principles in AA literature make Alcoholics Anonymous sound perfectly acceptable to many Christians. In fact, a number of statements by Bill Wilson even sound Christian. Spiritual principles of turning one's life over to God and following His will rather than self appear biblical on the surface. Therefore, the authors of *Serenity* assume that one can easily turn the Higher Power of AA into the God of the Bible. They say, "In Step 3, we recognize God as that higher Power and ask Him to assume control over and care of every aspect of our lives."[10]

Just as every major world religion has moral principles that may sound acceptable to many Christians (if they heard those principles outside the context of that religion), AA's Steps and Traditions sound very acceptable to unsuspecting Christians. Therefore, it is necessary to consider some of the doctrinal differences between AA and Christianity.

The Nature of God.

As stated earlier, the Triune God of Christianity—the Father, the Son, and Holy Spirit—is not the Higher Power of AA. According to AA, any deity will do. One AA pamphlet says:

> But if our concept of God is on the nebulous side, we are offered more concrete guidance on the subject of religion and spirituality.[11]

Such a statement sounds as if AA claims a spirituality superior to other religions even though AA's concept of God is "on the nebulous side."[12] Does that sound like Christianity or paganism?

The AA pamphlet goes on to quote various persons' definitions of religion. Here are just a few of them:

> "Religion is the **worship of higher powers** from a sense of need." —Allan Menzies. (Emphasis added. Note the plural: "higher powers.")

> "Religion shall mean for us the feelings, acts and experiences of individual men in their solitude, so far as they apprehend themselves to stand in relation to **whatever they may consider the divine**." —William James. (Emphasis added.)

> "Religion is that part of human experience in which man feels himself in relation with **powers of psychic nature, usually personal powers**, and makes use of them."—James Henry Leuba. (Emphasis added.)[13]

Do those quotations represent a Christian knowledge of the Most High? Or do they represent the fallen wisdom of men and religions of demons? At the end of the quotations, the pamphlet says: "One cannot but be impressed with the similarity of these definitions to our own Twelve Steps."[14] Indeed there is a great similarity, far more similarity than with Christianity!

In AA any god is acceptable as long as it does not diminish the value of the god of any other member of AA. Christians who say, "Jesus is my Higher Power," may have no trouble as long as their Jesus is not fully the Jesus of the Bible, because Jesus very clearly said that He is the only way. He is the exclusive God! According to the Bible all other deities are idols, false gods. Moreover, Jesus does not want His followers to be unequally yoked with unbelievers or idolaters.

> **Be ye not unequally yoked together with unbelievers**: for what fellowship hath righteousness with unrighteousness? and what communion

> hath light with darkness? And what concord hath
> Christ with Belial? or what part hath he that
> believeth with an infidel? **And what agreement
> hath the temple of God with idols**? for ye are the
> temple of the living God; as God hath said, I will
> dwell in them, and walk in them; and I will be their
> God, and they shall be my people. Wherefore **come
> out from among them, and be ye separate**,
> saith the Lord, and touch not the unclean thing; and
> I will receive you. (2 Corinthians 6:14-17; emphasis
> added.)

For a professing Christian to be a member of AA yokes him
with unbelievers and does so through calling any and all gods
a Higher Power. Furthermore, the Christ that a person finds
at AA may be the devil in disguise.

The God of the Bible is not only perfect love and perfect
power, He is also true and holy. His love is never separated
from truth. Therefore truth is as important as the other qual-
ities of love, such as mercy, grace, and forgiveness. God's holiness is an awesome and especially fearful thing. It includes
His righteousness, justice, and His judgment of sin and sinners. God's holiness also includes His holy will, which He has
revealed in His Holy Word. God's will is not identical to the
will of man. In fact, God's will is according to His good pleasure, not necessarily the good pleasure of any human.

The contrast between the holiness of God and the sinfulness of man forms so great a chasm that man cannot
approach God on the basis of his own power, righteousness,
love, or even need. A human cannot approach a holy God
without being justified and cleansed by the full payment for
the penalty of sin. God cannot be approached through any
Twelve-Step program or any other kind of human works.
Thus He provided a way of approach, through His Son. Jesus
is the only way to the Father. There is no other way.

The Nature of Man.

Explanations of the nature of man may vary among
members of AA and other recovery groups. However, most
believe that people are born good, but have been corrupted by

parents and society. As discussed earlier, many of the psychological purveyors of codependency/recovery therapies believe that people are motivated by an unconscious need for self-worth and that their basic problems come from unmet emotional needs. Many believe that people can find truth within a pure inner core. Some speak of a true self (the inner perfect essence of being) and a false self (distorted by parents, schools, religion, etc.).

Many contend that each person has a divine spark within him, but others go even farther and say that their inner being is god. The idea that man is by nature one with nature and one with God permeates many of the teachings. Nevertheless, most believe that the human family descended from apes, either through full-fledged faith in evolution or faith in a creative evolution.

The Bible does not support any of the above stated beliefs about the nature of man. God created man (male and female) in His own image, to live in relationship with Him and to reflect Him. Such relationship and reflection required obedience to the Creator. When Adam and Eve disobeyed, the relationship was altered and the reflection was marred, so much so that access to God could only be according to His stipulation: that sin be covered or washed away. The only way for sin to be covered or washed away is through the merciful provisions of God, received by the believer and acted upon by faith. The first covering for sin was in the Garden, when God clothed Adam and Eve with animal skins. A sacrifice was required, the death of animals to cover the sin of humans. Animals died in place of sinners who deserved immediate death, for indeed Adam and Eve deserved to die.

Adam and Eve's sins were covered by the sacrifice, but they retained their sinful natures, which they passed on to their children. Thus all are born sinners with a proclivity to sinning. Every person is totally depraved in that every part of his nature is infected with the deadly strain of sin. The Bible clearly states:

> There is none righteous, no, not one: There is none
> that understandeth, there is none that seeketh after
> God. They are all gone out of the way, they are

together become unprofitable; there is none that
doeth good, no, not one. . . . Therefore by the deeds
of the law there shall no flesh be justified in his
sight: for by the law is the knowledge of sin. . . . For
all have sinned, and come short of the glory of God
(Romans 3:11-12,20, 23).

Every person is a sinner, and sinners cannot approach the
Lord or draw near to Him on their own terms.

The Way of Salvation.

The way of salvation in AA is through subjective experience, attending AA meetings, and following a Twelve-Step
morality. The way of salvation for codependents is through
finding and regaining what Robin Norwood calls the "precious
self that has gotten buried beneath the external images and
the internal lies."[15] Self saves self through a psychospiritual
process presented in the numerous addiction and recovery
books, groups, programs, and treatment centers. However,
according to the Bible, humans cannot save themselves.
Though they may change their behavior, they are still lost.

In His mercy and grace, God provided a way of salvation.
Because their sinfulness and their multitude of sins stand
between themselves and a holy God, humans need to be saved
from their sinfulness and their sins. They need to be delivered from the condition of sin and the domination of sin.
Death and separation from God are the consequences of sin:
"For the wages of sin is death" (Romans 6:23). Thus God
provided a means of substitutionary sacrifice.

Before the incarnation of the Son of God and His sacrificial death on the cross, God required the sacrifice of animals
to cover the sins of His people until the coming of the
Messiah. Such sacrifice demonstrated the horror of sin, the
seriousness of disobeying God, sin's consequences of pain and
death, and God's execution of both justice and mercy. Justice
requires that the sinner pay the penalty of sin: death. Mercy
provides a substitute. Jesus' substitutionary death on the
cross is therefore essential to Christianity for "without shed-
ding of blood is no remission of sin" (Hebrews 9:22).

A person is saved when he confesses his sin and sinfulness deserving of death, believes that Jesus died in his place, and appropriates new life through faith in the resurrection of Jesus.

> For by grace are ye saved through faith; and that not of yourselves: it is the gift of God: Not of works, lest any man should boast (Ephesians 2:8-9).

This is necessary for establishing relationship with God. One does not attain this through any variety of religious experience (*a la* William James), no matter how dramatic or intense. While one may not understand the intricacies of salvation, a person is saved only through the death and resurrection of Jesus Christ. His sins are forgiven only on the basis of that sacrifice. When a person is saved he is given new life. He is indwelt by the Holy Spirit, who is revealed in the Bible (not a demon spirit as with Carl Jung, who was praised by Bill Wilson for his contribution to the establishment of AA). One cannot have the Holy Spirit of God unless he has been regenerated and put faith in Jesus Christ, as He is revealed in the Bible.

The only way to draw near to the Most High, Who has revealed Himself through the Bible, is by faith in the substitutionary sacrifice of Jesus Christ. And there is only one way to turn one's will over to the God of the Bible. It is through faith in Jesus, in His sacrificial death in the place of the sinner, which brings confession, repentance, and submission to Him as Lord in every area of life.

The AA religion is Christless and offers a counterfeit salvation without the sacrificial death of Jesus Christ. Seeking a Christless salvation through turning one's life over to a "God as we understood Him" has nothing to do with Christianity and everything to do with idolatry, false religions, and paganism. **And because of the many versions of God represented in AA, professing Christians are uniting themselves with a spiritual harlot when they join AA.**

The Christian Walk.

Another difference between Christianity and Twelve-Step religions is the way of life. A Christian lives by the very life of the Lord Jesus Christ. Paul states it this way:

> I am crucified with Christ: nevertheless I live; yet
> not I, but Christ liveth in me: and the life which I
> now live in the flesh I live by the faith of the Son of
> God, who loved me, and gave himself for me. I do
> not frustrate the grace of God: for if righteousness
> come by the law, then Christ is dead in vain. (Gala-
> tians 2:20-21.)

No longer does he try to gain righteousness (right standing
with God) through following the law or a code of ethics. Instead, he is as dependent upon the righteousness of Christ for
his daily walk as for his initial salvation.

> Wherefore, my beloved, as ye have always obeyed,
> not as in my presence only, but now much more in
> my absence, work out your own salvation with fear
> and trembling. For it is God which worketh in you
> both to will and to do of his good pleasure. (Philippi-
> ans 2:12-13.)

God performs the primary work in us. Ours is but to respond
in obedience by His enabling. Whereas the AA religion offers
a nebulous higher power (false god or idol of the mind) and a
code of rules, Christians are enabled to live by the very Word
of God by the indwelling Holy Spirit.

Because of his total identification with the death and resurrection of Christ, the Christian does not even belong to
himself. He belongs to Jesus and is a bond-servant of Christ,
because he was bought with a price, the sacrificial blood of
Jesus. At salvation he immediately comes under the Lordship
of Christ, not as an addition to salvation, but as an intrinsic
part. Before salvation we are all under bondage to the
lordship of self, sin, and Satan (Ephesians 2:2-3), but at the
moment of salvation we are translated out of the kingdom of
darkness and into the kingdom of light where Jesus is King of
Kings and Lord of Lords. As Paul reminded the Colossians,
God the Father "hath delivered us from the power of darkness, and hath translated us into the kingdom of His dear
Son: in whom we have redemption through His blood, even
the forgiveness of sins" (Colossians 1:13-14). Jesus is both

Savior and Lord. Thus the Christian is under the lordship of Christ. He is called to deny self, take up his cross, and follow Jesus (Matthew 16:24-26). He does this by grace through faith—not by self-effort.

Not only is there a **vast** difference between the Christian walk and working the Twelve Steps; the end result is the difference between heaven and hell. **It would be conceivable in AA for one to make a decision to turn one's will and life over to the care of Satan or Lucifer.** The legendary Dr. Faustus turned his will over to Mephistopheles (a devil). Simply deciding to turn one's life over to a Higher Power does not ensure right standing with the God of the Universe who will judge the living and the dead and who will assign some to heaven and some to hell. And while sobriety is important for an alcoholic, one may go to hell sober under the care of any "God *as we understood Him*" other than the Most High Creator who has revealed Himself in His written Word, the Bible. To turn one's will and life over to any other power than the Lord Jesus Christ has eternal consequences.

The Codependent and Step Three.

Codependency/recovery Twelve-Step programs also deny being religious, but they are religious in the same way as their model, Alcoholics Anonymous. Veronica Ray, author of *Design for Growth: A Twelve-Step Program for Adult Children*, even denies that such programs are moral. She says:

> It's a spiritual program, not a moral one. *Spirituality* can be defined as our relationship with our Higher Power. Morality, which is a specific code of moral rules and conduct, has nothing to do with the Twelve Step program.[16] (Emphasis hers.)

Even when a person reduces the morality to a permissive legalism it is still morality. People are still telling other people what to do and what not to do. For instance, Melody Beattie says:

> If we absolutely can't feel good about something we're doing, then we shouldn't do it—no matter how charitable it seems.[17]

Self-serving ethics are still a form of morality.

The movement takes the AA Step Three and makes it available for nearly every problem relationship that could possibly exist. Therefore, virtually all are called to turn their lives over to a nebulous higher power, a chameleon god that fits anyone's understanding or definition of deity. As Elizabeth Kristol notes, "There isn't a camel alive that couldn't get through the eye of this needle. The Higher Power is always in a good mood."[18] However, by changing one word, Co-dependents Anonymous goes one step further. The group has changed Step Three to say: "Made a decision to turn our will and our lives over to the care of God as we understood God." The masculine pronoun "Him" at the end of the statement is thus eliminated.

Wilson's understanding of God was evidently masculine, but since most codependents are women, they do not want to limit their range of possibilities. Indeed, with the explosion of goddess worship, there is a desire to keep the door as wide open as possible. Furthermore, if one's highest sense of good is god, then god might be "it." Or if one's highest sense of self is god and self happens to be feminine, the masculine pronoun "Him" just won't work.

Beattie discusses what it means for a "recovering codependent" to turn her will over to God. She says:

> We do not have to look around us too long or too hard to find God's will for us and our lives today. It is not hidden from the eye. **God's plan for us today is taking care of ourselves the way we want and choose**, within the framework of what's happening in our lives today.[19] (Emphasis added.)

Isn't that convenient! **Beattie's understanding of God's will is identical with her own.** When one turns one's life over to a god of one's own understanding (subjectively created in the mind), it is easy to create the character, words, and actions of that god (always affirming the person, no matter what). And it is easy to discover the will of that god.

There's no need to study the Bible to find out the will of Beattie's god. Notice that she can decide moment by moment what "God's will" is, since it is only "within the framework of what's happening in our lives today." This is even farther off the mark than situation ethics. "God's will" is whatever Beattie wants it to be at the moment and is limited by no standard beyond what she thinks is best for her. While she may use a smattering of the Bible and lots of God-talk, Beattie offers no body of truth from which a "recovering codependent" is to discover God's will.

And how does Beattie find "God's will"? She says:

> Usually we find God's will by becoming quiet, trusting God, and **listening to and trusting ourselves**.[20] (Emphasis added.)

What a wonderful boost to enhancing one's own ego! Just give self-will the stamp of "God's will" and one can do just about anything and feel righteous and justified. This method reflects the Oxford Group manner of obtaining guidance.

"Taking care of ourselves" is the theme of Beattie's books. Even her discussion of gratitude is self-serving. We would not argue with the importance of gratitude. After all that God has done for us day by day and especially through His Only Begotten Son, Christians should be thanking Him all day long. But, focus is to be on Him, because of what He has done.

For Beattie, gratitude is a technique to "make things work out well" and to "make us feel better while stressful things are happening." She says:

> Gratitude can help bring us to a point of surrender. It can change the energy in us and our environment. Gratitude diminishes the power of the problem and empowers the solution. . . . It breeds acceptance, the magic that helps us and our circumstances change.[21]

There is no hint that God deserves to be thanked, no hint of gratitude being a way to express our love for God. That's because a god created in the mind exists for the benefit of the human god-maker.

Even the so-called Christian books on codependency/recovery echo the theme of self. In their discussion of Step Three, the Christian authors of *Serenity* simply replace one

form of self-centeredness with another. Because of their commitment to humanistic need psychology, they say:

> Breaking out of bondage of self does not mean we
> ignore or deny our needs. In fact, quite the reverse
> is true. If we can discover healthy, God-directed
> ways to meet our emotional and physical needs,
> then we become less needy, less selfish, less self-
> preoccupied individuals. This is another recovery
> paradox. Discovering what our needs are and asking
> to have those needs met may be one of the most
> *unselfish* things we do. . . . Addictions, compulsions,
> and codependencies are counterfeit means of trying
> to meet our most basic physical, emotional, and
> spiritual hungers.[22]

These so-called emotional needs come from Maslow's hierarchy of needs, such as the need for self-worth, self-love, and
self-esteem. There is little distinction made between needs,
desires, wants, and lusts.

In his description of unbelievers Paul says:

> Wherein in time past ye walked according to the
> course of this world, according to the prince of the
> power of the air, the spirit that now worketh in the
> children of disobedience: Among whom also we all
> had our conversation in times past in the lusts of
> our flesh, fulfilling the desires of the flesh and of the
> mind; and were by nature the children of wrath,
> even as others. (Ephesians 2:2-3.)

God's remedy was not to supply the "desires of the flesh and
of the mind." His plan was to give new life. That meant doing
away with the old. Rather than meeting the "needs" of the old
man, He made us new. Thus Paul urged believers to "walk
not as other Gentiles walk, in the vanity of their mind"
(Ephesians 4:17). He said:

> But ye have not so learned Christ; If so be that ye
> have heard him, and have been taught by him, as
> the truth is in Jesus: That ye put off concerning the
> former conversation the old man, which is corrupt
> according to the deceitful lusts; And be renewed in
> the spirit of your mind; And that ye put on the new

man, which after God is created in righteousness and true holiness. (Ephesians 4:20-24.)

Desire for self-worth, self-esteem, self-love, self-significance and self-acceptance belong to the old man. Christians are to put off the old and "put on the new man, which after God is created in righteousness and true holiness."

For nearly 2000 years Christians have surrendered their lives to God for His plans and purposes, rather than for self-advantage. Paul describes what that entailed in his own life:

> Of the Jews five times received I forty stripes save one. Thrice was I beaten with rods, once was I stoned, thrice I suffered shipwreck, a night and a day I have been in the deep; in journeyings often, in perils of waters, in perils of robbers, in perils by mine own countrymen, in perils by the heathen, in perils in the city, in perils in the wilderness, in perils in the sea, in perils among false brethren; in weariness and painfulness, in watchings often, in hunger and thirst, in fastings often, in cold and nakedness. Beside those things that are without, that which cometh upon me daily, the care of all the churches. (2 Corinthians 11:24-28.)

Paul had a vision greater than taking care of himself. Jesus also came to serve others rather than himself. Jesus certainly could have turned the stones into bread (Matthew 4:3-4). He could have stepped down from the cross to save Himself, but He had a greater vision than taking care of Himself. He calls His followers to do likewise through His enabling.

Contrarily, Beattie's call to surrender is for self-empowerment. She says:

> Surrendering is how we become empowered to take care of ourselves.

> Turning our will and life over to the care of God takes the control of our life away from others. It also takes the control of others' lives away from us. It sets us free to develop our own connection to our Source and to ourselves, a connection free of the demands, expectations, and plans of another person. It can even set us free from our own demands, ex-

pectations, and plans.[23]

Again, taking care of self is foremost. Setting oneself free from "demands, expectations, and plans of another person" may **sound** like a good idea for a person who has been sinfully dominated. However, it gives license to excuse oneself from reasonable expectations and plans and legitimate obligations of relationship. There is also a strong possibility that the subtle demands, expectations, and plans of peers in a codependent support group will simply replace those of family and friends outside the group.

Victory in codependency/recovery thus sounds like this:

> As I changed, all hell broke loose in my marriage . . . My husband and I began to fight a lot. My changes threatened him. I kept getting better, but the healthier I got, the worse it got at home. . . . **I consider filing for divorce a real triumph in my recovery.**[24] (Emphasis added.)

Denying Self.

The way of victory in the Christian life is quite different. Not self, but Christ. Not self, but others. Relationship is both receiving and giving to others. When there is a short supply being given by others, the Christian amply receives from the Lord directly, through being strengthened and built up in the spirit. Therefore, while the Christian is to be a good steward of all that God has entrusted to him, including his body, which needs to be taken care of, **the emphasis is never on taking care of ourselves to the extent or in the ways that codependency/recovery literature demands.**

The way of life for any and all sinners who have been redeemed by Christ is through denying self, not catering to self.

> Then said Jesus unto his disciples, If any man will come after me, let him deny himself, and take up his cross, and follow me. For whosoever will save his life shall lose it: and whosoever will lose his life for my sake shall find it. For what is a man profited, if he shall gain the whole world, and lose his own

soul? or what shall a man give in exchange for his
soul? (Matthew 16:24-26.)

Following Jesus thus entails denying self and taking up one's
cross. Denying oneself involves losing one's life for Christ's
sake. It also means dying to all the old ways of the self. And
this must include denying oneself the self-teachings of
Twelve-Steppers who only know what it is to live after the
flesh. Codependency/recovery teachings, influenced by the
philosophies, psychologies, and religions of men are limited to
living after the flesh. They emphasize just the opposite from
denying self.

The denying of self that Jesus is talking about is denying
the will and desires of the self and following the will and
purposes of God. Death to self is for the purpose of living by
His life and will. It is coming under His rulership and obeying
His commandments, even to the very denial of self's pleasures, wants, and desires. Jay Adams explains:

> The words translated "self" and "life" (*heauton* and
> *psuche*) both mean "self" and refer to the same thing.
> . . . Christ is telling us not only to say no to ourselves
> and yes to Him ("follow me"), but He affirms that we
> must put self to death by "taking up our cross" (Luke
> adds "daily"). To take up the cross does not mean
> making some particular sacrifice, nor does it refer to
> some particular burden ("My husband is my cross").
> Anyone in that day, reading those words, would
> know plainly that taking up the cross meant one and
> only one thing: putting to death an infamous crimi-
> nal. Jesus, therefore, is saying, "You must treat
> yourself, with all your sinful ways, priorities, and
> desires, like a criminal, and put self to death every
> day." That says something about the self-image that
> Christ expects us to have![25]

Not all self-denial is biblical, however. People sometimes
deny themselves for the wrong reasons or with the wrong
attitudes and thus gratify themselves instead. Unbiblical
counterfeits of self-denial may be seen when a person puts
himself under the rulership of a spouse's habitual sin, rather
than under the rulership of Christ. In essence that is idolatry,

which is putting anyone or anything in the place of Jesus Christ as Lord. All idolatry is rebellion against God and directed at satisfying the self in one way or another. Even activities that are destructive to the person may be followed for self-satisfying reasons (such as excessive drinking, complaining, or playing the martyr). Predominant influences are lords of a person's life. These are activities of the self that must be denied.

Appearances of denying self are also unbiblical when any of the activities or attitudes involve disobedience to God, such as retaliation, bitterness, resentment, and a whole host of interpersonal sins. Self is not actually being denied in such external and internal activities. On the other hand, some activities, such as caretaking, may be involved in both biblical and counterfeit self-denial, but the purpose is different. Denying self for Jesus' sake is to serve and glorify God in all circumstances.

The battle between the flesh (the ways of the old self) and the Spirit (living in the believer) is ongoing and cannot be ignored. Self is always ready to assume center stage even in the lives of dedicated Christians. That is why the self-teachings of recovery therapists, groups, and guides who are still living under the influence of Satan (Ephesians 2:2) are so dangerous. And that is why Christians must daily deny themselves, take up their cross, and follow Jesus. They must diligently put off the old self and put on the new. What must constantly be denied is the old authority of self ruling the life, of self having its own way, and of self living in such a way as to please itself. It boils down to putting God's will and interests before one's own.

Denying self, rather than esteeming self, equips people to say "No" to habitual sin when they are indwelt by the Holy Spirit. Instead of building up the self, following Jesus and thereby denying the self is the biblical antidote to alcohol, drugs, and other sinful patterns of living. Self-control, not self-love, is a fruit of the Spirit.

Placing the emphasis on taking care of self in codependency/recovery programs is even farther off the mark than AA's Step Three. Both turn the will and life over to a "God as we understood God." The alcoholic does it for the sake of sobriety. The codependent does it for the sake of self. Surely another god is being proclaimed and another gospel is being preached by the promoters of recovery steps and programs. Indeed they may recover their own lives but lose their souls.

7

HERE'S LOOKING
AT ME

Step Four: "Made a searching and fearless moral inventory of ourselves."[1]

If Step Four were taken in the context of Christianity with One Lord and Savior Jesus Christ and one standard rule, the Bible, by which to make the "searching and fearless moral inventory," for repentance and confession by the power of the Holy Spirit, this could indeed be useful. However, as helpful as this may appear, Step Four is part of a Christless system that lacks a universal unchanging standard. And, adding Christ to a Christless system does not make it Christian. Furthermore, the purpose, as brave and righteous as it seems, is once again self-serving. It is to better self rather than to please God and conform to the image of Jesus Christ.

Because of Bill Wilson's exposure to the Oxford Group, some of what he says sounds biblical, but at base he avoids the idea of sin as much as possible. There is no hint of total depravity. Instead, he gives the impression that people are born good, or at least neutral. Rather than being born in sin, he says that everyone is born with personal and social instincts that are good in themselves. However, he contends that when they are misdirected, "our great natural assets, the instincts, have turned into physical and mental liabilities."[2] Therefore, no one need feel guilty or undermined by Step

Four because the "searching and fearless moral inventory"
only has to do with liabilities. It simply has to do with "how,
when, and where our natural desires have warped us."[3] He
further explains that "alcoholics especially should be able to
see that instinct run wild in themselves is the underlying
cause of their destructive drinking."[4] All of this sounds passive, something done **to** the alcoholic rather than **by** the alcoholic.

Wilson then discusses difficulties that one might face in
taking Step Four. First, he says that those "on the depressive
side" may be "apt to be swamped with guilt and self-loathing."[5] He warns against guilt and self-loathing, calling them
"pride in reverse," and advises workers to "comfort the melan-
choly one by first showing him that his case is not strange or
different, that his character defects are probably not more
numerous or worse than those of anyone else in A.A."[6] Sin is
thus minimized.

On the other hand, Wilson warns against the self-righteousness of blaming everything on excessive drinking or on
the behavior of other people.[7] He says:

> For most of us, self-justification was the maker of
> excuses. . . . We thought "conditions" drove us to
> drink. . . . It never occurred to us that we needed to
> change ourselves to meet conditions, whatever they
> were.[8]

Here is the idea that we change ourselves rather than putting
off our old sinful ways and putting on Christ through the
power of the Holy Spirit. While Wilson correctly points out
that "something had to be done about our vengeful resent-
ments, self-pity, and unwarranted pride,"[9] the something he
offers is another religion empowered by self-effort.

After easing into the topic of a "searching and fearless
moral inventory" of instincts that became liabilities, Wilson
adds stronger language as he progresses in his essay on Step
Four. He says there are different degrees of "personality
defects" and says that "those having religious training" might
refer to them as "serious violations of moral principles." He
says, "Some will become quite annoyed if there is talk about

immorality, let alone sin."[10] Nevertheless, he takes the plunge and uses the word *sin*, but really only for a convenient framework set forth by the "Seven Deadly Sins," which he calls "major human failings." He says:

> To avoid falling into confusion over the names these defects should be called, let's take a universally recognized list of major human failings—the Seven Deadly Sins of pride, greed, lust, anger, gluttony, envy, and sloth.[11]

Wilson then makes an amazing statement which thoroughly contradicts his disease notions about alcoholism. He says:

> By now the newcomer has probably arrived at the following conclusions: that his **character defects**, representing instincts gone astray, **have been the primary cause of his drinking and his failure at life**; that unless he is now willing to work hard at the elimination of the worst of these defects, both sobriety and peace of mind will still elude him; that all the faulty foundation of his life will have to be torn out and built anew on bedrock.[12] (Emphasis added.)

That is why the Twelve Steps present a moralistic, religious program—because heavy drinking **is** caused by moral failure (*sin*, to be more exact), not some kind of "allergy."

While taking a "searching and fearless moral inventory" may indeed reveal "character defects" and even the "Seven Deadly Sins," there is no mention of sinning against a Holy God by disobeying His Word and rebelling against His love and sovereignty. Step Four is man-made, man-powered, and man-centered.

The Codependent and Step Four.

The wording of Step Four is identical for Co-Dependents Anonymous, but only parts of the process are the same. Beattie describes what codependents must look for in this "searching and fearless moral inventory." She says:

> We look for what is right about ourselves and our values. We look for the wrongs we have done, too.

> But also included in this moral inventory are our
> self-defeating behaviors and the moral issue of
> whether or not we love ourselves.[13]

For Beattie, the "moral issue of whether or not we love ourselves" is as central to her religion as the issue of whether or
not we love God is central to Christianity. Self is central
throughout her writings.

Codependency/recovery Step Four emphasizes looking
within oneself to expose the pain that has supposedly been
hidden in unconscious repression and denial. Beattie says:

> We look for anger, fear, pain, rage, and resentment,
> including anger at God. We look for victimization. . .
> We look for painful repressed memories.[14]

Just as Step Four is man-made, man-centered, and man-powered for AA, Step Four is self-centered and self-saving for the
codependent. Beattie explains why Step Four is important:

> We do this to set ourselves free from the past. We do
> this to hold ourselves accountable for our own heal-
> ing and to achieve the highest level of self-responsi-
> bility and self-accountability possible.[15]

Notice that self is savior and self is central.

Beattie also says that "the core of recovery" is "self-responsibility."[16] Being responsible for oneself sounds good as
long as this means to be personally responsible to do what is
right. However, throughout the codependency/recovery literature, "being responsible for myself" generally means to put
my needs first.

Dr. Bernie Zilbergeld says, "The doctrine of responsibility
is seductive because it implies power." He quotes Will Schutz
as saying, "Once we accept responsibility for choosing our
lives, everything is different. We have the power. We decide.
We are in control." Zilbergeld says that idea expressed by
Schutz "feeds fantasies of omnipotence. We don't have to bear
any burden or put up with anything we don't like. We've
chosen it and therefore can change it."[17]

Beattie declares: "Honestly facing ourselves and taking
responsibility for ourselves is where our true power lies."[18]

Self comes first and foremost and self is empowered to do what it pleases and chooses.

Codependent Characteristics.

A major activity of Step Four is to look at the characteristics which have been identified with codependency to see how one fits into the picture. Every book about codependency has lists of theoretical symptoms, feelings, actions, and other descriptions. There are authoritative-sounding lists written by psychologists who speak as if they thoroughly understand the problem, even though they are simply applying their own combinations of favorite theories and notions. Lists for self-diagnosis include such questions as these:

> Have you become so absorbed in other people's problems that you don't have time to identify , or solve, your own?
>
> Do you care so deeply about other people that you've forgotten how to care for yourself?[19]

Moreover there are numerous personal anecdotes and stories that seem to lend reality to the notions promoted by the various so-called experts on codependency.

The descriptive phrases on the various lists often have to do with feeling, as well as with thinking and doing. Items on the lists are by no means limited to the so-called codependent. Nor will anyone have all of the characteristics or behaviors. In this section we will discuss a few of the most often described characteristics of so-called codependents. Each section will include descriptive phrases from codependent literature, a brief biblical analysis of the behavior, a psychological and/or Twelve-Step solution, and a biblical solution.

Responsibility and caretaking are given a bad name in codependent literature. Such activities as setting aside one's own routine to meet someone else's need, trying to please others more than self, and being concerned about other people are seen as symptoms of codependence. In contrast, loving and caring for others are virtues from a biblical perspective. To love neighbor as self follows the Great Commandment to love God (Matthew 22:37-40).

Christians are taught concern for others. For instance, Philippians 2:4 says, "Look not every man on his own things, but every man also on the things of others." Throughout Scripture, parents are held accountable for training and nurturing their children (Ephesians 6:4). Their responsibility for the well-being of their spouses is described in Ephesians 5:22-33 and other passages. They are given a measure of responsibility in caring for the poor (James 2:14-16) and for orphans and widows (James 1:27). Jesus' example was one of selfless love. He gave Himself for others.

On the other hand, sinful pride and interference in another person's area of responsibility can occur when a person usurps or undermines the personal responsibility of another person. Here, the sin (most codependent literature does not call any of this sin) is the proud illusion of power and self-righteousness. While one may influence another person for good, one cannot be directly responsible for the choices another adult makes, unless it is by coercion. Also, when feeling responsible for someone else's choice takes precedence over one's own responsibilities for obeying God, a person may tend to blame that other person for his own attitudes, words, and actions.

An example of making this delineation of responsibility, outside the realm of codependency, is when a person witnesses for Christ and shares the Gospel with an unbeliever. While the Christian is responsible to the Lord, he is not responsible for the unbeliever's response to the gospel. That is between God and the unbeliever. If the Christian who testifies for the Lord without apparent results thinks it's his fault the listener is not converted, he is limiting the sovereignty of God and taking responsibility beyond his capability. Likewise, if a spouse or friend assumes responsibility beyond what God has given, he is operating outside his own area of obedience to the Lord. When that happens, he may tend to discontinue obeying God, since he is unsuccessful in accomplishing the responsibility given to others.

Other attitudes and actions accompany wrongfully attempting to usurp authority and responsibility. They include: resentment, anger, and bitterness against the person being helped when that person does not respond as hoped; assuming the guilt of another person instead of admitting and confessing one's own sin; feeling hurt and bitter over not being appreciated; and proudly thinking self is more responsible and capable and therefore better than the other person. Feelings of hopelessness, despair, and depression also come into play after numerous attempts to help turn into absolute failures.

The remedy for all of this in the codependent literature is becoming responsible for oneself rather than for others. And, as mentioned earlier, being responsible for oneself in recovery jargon generally means: putting personal feelings, needs, and even desires first; thinking of what is best for self; and learning to love and care for self more. Codependent writers attempt to help people shift their focus and effort from other people to self. This merely exchanges one form of idolatry for another because whoever or whatever is the unbiblical focus of one's life is that person's idol. Therefore, the self-focus, self-pleasing, and self-loving of this kind of self-responsibility puts self in the place of God.

God's way of clarifying responsibility is through His Word. God's Word is true and sets the prisoner (to self and others) free. Responsibility is in reference to Him, not self. Responsibility comes from responding to God Himself and to His grace and His Word. Biblical responsibility is the response to love, obey, and please God, not self. Rather than self in control, one is to die to self, deny self, and live in obedience and submission to God by grace.

Control is another characteristic assigned to the codependent. Research shows that people tend to develop positive illusions about their own control over self, circumstances, and the future.[20] Such illusion may also be propped up by vain wishes and empty promises in sinful relationships. And with the illusion of control comes a sense of responsibility for keeping everyone and everything under control.

On the other hand, self-control is a fruit of the spirit. It is placing self under the rulership of the Holy Spirit. Christians may also influence one another for good through attitudes and actions that come from the fruit of the Spirit (love,

joy, peace, longsuffering, gentleness, goodness, faith, meekness, temperance). Furthermore, parents are responsible to
control aspects of their children's behavior during their early
years of training. Thus, influence and control are not wrong
in themselves. However, sinful attempts to control others
through domination, intimidation, manipulation, threats,
lies, physical force, helplessness, blame, or nagging are biblically wrong whether they are done by so-called codependents,
substance abusers, or any other human being.

Sinful attempts to control may come from a lust for
power or from unsuccessful attempts to correct problem situations. Underneath sinful attempts to control or manipulate is
the deadliest sin of all: pride. It is pride that puts self, self's
interests, desires, plans, and ideas first. It is often the self-
righteous pride of thinking that self knows what is best. Conflict over control often enters into human relationships and
can bring great devastation.

The answer given by "recovering codependents" and other
writers in the field is simply to control self rather than
others. If the self control is a fruit of the spirit, the person is
moving in a godly direction. However, in the codependency/re-
covery movement, this easily degenerates into a self-centered
activity of looking after number one and arranging self-pleasing circumstances.

Letting go of trying to control or change other adults may
also be admirable. But what is often implied is abandoning
unsuccessful relationships and focusing on controlling oneself
through changing circumstances. While this may be good advice in noncommitted relationships, it has also led to divorce
and abandonment of family members. Anyone, for instance,
who is dating a person with whom there is a sinful relationship of wrongful control, manipulation, intimidation, or any
other kind of cruelty should break the relationship unless
there is a drastic change. On the other hand, unbiblical divorce is never an acceptable solution. Yet divorce is a viable
option according to codependency/recovery authors, some of
whom have solved their own relationship problems that way.
Again the codependency/recovery answer is limited to self, to
self in control. Only the objects of control may change.

What is God's answer to control in relationships? It is the Lordship of Christ in every situation and every relationship. Anyone who is not under the Lordship of Christ is under the domination of self, sin, and Satan. Paul's letter to the Ephesians clearly reveals the condition of unbelievers:

> Having the understanding darkened, being alienated from the life of God through the ignorance that is in them, because of the blindness of their heart: Who being past feeling have given themselves over unto lasciviousness, to work all uncleanness with greediness. (Ephesians 4:18-19.)

Unbelievers are in bondage. But what about Christians who sinfully attempt to control another person? They are to come under the Lordship of Christ. Jesus said:

> As the Father hath loved me, so have I loved you: continue ye in my love. If ye keep my commandments, ye shall abide in my love; even as I have kept my Father's commandments, and abide in his love. These things have I spoken unto you, that my joy might remain in you, and that your joy might be full. This is my commandment, That ye love one another, as I have loved you. Greater love hath no man than this, that a man lay down his life for his friends. (John 15:9-13.)

Jesus put it more strongly:

> If any man will come after me, let him deny himself, and take up his cross, and follow me. For whosoever will save his life shall lose it: and whosoever will lose his life for my sake shall find it. (Matthew 16: 24-25.)

Denying self may not sound very appealing to a person who is accustomed to trying to control other people, but it is God's remedy with great reward, both for now and eternity. Putting every aspect of one's life under the Lordship of Christ will correct wrongful attempts to control others.

Preoccupation with others often accompanies caretaking, feeling responsible for others, and attempting to control them. And of course the answer given by the "experts" centers in being occupied with oneself rather than others. In contrast, the biblical way is be to be occupied with the Lord and others, since we are all naturally occupied with ourselves in one way or another.

Numerous other behaviors and attitudes which supposedly characterize a codependent include guilt, anxiety, dishonesty, finding meaning in other persons rather than self, poor communication, and fear. Remedies are offered, most of which center in self according to the wisdom of men, rather than on God according to His Word. Even the remedies offered by Christians in the field generally reflect those offered by non-Christians. While the Bible is added, it is not treated as the exclusive, authoritative word on the matter. And while Christ is permitted to be the "Higher Power," He cannot be given exclusive Lordship in a program that is based on the worldly wisdom of men rather than on the Word of God.

"Wrongs Others Have Done to Us."

While a so-called codependent may discover things he did to foster the "unhealthy" (actually *sinful*) relationship, there is generally no fault-finding with self, unless it is not having been good enough to self. Instead, the blame and fault-finding land on the person's parents for not having loved enough or just right. Therefore, in practice, Step Four becomes: "Make a searching and fearless moral inventory of my parents."

A major part of looking at characteristics of "recovering codependents" has to do with "denial" and "repression." Denial and repression are so-called ego-defense mechanisms created by Sigmund Freud as part of his theory of the unconscious. According to Freudian theory, people are driven by their unconscious rather than by conscious volition. He believed that people do what they do today because of what happened to them as young children. Thus, in codependency/recovery, the "searching and fearless moral inventory" focuses on the wrongs of others.[21] People are encouraged to reconstruct their past to change the present.

Freud believed and taught that there are three parts to the personality: the *id, ego,* and *superego*.[22] He believed that behavior is motivated by the conflict between id impulses (mainly sexual and aggressive instincts) and the restraints of the ego and superego.[23] According to Freud's system, anxiety comes from restraining the "sexual and aggressive instincts," and defense mechanisms are the means of reducing that anxiety.[24] In their description of Freudian theory, Ernest Hilgard et al explain:

> Freud used the term *defense mechanisms* to refer to unconscious processes that defend a person against anxiety by distorting reality in some way. . . they all involve an element of self-deception.[25] (Emphasis theirs.)

Of course, according to Freud, the person is not aware of his defense mechanisms because they work from the unconscious. They are motivated by so-called unconscious conflicts and unconscious memories of early childhood.

Many Christians assume that they are motivated by an unconscious filled with drives, conflicts, and childhood memories. Nevertheless, Freud's theories of the unconscious and repression have come into disrepute. After carefully analyzing Freud's arguments for his theory of personality and therapy, Dr. Adolf Grunbaum, who is the Andrew Mellon Professor of Philosophy and Research Professor of Psychiatry at the University of Pittsburgh, finds Freud's "cornerstone theory of repression to be clinically ill-founded."[26] Grunbaum faults Freud's theory for failing the test of science. Likewise, Dr. David Holmes reviewed numerous research studies having to do with the possible existence of repression. He concludes that concerning repression "there is no consistent research evidence to support the hypothesis."[27] He further comments on the failure of numerous studies to support the reality of this Freudian notion and then says, "At present we can only conclude that there is no evidence that repression does exist."[28] Individuals should be aware that the defense mechanisms are both unscientific and unsubstantiated.

Moreover, there is no biblical support anywhere for the Freudian unconscious. And since the defense mechanisms depend upon the Freudian theory of the unconscious, there can be no support for them in Scripture either. Freud created defense mechanisms to explain the condition of man because he refused to believe what the Bible says about God's sovereignty, His law, the sinful condition of man, and God's provision for salvation and sanctification through Jesus Christ.

Simply ignoring our own faults or excusing our sin or even forgetting about it does not make it unconscious denial. The human tendency, according to the Bible, is for people to see themselves in a biased manner (Proverbs 16:2). Furthermore, one cannot equate the spirit of man with the unconscious. Paul made this clear when he wrote: "For what man knoweth the things of a man, save the spirit of man which is in him? Even so the things of God knoweth no man, but the Spirit of God" (1 Corinthians 2:11). This verse compares the relationship of the spirit of man with man himself and the relationship of the Spirit of God with God Himself. Therefore, if one were to equate the spirit of man with the unconscious, one would also be saying that the Spirit of God is His unconscious, which would be perfectly ridiculous.

Later theorists, such as Alfred Adler, continued to believe in a Freudian type of unconscious that motivates behavior.[29] However, he believed that people are motivated by a striving for superiority and self-worth rather than by id impulses. Adler and subsequent therapists encourage people to remember instances in the past where so-called needs for self-worth were not met, to feel the pain they experienced as children, and to build one's own self-worth through putting new beliefs into the unconscious.

Because of the heavy influence of both Freudian and humanistic psychology on those who write about and attempt to treat codependents, this "searching and fearless moral inventory" eventually lands in the past and focuses on wrongs that others committed against the codependent's so-called "inner-child-of-the-past." In fact, Hemfelt and Fowler suggest that all addictions arise out of adverse relationships with parents:

> Perhaps our most basic needs for love and nurturing were not met in those early family encounters. . . . This early codependent vacuum becomes the root of our later adult addictions.[30]

What these professing Christians are saying is that the reason for addiction is early childhood deprivation, not simply a sinful nature successfully tempted to sin.

In essence they are saying that people cannot help the way they are and what they do and can therefore say, "I am the way I am because of someone else." Nevertheless no one has ever proved that to be so. While we cannot include research about all "adult addictions" in this book, we will mention research about the one addiction that started the whole movement, alcoholism. *The Harvard Medical School Mental Health Report* gives the following "somewhat unexpected" results:

> For the great majority of alcoholics, there is no good evidence that they began abusing alcohol because they were anxious, depressed, insecure, poorly brought up, dependent on their mothers, subjected to child abuse, raised in unhappy families, or emotionally unstable in childhood and adolescence.[31]

While children are indeed innocent of the wrongs committed by adults, they are by no means pure and sinless. They, too, have been born in sin and sin. They, too, have a sinful nature. To attempt to "reparent" or fix up an innocent inner child is to engage in activity that is nowhere suggested or condoned by Scripture. When Paul declared that he was crucified with Christ, he meant his entire self, including who he was as a child. When he counted his past as dung, he even included his infancy (Philippians 3:4-8). He did not mention an "inner child of the past." Nor did he attempt to fix up the past. Instead, he knew that he deserved the penalty of death and that Christ had died in his place. He identified with that death and then received new life in Jesus.

Jesus gives new life, His own life in the believer, rather than healing the so-called inner child. When a believer identifies with the death of Jesus and reckons himself "to be dead indeed unto sin, but alive unto God through Jesus Christ our Lord," he should not try to hold on to a supposedly pure inner child. There is no pure inner child! That is a secular humanistic, not biblical, idea. Every person was a sinner even when he was a child. Christ died in the place of sinners, including adults and children.

Parent Bashing.

In the codependency/recovery movement, especially in ACOA (Adult Children of Alcoholics), the child is looked upon as innocent and parents are blamed for their grown-up off-springs' present problems. A good example of this is Alice Miller's book *The Drama of the Gifted Child*, which inspired the "inner child" movement.[32] While this book is about damage to children as a result of early "dysfunctional" parenting, inappropriate mothering is really its focus.

In her article "Adult Children: Tied to the Past," Melinda Blau says, "Dumping your sorrows on your parents is not the way to grow up." Blau discusses the pattern of early life blame on parents and the way such individuals see themselves as victims. She quotes one victim as saying, "It's very painful. The way I feel has to do with things done *to me*—not because of who I am as a person."[33] (Emphasis hers.) Blau describes the movement in this way: "Blaming parents for what they did or didn't do has become a national obsession—and big business."[34] Blau says, "Those Adult Children are looking for the Answer—and many think their parents are *it*."[35] (Emphasis hers.)

Family mobiles and diagrams are often used to visually demonstrate that a person's present problems are because of the past behavior of other people. Therapists and others into Family Systems create mobiles to illustrate the paradigm of "dysfunctional" families. These mobiles have various figures represent family members. When weight is added to one member, the others shift to balance the family. As appealing as the visual aid is, it actually misrepresents real life, because it ignores individual differences, relationships with friends, the influence of school, teachers, babysitters and other adults, and even the effects of watching TV. As children mature, they progressively have less to do with their parents and more to do with their own lives, interests, and peers.

Extensive family diagrams, popularized by John Bradshaw, may appear scientific, but they carry the same flaws as the unbalanced mobiles. One cannot use them to **predict** the future of family members. Therefore, they are inadequate to explain the present.

Elizabeth Kristol reports:

> The original Adult Children of Alcoholics movement focused on creating a paradigm of the alcoholic home, in which every family member was entwined in a web of addiction, conspiracy, and silence.[36]

The purpose was to indicate what destructive ways of thinking and behaving they learned in their family. However, in focusing on what happened in the past, there is a strong tendency to think that whatever is done in the present can be blamed on the past. It can turn into a convenient excuse for present behavior with blameshifting rather than simply looking at present patterns of behavior, repenting according to 1 John 1:9, and learning new ways by the grace of God according to His pattern outlined in 2 Timothy 3:16-17.

In addition to the original intent of ACOA, there has been a broad expansion to include everyone from any kind of background. Parental blame has been around for a long time. Blameshifting began immediately after the Fall and has been a sinful tendency ever since. In fact, God's commandment for children to honor their parents was a command against blaming parents. Furthermore, the breaking of that commandment has serious eternal consequences (Mark 7:9-10). However, since the rise of Freud, parent blaming and parent bashing have increased immeasurably.

Parent bashing in the codependency/recovery movement occurs as a result of a perceived early life "dysfunctional" (why not call it *sinful?*) family. However, the parent bashing is generally a euphemism for mother bashing. But bashing of either or both parents is a violation of the commandment to "Honor thy father and thy mother: that thy days may be long upon the land which the Lord thy God giveth thee" (Exodus 20:12).

Whether the codependency/recovery people know it or not, parent bashing is a direct result of Freudian psychology. According to Freud's theory of infantile sexuality, the first five or six years of life pretty much determine the rest of a person's life. Freud's theory of infantile sexuality is also related to his theory of psychic determinism, both of which are within his theory of the unconscious. According to his theory of psychic determinism, each person is what he is because of the effect of the unconscious upon his entire life. Freud believed that "we are 'lived' by unknown and uncontrollable forces."[37] He theorized that these forces are in the unconscious and control each person in the sense that they influence all that the person does. Thus, he saw people as puppets of the unknown and unseen unconscious, shaped by these forces during the first six years of life.

Mothers are blamed for being overprotective during their children's early years. If fathers are blamed for anything, it's for not being there. In addition to being blamed for overprotectiveness, mothers are blamed for emasculating fathers. This is all compounded by Freud's accusation of women being masochistic and envying men for what Freud regarded as having the superior sex organ. So mothers are overprotective, emasculative, masochistic, and envyistic. While none of this has been proved in research, much of it is behind contemporary codependency/recovery programs. **The misogynistic psychology of Freud, slightly modified and greatly disguised, becomes the new persona of a movement that pathologizes and psychologizes women's behavior.**

Like Freud's Oedipus Complex, the codependency/recovery programs are a product of Western minds. Asians are definitely not interested in such programs for two important reasons. Because of the family's sacrosanct character in the East, parent bashing is taboo. Also in the East, expression and individuality are signs of self-centered immaturity. Relationship is Eastern; individuality is Western. For Orientals to be interested in codependency/recovery programs, they must suffer a great fragmentation in family life, as has happened in America, and they must become narcissistic and self-centered, as is the case of Americans.

Dangers of Delving into the Past.

Many of the codependency/recovery therapies encourage

people to remember painful incidents in their childhood and to reexperience those memories with heightened emotion. In outlining the recovery process, the Christian authors of *Love is a Choice* say, "You will explore your past and present to discover the truth about you."[38] But what kind of truth does a person find? Besides learning theoretical explanations which are fabrications of men's minds, they may actually recall fictitious or distorted events. Therefore, they may not even be certain of finding facts, let alone truth. Nevertheless, this is the underlying, unfounded promise of regressive therapy.

With the help of a therapist, the person is led step by step into recall and sometimes visualization. And with an external voice directing the process through questions and suggestions, the person may actually recreate events and add into the memory false information, events that never actually happened, and strong emotions related to the reconstructed memory. Thus, while memories of actual events may be recalled in therapy and group sessions, they may be distorted through present recall, and false memories may even be implanted. Because of the highly suggestible state of the person in such sessions, neither the participant nor leader may be able to distinguish true memories from false memories that arise during sessions of recalling childhood incidents.

As a result of such regression, some adult children are recalling events that never even happened. A number of parents have reported receiving phone calls and correspondence from their children that plunge them into a nightmare of accusations of abuse and incest. These are grown children who throughout their lives had no recollection of being sexually molested. Now, seemingly out of the blue, their bizarre stories are stunning their parents. These adult children, usually daughters, now claim to remember precise details of one of their parents sexually abusing them. Some even accuse their parents of involving them in such unlikely activities as satanic rituals and human sacrifice. Where do they get such ideas? Where do those sordid memories come from? What brings them to the surface? Regressive-type witch hunting, used in codependency/recovery, lurks behind this surge of family horror stories.

At first the parents are stunned. They are being accused of sexual exploits they declare they would never even think of doing. But when they try to talk to their adult child, their words fall on deaf ears. They are accused and condemned without a trial—all based upon alleged memories discovered through regressive therapy. And now they are helpless in their concern over the welfare of their adult child who will have nothing to do with them.

With the media accentuating and exaggerating the numbers of women who have been molested, nearly anyone who cries "incest" is believed without question. And why should anyone doubt a grown woman's sudden "recall" of a memory hidden in her unconscious? After all, most people believe that the memory, like a tape recorder or computer, faithfully records and retains every event in some deep subconscious vault of the mind. However there are some serious problems with those assumptions.

The Brain and Memory.

When the "moral inventory" involves going into the past, it relies on the false assumption that the brain accurately records past incidents and that such memories can be recalled accurately and intact. While many writers of pop psychology continue to equate the human mind with a tape recorder or computer, those are poor and misleading analogies. Dr. John Searle, in his Reith Lecture, "Minds, Brains, and Science," says:

> Because we don't understand the brain very well we're constantly tempted to use the latest technology as a model for trying to understand it.[39]

But Searle explains that the brain is neither a mechanical piece of technology nor a repository of solid material.

Medical doctor-researcher Nancy Andreasen, in her book *The Broken Brain*, declares that "there is no accurate model or metaphor to describe how [the brain] works." She concludes that "the human brain is probably too complex to lend itself to any single metaphor."[40]

Current research demonstrates that computer memory

and biological memory are significantly different. In his book *Remembering and Forgetting: Inquiries into the Nature of Memory*, Edmund Bolles refers to the human brain as "the most complicated structure in the known universe."[41] He says:

> For several thousand years people have believed that remembering retrieves information stored somewhere in the mind. The metaphors of memory have always been metaphors of storage: We preserve images on wax; we carve them in stone; we write memories as with a pencil on paper; we file memories away; we have photographic memories; we retain facts so firmly they seem held in a steel trap. Each of these images proposes a memory warehouse where the past lies preserved like childhood souvenirs in an attic. This book reports a revolution that has overturned that vision of memory. **Remembering is a creative, constructive process. There is no storehouse of information about the past anywhere in our brain.**[42] (Emphasis added.)

And the creative aspect of remembering is highly charged in counseling or group work that delves into the past. It becomes a joint creativity of the counselor or group leader asking leading questions and making suggestions and the counselee or group participant cooperating and thereby incorporating new material or making new connections.

Is Memory Reliable?

Unlike a computer, **the memory does not store everything that goes into it**. First, the mind sifts through the multitude of stimuli that enters it during an actual event. Then time, later events, and even later recall color or alter memories. During the creative process of recall, sketchy memories of events may be filled in with imagined details. And, an amazing amount of information is simply forgotten—gone, not just hidden away in some deep cavern of the mind. Memory is neither complete nor fixed. Nor is it accurate. As researcher Dr. Carol Tavris so aptly describes it:

> Memory is, in a word, lousy. It is a traitor at worst,
> a mischief-maker at best. It gives us vivid recollec-
> tions of events that could never have happened, and
> it obscures critical details of events that did.[43]

Yes, memories can even be created, not from remembering
true events, but by implanting imagined events into the
mind. In fact, it is possible for implanted and enhanced memories to seem even more vivid than memories of actual past
events.

Under certain conditions a person's mind is open to
suggestion in such a way that illusions of memory can be
received, believed, and remembered as true memories.
Exploring the past through conversation, counseling, hypnosis, guided imagery, and regressive therapy **is as likely to
cause a person to dredge up false information as true
accounts of past events**. In a state of heightened suggestibility a person's memory can easily be altered and enhanced.
This can readily happen during codependency/recovery
"moral inventories" that search out early life experiences.

The Power of Suggestion.

Because the power of suggestion is so very strong in
regressive explorations and in groups that encourage remembering and reliving the past, some of the same things happen
as in hypnosis. Bernard Diamond, a professor of law and clinical professor of psychiatry, says that hypnotized persons
"graft onto their memories fantasies or suggestions deliberately or unwittingly communicated by the hypnotist."[44]

Not only may they have new memories, but Diamond
declares that "after hypnosis the subject cannot differentiate
between a true recollection and a fantasy or a suggested
detail."[45] He notes that court witnesses who have been hypnotized "often develop a certitude about their memories that
ordinary witnesses seldom exhibit."[46] That certitude is strong
for memories that have been enhanced during any kind of
highly suggestible regressive therapy. Even in instances
where there are eye witnesses to the past events with material such as photographs and other reliable records (such as

medical records), the person with such engrafted memories may well deny the evidence and stick with the false memory.

The certainty of pseudomemories and the uncertainty of real memories render such activities as hypnosis and regressive explorations questionable at best and dangerous at worst. Because memory is so unreliable and pliable under suggestion, methods of cure that rely on unearthing so-called hidden memories may even expose the mind to demonic suggestion. While a hypnotist, therapist, or group leader may wish to protect the person from receiving false material, he cannot avoid implanting human suggestion. Nor can he prevent demonic suggestions from entering the vulnerable mind of the person who is in a heightened state of suggestibility.

It is **very possible** that people who remember verbal abuse, physical abuse, sexual abuse, or incest by regressing are remembering an illusion or distortion of reality, a destructive suggestion accidentally placed there by another person, or created through a combination of stimuli, such as from a nightmare, or worse yet, implanted by demonic influence. The pain and agony of false memories and then the extended pain and agony of reliving false or enhanced memories add more pain and agony that must later be resolved in one way or another. That is why regressive explorations, which are often used in so-called "moral inventories," go on for such extended periods of time.

Worse yet, such people have **no doubts** about their newly discovered dark memories. In fact, the certainty of the alleged memory has the mark of an hypnotically engrafted memory rather than of a distant reality. And who can or will reveal the truth to them? Probably not their church or other Christians who believe in psychotherapy and Twelve-Step programs.

The tragedy of people with newly unearthed "memories," caught in a black hole of anger, resentment, unforgiveness, accusations, separation, and confusion, is part of the picture of the damage wrought by those who honestly believe they are helping people. Regressing into the past, rummaging about in the unconscious for hidden memories, conjuring up images, experiencing the agony of such nightmares, and believing lies resemble the work of Satan, **not** the Holy Spirit. An imaginary memory created in a highly suggestible activity or environment will only bring imaginary healing. It may also plunge people into a living nightmare.

Even if the memories were truly reliable, the solution to the problem does not lie in the past or in what other people have done to us. It is not the sins of others that separate us from God and ultimately from each other. It is our own sin and our own sinful reactions. It is our own sin that brings separation, guilt, fear, and a whole host of other problems.

Cause or Temptation?

One reason why the past is so important to therapists and codependency/recovery books and programs is because people are looking for the why's and wherefore's of present behavior. They hope that going into the past will provide keys for understanding and therefore changing present feelings and behavior. It is also a way to avoid or lessen the issue of human depravity and sin.

Psychologists generally assign a cause and effect relationship to behavior, as if someone or something (parents, society, circumstances) causes a person to behave in a certain way. Cause and effect behavior began in the Garden of Eden when Adam blamed Eve and Eve blamed the serpent. Even though many reasons are given for sinful behavior, responses, and habits, the biblical reason is the combination of a person's sinful nature and temptation.

The popular codependency/recovery movement places the reason for a whole host of behaviors on other people and relationships. Since behaviors which would be identified as sin in the Bible are relabeled "codependent behavior," the answer is not Christ and Him crucified, confession, forgiveness, and repentance. The answer given by the sirens of codependency/recovery is to change yourself by taking care of yourself, "reparenting yourself," and putting your own needs first. Thus people identified as "codependents" are simply urged to move from one form of self-centeredness to another, rather than from self to God.

While certain behavior patterns are called "codependent"

they are not unique in themselves, even though there may be similarities of sinful responses to similar temptations. God's Word applies to such temptation:

> There hath no temptation taken you but such as is common to man: but God is faithful, who will not suffer you to be tempted above that ye are able; but will with the temptation also make a way to escape, that ye may be able to bear it (1 Corinthians 10:13).

Hope for the Present (and the Future).

Parents are to bring up their children in the nurture and admonition of the Lord. If they do not, they stand guilty for their own sin. Children who have not had godly parents and children who have had godly parents stand equally guilty before God for their own sins. They are not excused on the basis of parental failures (Ezekiel 18:20). The same remedy applies: death to the old man (including the so-called hurt inner child) and new life in Jesus.

Whether people have learned good or bad ways of interacting in relationships while growing up, they will sin in relationships. The answer to **all** sinful relationships is relationship with Jesus and learning godly ways of interacting with other people through the Word of God, work of the Holy Spirit, and fellowship in a local body of believers. The answer is **not** healing the so-called child within, but taking the whole person (one's childhood and all) to the cross.

A major problem with many codependency/recovery books is the belief that going back to childhood to find the why's of present feelings and behavior and even to find where patterns developed will bring relief and transformation. For instance, in *Love Is a Choice* the authors reveal their psychological assumption that the past is causing present problems. They say:

> Codependents characteristically have an excess load of guilt and magical thinking. These two factors (among others) play an important role in this perpetuation of the original family, as codependents feel the intense need to replicate the past even more so than most of us. It is said that twenty percent of

> our decisions come from the conscious, reasoning
> mind. The rest come from deep within. And the
> depths within the codependent have been skewed
> like the lightning-struck tree.[47]

There is not a shred of research evidence to support the above
statement. The Lord holds us responsible for all our decisions
and actions. There is neither biblical nor scientific support for
saying that most decisions come from deep within, unless one
is speaking of learned habitual ways of acting, such as
opening a door before entering a room without going through
a long process of deciding whether to open the door. Those
who major on exploring the past believe the Freudian myth
that the unconscious is a vast reservoir of motivation that is
filled with past determinants of behavior.

The following is an example of a therapist speaking with
a client in *Love Is a Choice*:

> On your last visit, Gladys, we talked about your
> father and the influence he worked on you . . . the
> fact that he never listened, was never there for you.
> I suggested then that you've applied your father's
> obtuseness to John—even though John is not
> obtuse. Have you been thinking about that?[48]

Notice the strong generalizations, "the **fact** that he **never**
listened, was **never** there for you." How can the therapist
make such all-encompassing statements? He was not there.
Even if this is the impression the woman has of her father,
the therapist is making a strong assumption that may or not
be true. Moreover, whether the assumption is true will not
make the difference. The woman can only make present
choices. She is the one who may have to change habitual
ways of thinking, acting, and reacting to others. In fact, the
woman resists the therapist's suggestion and does not see a
connection.

The authors counter her resistance to their suggestion
from their superior position of authority by saying that
"counselors are trained to hear and listen exactly."[49] There is
no evidence for such a statement. Instead, counselors are
trained to listen for what will fit into their psychological

theories. In other words, they are looking for something when they are listening. While they are doing that, they may miss valuable information. In fact, they may totally overlook the obvious.

Fossicking about in the past to hunt for reasons for present behavior to produce change denies the work of the cross, which is the only remedy for the guilt and domination of sin. Indeed, more needs to go to the cross than a person's "shortcomings"! The old self must be crucified (Galatians 2:20). To go back does not free anyone from self or from present or past problems. Instead, there is a strong possibility that the person will become a prisoner of the past by dwelling on it and in further bondage to self through blameshifting.

Instead of attempting to understand the depth of our own depravity as a reality, not just as a theological concept, we spend most of the time trying to minimize our own natural depravity. Then when we get glimpses of it, we wonder why we are the way we are and look for some external reason, such as a negative childhood, parents, or spouse. The Epistle to the Romans teaches that all stand guilty before God (Romans 3:10-12, 23). But Jesus died for sinners. Through His death and resurrection He opened the way of new life through faith in Him (Romans 5:8-10).

When a person is regenerated he is to count his old self dead and walk in newness of life (Romans 6:3-11). However, even then he encounters the problem of old habits and patterns of sin lodged in his flesh. Paul found that it was impossible to do the right thing just by wanting to (Romans 7:14-23). He needed more than himself or his own will to overcome temptation. He cried out, "O wretched man that I am! Who shall deliver me from the body of this death?" But he did not stop there. His devastating realization of his own sinfulness was met by the conclusion of Romans 7: "I thank God through Jesus Christ our Lord. So then with the mind I myself serve the law of God; but with the flesh the law of sin." And that introduces Paul's discourse on being spiritually minded and walking according to the Spirit of Life in Christ Jesus rather than the flesh (Romans 8).

Jesus came to save us from our past sins and He came to

save us from sinning now. He does it through enabling us to resist temptation through His own life at work in us—through a love relationship that enables the obedience He calls us to. When Christians do sin, they have an advocate with the Father, who intercedes on their behalf and provides a way for present forgiveness and cleansing (1 John 1:9-2:1). Therefore the diagnosis of sin is not to be avoided. Jesus came to save sinners and to set them free from their own sinfulness and to give them eternal life. Rather than "making a searching and fearless moral inventory," David prayed:

> Search me, O God, and know my heart: try me, and know my thoughts: And see if there be any wicked way in me, and lead me in the way everlasting (Psalm 139:23-24).

8

JUDGING BY WHAT STANDARD?

Step Five: "Admitted to God, to ourselves, and to another human being the exact nature of our wrongs."[1]

Step Five looks good on the surface. After all, 1 John 1:9 says, "If we confess our sins, He [God] is faithful and just to forgive us our sins, and to cleanse us from all unrighteousness." However, lest anyone think Step Five is equivalent to biblical confession of sin, we must remember that in AA God can be any form of higher power, and admission in itself is not what saves. Only the God of the Bible can save and forgive sin, because it was committed against Him; in actuality, every sin is ultimately against Him. According to the Bible, freedom from sin comes from God's forgiveness and cleansing, not from admission to any god, self, or another person.

According to Bill Wilson, a person does not have to be a Christian to benefit from Step Five. He says:

> This practice of admitting one's defects to another person is, of course, very ancient. It has been validated in every century, and it characterizes the lives of all spiritually centered and truly religious people. But today religion is by no means the sole advocate of this saving principle. Psychiatrists point out the deep need every human being has for practi-

cal insight and knowledge of his own personality
flaws and for a discussion of them with an understanding and trustworthy person.²

Therefore the God of Creation who revealed Himself in the
Bible is not even necessary for Step Five. Instead of this
being a recognition of sinful rebellion against God the Father
and the Lord Jesus Christ, this step is for "practical insight"
and self-knowledge. It is for a sense of relief, of feeling forgiven, and of being accepted by the paid professional or by
members of a support group. Nevertheless, it is a counterfeit.
Without Jesus there is no forgiveness of sin. People may forgive people. But all continue under the condemnation of sin
until they are cleansed by the blood of the Lamb by faith in
Jesus dying in their place. But according to the Twelve Steps
it doesn't matter what god is involved. What matters is finding an accepting, affirming, supportive listener.

In spite of the seeming good intentions of admitting "the
exact nature of our wrongs," two roadblocks stand in the way
of such an admission. First of all, the moral code of a person
who follows a nebulous higher power will be equally nebulous. It will resemble the person's own sliding scale of situation ethics or whatever moral code he happens to subscribe to.
Second, self-deception is a strong component, especially when
a person has been under the domination of habitual sin. That
is why the "exact nature of our wrongs" will certainly exclude
many facets of sin and even might, on the other hand, include
admirable behavior, such as putting others before self.

The Subjective Standard of Self.

The lamentable last words in the book of Judges are
these: "In those days there was no king in Israel, every man
did that which was right in his own eyes" (Judges 21:25). And
this is the grievous condition today. Unless Jesus is the sover-
eign king in a person's life, that person does "that which [is]
right in his own eyes." The Israelites did so even though
God's Law had already been given to them through Moses.
People continue to do what seems right in their own eyes
today even though they have God's law and gospel in the

Bible. Therefore, for a person to admit to a god of his own understanding, to himself, and to others the exact nature of his wrongs, he must rely on his own subjective knowledge of good and evil.

Subjective knowledge of good and evil is appealing to the fallen nature of man. Atheists, agnostics, secular humanists, religionists, and even many who profess Christ live by their own subjective code—their own personal understanding of good and evil. This is especially true in the religions of recovery. If they create a god of their own understanding, they can create their own subjective knowledge of good and evil. In doing so they are simply following the example of Adam and Eve in the Garden of Eden.

The forbidden fruit from the tree of the knowledge of good and evil birthed a sinful self that would live by subjective standards and seek personal fulfillment and gratification. The tempter seduced Eve away from trusting God and into trusting self and Satan. When the serpent asked Eve about the restriction in the Garden, Eve answered:

> We may eat of the fruit of the trees of the garden: but of the fruit of the tree which is in the midst of the garden, God hath said, Ye shall not eat of it, neither shall ye touch it, lest ye die. (Genesis 3:2-3.)

She knew the command of God, but the enemy of her soul was not daunted. He boldly declared, "Ye shall not surely die" (Genesis 3:1, 3), and then implied that God was withholding good from her by saying:

> For God doth know that in the day ye eat thereof, then your eyes shall be opened, and ye shall be as gods, knowing good and evil (Genesis 3:4).

This has been Satan's ploy all along—offering personal enlightenment, power, and subjective knowledge of good and evil in opposition to God's revelation, sovereignty, and truth.

This was the first offer to become one's own bearer of truth, evaluator of right and wrong, and personal benefactor. Eve was fascinated at the prospect. Her eyes shifted from trust in God to the seductive promise of the forbidden fruit.

> And when the woman saw that the tree was good for
> food, and that it was pleasant to the eyes, and a tree
> to be desired to make one wise, she took of the fruit
> thereof, and did eat, and gave also unto her husband
> with her; and he did eat (Genesis 3:6).

Eve's confidence in God's character, truthfulness, love, and spoken word wavered. Rather than waiting on God in trust and obedience, she took the first step towards self-direction, self-empowerment, self-love, self-gratification, and self-fulfillment.

Eve shared her new-found knowledge with Adam and he ate as well, in full recognition that he was disobeying God's command. This was the beginning of trusting self rather than God and the beginning of loving self more than God. Adam and Eve became their own little gods, knowing good and evil from their own subjective perspective. Their vision of God dimmed and their vision of self and each other became distorted. This was the beginning of the darkness spoken of by Paul when he described how the Gentiles walk, "in the vanity of their mind, having the understanding darkened, being alienated from the life of God through the ignorance that is in them, because of the blindness of their heart" (Ephesians 4:17, 18). It all began with a focus on self.

Partaking of the tree of the knowledge of good and evil did not bring godly wisdom. It brought guilt, fear, and separation from God. Thus, when Adam and Eve heard God approaching, they hid. When God asked, "Who told thee that thou wast naked? Hast thou eaten of the tree, whereof I commanded thee that thou shouldest not eat?" (Genesis 3:11), they justified themselves and cast blame.

Adam blamed Eve and God, and Eve blamed the serpent. The fruit of the knowledge of good and evil spawned the sinful self with all of its self-determined values, self-salvation techniques, self-love, self-esteem, self-acceptance, self-righteousness, self-denigration, self-pity, and other forms of self-focus and self-centeredness. It was also the beginning of blameshifting.

The present recovery movement is thus rooted in Adam and Eve's sin. Through the centuries mankind has continued to feast at the tree of the knowledge of good and evil, which has spread its branches of worldly wisdom. It has branched out into the vain philosophies of men and, more recently, the "scientized" philosophies and metaphysics of modern psychology. The four branches of psychology which seek to supplant the Word of God are the psychoanalytic, the behavioristic, the humanistic, and the transpersonal. Those kinds of psychology are neither objective nor scientific. They are bound to subjectivity and bias and are built on presuppositions which often conflict with the revealed Word of God. They consist of the worldly wisdom of men, which Jesus, the prophets, and the apostles rejected (1 Corinthians 2). They are part of the world referred to in 1 John 2:

> Love not the world, neither the things that are in the world. If any man love the world, the love of the Father is not in him. For all that is in the world, the lust of the flesh, and the lust of the eyes, and the pride of life, is not of the Father, but is of the world (1 John 2:15-16).

Existentialism along with secular humanism undergirds the great emphasis on the self. Personal subjectivity and feelings are the hallmarks of existential humanism. The self is the center and evaluator of experience, the determiner of right and wrong, and its needs must be met. Add the spiritual dimension of a higher power and a mystical experience and you have a perfect combination of transpersonal psychology in Twelve-Step recovery programs, along with the basic tenets of psychoanalytic and humanistic theories.

"The exact nature of our wrongs" is tied to a subjectivity that began in rebellion, a subjectivity that sets self up as the standard. Furthermore, the analysis of "the exact nature of our wrongs" comes from the popular concepts of secular psychology, made palatable to each person's subjective understanding of God and of right and wrong. While this could lead to anarchy, it is held in check by a hierarchy of opinion and power through professional therapists and support group peer pressure. Thus, while each person has great freedom in creating his own god, there is a moral code that is taught throughout the recovery literature. The thrust of that moral code, especially in codependency/recovery programs, centers in loving self.

Subjective Feelings and Self-Deception.

Self-deception is not only a strong component in those whose lives are dominated by habitual sins, such as "alcoholism" and other "addictions"; it is also common among all people because of the fallen nature. The Bible calls the heart deceitful: "The heart is deceitful above all things, and desperately wicked: who can know it?" (Jeremiah 17:9.) This does not refer to an unconscious, but rather to subtle but intentional self-deception. Self-bias prevails even among those people who engage in feelings of self-hatred because underneath it all, everyone loves himself.

Recent studies of self-deception have to do with what are called "positive illusions" in contrast to "accurate self-knowledge." Dr. Shelley Taylor and Dr. Jonathon Brown, in an article titled "Illusion and Well-Being: A Social Psychological Perspective on Mental Health," propose that "accurate self-knowledge may be negatively related to psychological health."[3] In other words, they are suggesting that "positive illusion" (self-deception) may be good for people. They discuss research that challenges the traditional view of mental health. In a summary they say:

> Many prominent theorists have argued that accurate perceptions of the self, the world, and the future are essential for mental health. Yet considerable research evidence suggests that overly positive self-evaluations, exaggerated perceptions of control or mastery, and unrealistic optimism are characteristic of normal human thought. . . . These strategies may succeed, in large part, because both the social world and cognitive-processing mechanisms impose filters on incoming information that distort it in a positive direction; negative information may be isolated and represented in as unthreatening a manner as possible.[4]

They are suggesting that self-deception is normal and

healthy. Taylor discusses these same issues in her book *Positive Illusions: Creative Self-Deception and the Healthy Mind.*[5]

Taylor and Brown use the following definition of *illusion*:

> . . . a perception that represents what is perceived in a way different from the way it is in reality. An illusion is a false mental image or conception which may be a misinterpretation of a real appearance or may be something imagined. It may be pleasing, harmless, or even useful.[6]

And they distinguish illusion from error and bias by saying:

> *Error* and *bias* imply short-term mistakes and distortions, respectively, that might be caused by careless oversight or other temporary negligences. *Illusion*, in contrast, implies a more general, enduring pattern of error, bias, or both that assumes a particular direction or shape.[7]

In summary they say the research:

> . . . documents that normal individuals possess unrealistically positive views of themselves, an exaggerated belief in their ability to control their environment, and a view of the future that maintains that their future will be far better than the average person's.[8]

Taylor and Brown demonstrate that most people do, in fact, have unrealistically positive views of themselves, their ability to control their environment, and their future. In contrast, those who have a realistic view tend to be moderately depressed. They call the ability and propensity to deceive oneself as an "enviable capacity."[9]

In her book *Positive Illusions*, Taylor gives much research evidence to support the idea that positive illusions and self-esteem begin early in life and may be part of the fabric of being human. She says:

> Mild positive illusions appear to be characteristic of the majority of people under a broad array of circumstances. . . . The evidence from studies with children suggests that positive illusions may actually be

wired in, inherent in how the mind processes and as-
cribes meaning to information. The fact that positive
illusions are typically so much stronger in children
than in adults argues against the idea that they are
learned adaptations to life.[10]

Taylor says that while people may learn more complex
ways of deceiving themselves, such self-deception is not a
learned behavior:

> Rather, the basic form of positive illusions—seeing
> the self, one's potency, and the future in a falsely
> positive manner—may not have to be learned. In
> fact, the opposite appears to be true. Positive illu-
> sions may actually have to be unlearned, at least to
> a degree, for people to function effectively in the
> adult world.[11]

Nevertheless, Taylor and Brown believe that:

> . . . the capacity to develop and maintain positive il-
> lusions may be thought of as a valuable human re-
> source to be nurtured and promoted, rather than an
> error-prone processing system to be corrected.[12]

The codependency/recovery movement, along with the
self-esteem, self-love industry, is based upon people's desire
to feel good about themselves. And if one wants to feel good
about himself, there will be plenty of opportunities to develop
that natural propensity of self-deception. Perhaps one of the
reasons so much attention is given to cultivating the "inner
child of the past" is because of this tendency to deceive oneself
into thinking of oneself as good, perfect, wise, and innocent.
The "inner child of the past" fulfills this role.

The apparent purpose of Taylor's book *Positive Illusions*
is to justify and promote self-deception, because she seems to
believe that self-esteem is more important than truth. What
this research actually demonstrates is that the fruit of the
knowledge of good and evil is laced with lies and that fallen
humanity has followed the footsteps of Satan, who is the de-
ceiver and the father of lies. Any system that promotes self
evaluating self on the basis of self or any other human standard is bound to error, bias, deception, and ultimately evil.

The Only True Standard.

In contrast to the self-deceptive ways of the world, the flesh, and the devil, Jesus said, "If ye continue in my word, then are ye my disciples indeed; and ye shall know the truth, and the truth shall make you free" (John 8:32). The issue at stake is truth. Truth is extremely important to God. So much so that Jesus promised to send the Spirit of Truth to indwell His disciples (John 14:16-17).

The Bible is God's revelation of truth to mankind. Jesus prayed to the Father: "Sanctify them through thy truth: thy word is truth" (John 17:17). Believers are saved by this "word of truth, the gospel of your salvation" (Ephesians 1:13).

Jesus is the very life of the believer. He is also the standard and the model. A number of years ago Charles Sheldon wrote a book titled *In His Steps*.[13] It is a story that explores the challenge of doing what Jesus would do in every situation. In the story people are challenged with this question, "What would Jesus do?" Those who accepted the challenge and asked themselves that question at decisive points in their lives met with tremendous adventures. The book has been reprinted and been a challenge to others. However, that question often gets lost in the flurry of events and in the convenience of living in an affluent society. Nevertheless, it is a question that drives us to the standard: Jesus Christ.

One does not have to guess how Jesus would act. The Bible is the decisive, authoritative book which both reveals and reflects Jesus. The Bible is God-breathed and works together with the Holy Spirit for direct application. It is the only authoritative standard that perfectly matches Jesus. Both Jesus and the Bible are called the Word of God. Therefore, the Bible is the standard by which to live, to judge thoughts and behavior, and to change.

> All scripture is given by inspiration of God, and is profitable for doctrine, for reproof, for correction, for instruction in righteousness, That the man of God may be perfect, throughly furnished unto all good works. (2 Timothy 3:16-17.)

First of all, the Bible is absolutely true and accurate because it is inspired by God and therefore is His revelation of right and wrong. It is His written guide for faith and practice. It is neither culturally bound nor vacillating. It is universal and permanent (1 Peter 1:25).

The Bible is "profitable for doctrine." The doctrine of the Bible is its authoritative teachings. Bible doctrine teaches about God and man and tells him everything that he needs to know to live in a manner pleasing to God. Doctrine gives the basic commands and guidelines for behavior.

The Bible is also "profitable . . . for reproof." The Bible reproves of sin because it is not simply a written word. It is a living Word:

> For the word of God is quick, and powerful, and sharper than any two-edged sword, piercing even to the dividing asunder of soul and spirit, and of the joints and marrow, and is a discerner of the thoughts and intents of the heart (Hebrews 4:12).

The Bible is "profitable . . . for reproof" because such reproof brings believers to repentance and confession and therefore correction. Reproof is pointing out sin.

The natural man does not like reproof from the Word of God. He wants affirmation, compliments, and praise. Yet, in His love, the Lord reproves His children with His Word. Reproof is something to be embraced by a Christian, not avoided.

> Whoso loveth instruction loveth knowledge: but he that hateth reproof is brutish (Proverbs 12:1).

> A wise son heareth his father's instruction: but a scorner heareth not rebuke (Proverbs 13:1).

> The ear that heareth the reproof of life abideth among the wise (Proverbs 15:31).

The response of a Christian is to agree with the reproof, the conviction of sin. That is what confession really is. God's forgiveness then cleanses him from sin so that he can start out all over again with a clean slate. He is then free to change his direction in that he is free to act according to the Life of Jesus within him, rather than according to his old sinful ways.

The Bible is "profitable . . . for correction." Corrections from the Lord may not be easy. It takes diligence to overcome old habits with godly habits. It is a continual process of putting off the old ways of the self with the new ways of the Lord. Even though change may be difficult, the Lord's correction brings with it His promise to work in us. As we choose to change according to His plan, He enables us to do so by His grace. The Lord's correction brings hope rather than discouragement or despair, because He is able to do what He has promised. He is working in every believer to conform him to the image of Jesus Christ.

> Now the God of peace, that brought again from the dead our Lord Jesus, that great shepherd of the sheep, through the blood of the everlasting covenant, Make you perfect in every good work to do his will, working in you that which is wellpleasing in his sight, through Jesus Christ; to whom be glory for ever and ever. Amen. (Hebrews 13:20-21.)

Further instruction in righteousness follows the doctrine, reproof, and correction. This is the daily practice of living by the Word of God. A good description of this daily practice is described in 2 Peter 1. Peter first declares that God has given believers all that they need to live the Christian life. He says:

> Grace and peace be multiplied unto you through the knowledge of God, and of Jesus our Lord, according as his divine power hath given unto us all things that pertain unto life and godliness, through the knowledge of him that hath called us to glory and virtue: Whereby are given unto us exceeding great and precious promises: that by these ye might be partakers of the divine nature, having escaped the corruption that is in the world through lust. (2 Peter 1:2-4.)

After Peter says that Christians have been given all they need to live the Christian life, he gives them instruction for their part:

> And beside this, giving all diligence, add to your faith virtue; and to virtue knowledge; And to knowl-

> edge temperance; and to temperance patience; and to patience godliness; And to godliness brotherly kindness; and to brotherly kindness charity. For if these things be in you, and abound, they make you that ye shall neither be barren nor unfruitful in the knowledge of our Lord Jesus Christ. (2 Peter 1:5-8.)

Notice the great importance of the knowledge of Jesus Christ in all of this. He is indeed our model and standard, as well as our life. Also notice the importance of diligence and perseverance in continuing in "doctrine, reproof, correction, and instruction in righteousness."

> But he that lacketh these things is blind, and cannot see afar off, and hath forgotten that he was purged from his old sins. Wherefore the rather, brethren, give diligence to make your calling and election sure: for if ye do these things, ye shall never fall: For so an entrance shall be ministered unto you abundantly into the everlasting kingdom of our Lord and Saviour Jesus Christ. (2 Peter 2:9-11.)

The standard of the Bible is "profitable . . . that the man of God may be perfect, throughly furnished unto all good works" (2 Timothy 3:17). In other words, the Bible is a perfect and living standard that not only shows the way, but also enables the person to follow the way. Each child of God is "his workmanship, created in Christ Jesus unto good works, which God hath before ordained that [he] should walk in them" (Ephesians 2:10).

The standard for truth is not simply an external standard, as many who criticize biblical Christianity say. Neither is it the inner unregenerate person. The standard of truth is both objective and external as a written document and an internal living reality through the indwelling Holy Spirit. Christians are vitally connected to their standard, Jesus Christ. In fact, Jesus emphatically declares:

> Abide in me, and I in you. As the branch cannot bear fruit of itself, except it abide in the vine; no more can ye, except ye abide in me. I am the vine, ye are the branches: He that abideth in me, and I in him, the same bringeth forth much fruit: for without

me ye can do nothing. (John 15:4-5.)

As Paul testifies, the mystery of the Christian life is "Christ in you, the hope of glory" (Colossians 1:27).

The Word of God is the sole standard of authoritative truth for living in a manner pleasing to God. It is also a powerful spiritual Word, which enables believers to live by its standard. The Word of God gives wisdom and guidance. It cleanses and sanctifies (John 15:3 and 17:17). It strengthens, sustains, and comforts. And it is the only true standard of righteous judgment and godly living.

Oh that Christians would return to the blessed Word of God for help in time of need, for wisdom in confusing circumstances, for light in dark places, and for refreshing in times of spiritual drought! Oh that Christians would not be deceived by the ways of men and the wiles of the devil in these treacherous times! Oh that Christians would once again declare with their Savior that they "shall not live by bread alone, but by every word that proceedeth out of the mouth of God" (Matthew 4:4). There is only one way to discern the "exact nature of our wrongs" and that is through the Word of God. May He give us grace to abide by His Standard revealed in His Holy Bible!

Toxic Substitutes.

In spite of all that the Lord has given to His children through His Word and Holy Spirit, Christians continue to look elsewhere to solve their problems of living. Pastors and theologians have delegated much of their leadership and responsibility for God's flock to psychologists. First they lost confidence in the Word of God for counseling and added the theories and therapies of the world. Then they reneged on their responsibility to counsel and either sent their flock out to a "Christian psychologist" or brought such professionals on staff. Professional psychological counselors are now therapizing and "discipling" the flock. Indeed they are teaching whole congregations how to live. Today pastors and theologians are being stripped of their authority in spiritual, theological matters. The "Christian psychologists" are now the authorities on what constitutes true faith and what is "religious addiction."

Secular psychologists have been suspicious of and antagonistic to biblical Christianity all along. Freud contended that religion is "the obsessional neurosis of humanity."[14] The book *Rorschach Interpretation: Advanced Technique* reveals the anti-religious bias of psychological diagnosis:

> Religion contents are virtually never present in the records of normals. Their occurrence is associated with profound concern about the problems of good and evil, concern which, almost always, is a screen for and displacement of guilt induced by sexual preoccupation. Religion content may be used to infer critical and unresolved problems of sexuality.[15]

The humanistic psychologists repudiated Christianity, but wanted the lion's share of the spiritual life. Abraham Maslow contended that "spirituality was a legitimate focus of psychology."[16]

One of the most rapidly growing branches of psychology is transpersonal psychology, which is any blend of psychology and religion. Today psychologists incorporate whatever faith system or parts of faith systems they desire. They have not only become the spiritual mentors of the New Age and the addiction/recovery movement; they have also become the spiritual mentors in the church. Thus from their position as psychologists, both Christians and nonChristians are speaking authoritatively about what constitutes "religious addiction," or what two Christian authors have labeled "toxic faith." Christian psychologists have joined their secular colleagues in criticizing fellow believers for being rigid, fundamental, or excessively religious. But their subjective evaluations have swerved from the only true standard by which to judge. Therefore they judge what is rigid and what is right, what is narrow and what is fundamental, according to their own psychological persuasion and personal opinion.

An example of this is the book *Toxic Faith* by Stephen Arterburn and Jack Felton. One of their examples of "toxic faith" is faith in the Bible alone instead of faith in the Bible

and psychology. They attempt to make a case for the integration of psychology and the Bible. According to their own "toxic" reasoning, they set up a straw man as follows:

> The battle between religion and psychology has been waged on this toxic belief for years. Many have nothing to do with anything relating to emotions unless it is in Scripture. Their train of thought goes like this: *If there is not a Scripture to back the idea, it must be harmful.* This is close to the truth but not quite on the mark. True faith means that a person should not do anything that goes against something from God's Word. It doesn't mean that *every* behavior or insight into life is going to be found there.[17] (Emphasis theirs.)

The straw man erected by these authors is that individuals who are opposed to the integration of psychology and the Bible believe that: "If there is not a Scripture to back the idea, it must be harmful." Someone once said, "There is nothing so uncommon as common sense." However, common sense would dictate that no one literally holds such a point of view. There are numerous ideas not in Scripture that may be neutral or even beneficial that do not usurp the exclusive role of Scripture.

We, along with numerous others hold the view that according to 2 Peter 1:2-4, the Lord has given people all they need to know to lead a life pleasing to God. We contend that the Bible is sufficient for problems of living as it works together with the Holy Spirit to discern the thoughts and intents of the heart and to guide in all matters of the nonphysical aspects of life (the soul and spirit). We further believe that psychological theories and therapies based upon the philosophical assumptions of unregenerate men (who originally developed such theories) intrude upon an area that exclusively belongs to Scripture and thereby subvert the Word of God to being simply one of many sources of wisdom. As Thomas Ice and Robert Dean clearly state in their book *A Holy Rebellion*:

> Second Timothy 3:16, 17 tells us that "all Scripture is God-breathed and profitable for teaching, for

reproof, for correction, and for training in righteousness, that the man of God may be adequate,
equipped for every good work." This passage gives
us some valuable information about the Scriptures.
First, it tells us that the source of the Bible is God.
. . .

Second, because the Bible is absolute truth, it is
profitable to teach us, to correct our thinking, to
reprove or reprimand us for wrong thinking and living, and to instruct us. Our Lord said in His prayer
for the disciples the night before He was crucified,
"Sanctify them in the truth; Thy word is truth"
(John 17:17). It is *the Word of God alone* which gives
us the truth we need to live for Him.

The third point we want to emphasize from 2
Timothy 3:16, 17 is the purpose for the Word of God.
It is to make the believer, the man or woman of God,
completely equipped for every good work. The word
translated "adequate" is the Greek word *artios*,
which means "fit, complete, capable, sufficient."
This means that the Word of God gives us the information or guidelines needed to meet every situation
we face in life. . . . The point is that the Bible claims
not only to give us true and accurate information
but *all* the information we need to handle *any and
every* situation that might arise in our lives.[18]
(Emphasis theirs.)

The difference between those of us who believe in the
sufficiency of Scripture and the authors of *Toxic Faith* is simply that. We believe that the Scriptures are sufficient for
problems of living and for correcting erroneous thinking and
for overcoming life-dominating sinful habits. They do not; else
why would they offer a substitute?

We do not claim, as the authors of *Toxic Faith* suggest,
that "every behavior or insight into life is going to be found
there." Neither do Ice and Dean. They say:

Whenever we have taught this principle that the
Scriptures are totally sufficient for every need and
situation in the believer's life, someone inevitably
asks why, if this is true, should we even go to school

or pursue studies in any other area. . . .

This question arises because people do not realize how the truth of God's Word impacts all the different realms of life. In this book we are talking about the sufficiency of God's Word in enabling us to live a life pleasing to God. God's Word does not claim to be a textbook about oceanography or accounting or engineering, though it does contain some broad information about these areas of study.

What the Bible claims to provide is *absolute truth in all areas of Christian life and spirituality.*[19] (Emphasis theirs.)

Ice and Dean's book deals with spiritual warfare and that includes resisting temptation, overcoming devastating life-dominating sins, and walking in the spirit rather than according to the world, the flesh, and the devil.

Another Christian leader who reveals a high view of Scripture says about the Word of God:

It is complete, there is nothing left out. It is comprehensive, it does everything that we need it to do. There is no part of your life, no problem that you will ever face in your life, no question, with which you will ever be troubled, that the Word of God does not speak to and illuminate and meet.[20]

Like those who "do not realize how the truth of God's Word impacts all the different realms of life," the writers of *Toxic Faith* try to build an argument for using psychological theories and therapies with the same kinds of illogical arguments. They say:

The Bible is not a manual for brain surgery. It does not tell us not to smoke crack cocaine. There is no Scripture on what music is bad or good. How to operate a computer has been left out.[21]

The extension of their argument is that since the Bible does not contain all of the information necessary for various activities in life, it is certainly permissible and even advisable to supplement it with psychological theories and therapies. We say this is "toxic" reasoning. They began with the mental-emotional realm, and specifically throughout their argument they make a case for integrating psychology and the Bible. Yet they use an example from the medical realm (brain surgery). To confuse it even further, they mix in "what music is bad or what is good." And end up with "how to operate a computer."

Their parallel of performing surgery on the brain and using psychological theories and therapies is erroneous. Equating the practice of medicine with the practice of psychology shows little sensitivity to the gross errors involved in this mistaken logic. Nevertheless, psychologists often use the medical model to justify the use of psychotherapy. By using the medical model, many assume that "mental illness" can be thought of and talked about in the same manner and terms as medical illness. After all, both are called "illnesses." However, in the medical model, physical symptoms are caused by some pathogenic agent, such as viruses. Remove the pathogenic agent and the symptom goes as well. Or, a person may have a broken leg; set the leg according to learned techniques and the leg will heal. One tends to have confidence in this model because it has worked well in treating physical ailments. With the easy transfer of the model from the medical world to the psychotherapeutic world, many people believe that mental problems are the same as physical problems.

Applying the medical model to psychotherapy originated with the relationship between psychiatry and medicine. Since psychiatrists are medical doctors and since psychiatry is a medical specialty, it seemed to follow that the medical model applied to psychiatry just as it did to medicine. Furthermore, psychiatry is draped with such medical trimmings as offices in medical clinics, hospitalization of patients, diagnostic services, prescription drugs, and therapeutic treatment. The very word *therapy* implies medical treatment. Further expansion of the use of the medical model to all psychological counseling was easy after that.

Additionally, the medical model supports the idea that every person with social or mental problems is ill. When people are labeled "mentally ill" and their problems of living are categorized under the key term *mental illness*, it is easy for people to assume that addictions are diseases and that thinking and behaving are "toxic."

Those who believe this do so because they have been influenced by the medical model of human behavior and are confused by the terminology. They think that if one can have a sick body, it must follow that one can have a sick mind. But, is the mind part of the body? Or can we equate the mind with the body? The authors of the *Madness Establishment* say, "Unlike many medical diseases that have scientifically verifiable etiologies and prescribed methods of treatment, most of the 'mental illnesses' have neither scientifically established causes nor treatments of proven efficacy."[22]

The authors of *Toxic Faith* have fallen into the error of equating brain with mind. Their error is further extended when by inference they equate working with a computer with living a life pleasing to God. The Bible does not purport to be a scientific or medical textbook. It does claim to be sufficient for doctrine, reproof, correction, and instruction in righteousness so that a person may live pleasing to God. Brain surgery is a physical activity, which should be under the moral and spiritual restraint of Scripture in that no harm be done, such as in the horrendous cases of frontal lobotomy. But, the Bible plays a far greater role than that of authority in the nonphysical realm; this is the realm of scriptural exclusivity.

The Bible is not only the authoritative guard and guide as should be the case for scientific inquiry and technological advances; but Scripture is the exclusive source of truth for understanding the condition of man and for knowing how to overcome sin and live a life pleasing to God. Psychological therapy and any other psycho-religious system, such as Twelve-Step programs, operate in the nonphysical realm. But psychological theories and therapies advanced by both secularists and Christians are intruders in the nonphysical realm because they did **not** originate from Scripture. They originated elsewhere, in the imaginations of men's minds and from subjective observations based upon unbiblical presuppositions.

The Bible was not written as a science text on physical

aspects of the universe. Rather, it was written for the express purpose of revealing to man what he needs to know about living in relationship to God and to others. Within that revelation comes the knowledge of the Fall, the sinful condition of unredeemed man, God's provision for salvation, and how a redeemed person is to live in relationship to God and man through the new life in Jesus Christ. Between the Bible's covers lie "exceeding great and precious promises, that by these ye might be partakers of the divine nature" (2 Peter 1:4). The Word of God is revealed truth about mankind, with no error or bias.

In their defense of psychology, the authors of *Toxic Faith* give an extreme example of a woman on medication for depression, who went to a church that frowned on that kind of medication. They say that she stopped her medication and "in a fit of depression she slit her wrists."[23] If one were to make a general case from extreme examples, one would have to repudiate the toxic faith of Arterburn and Felton. Much harm has been done through psychotherapy and there are numerous hideous skeletons in the psychological closets, such as those recorded in such books as *The Victim is Always the Same*[24] and *"If I Die, Will You Love Me?"* [25]

Richard Stuart's book *Trick or Treatment: How and When Psychotherapy Fails* is filled with case studies that reveal "how current psychotherapeutic practices often harm the patients they are supposed to help."[26] At the end of his book Stuart says:

> The extensive research reviewed in this book has shown that, compared with patients who receive no treatment or very limited treatment, those who receive both in- and out-patient treatment have a small chance of experiencing marked improvement, a very great chance of experiencing little or no change and a small chance of experiencing deterioration.[27]

Negative effects from psychological therapy have been verified by other research. Harm rates range from small to great with the average being about ten percent.[28]

We have numerous cases in our files of the harmful

results from Christian therapists and treatment centers that would make cases recited by Arterburn and Felton in their book pale by comparison. However, it is not upon the extreme cases that we rest our case; we rest it upon the Scriptures. We include the additional scientific research for the sake of those who do not fully trust the Bible. Our differences with the *Toxic Faith* authors are based upon the issue of the sufficiency of Scripture. We hold to the sufficiency view; they hold an insufficiency view of Scripture or they would not use the opinions of men masqueraded as science in order to commercialize a business.

Arterburn is the Chief Executive Officer of New Life Treatment Centers. Charles Todd, Robert Schuller's attorney, reported that Arterburn "approached the [Schuller] ministry and indicated his desire to establish an inpatient-treatment facility based upon Christian principles. . . . He felt that Dr. Schuller's positive theology, combined with the gospel of Jesus Christ, would provide an excellent Christian treatment program."[29] Of course all such treatment programs are psychologically-based, so this would be a combination of psychological theories/therapies, positive thinking, and a version of the gospel that would fit.

The book *Toxic Faith* is not our main subject. However, we did want to give at least one example of how a "toxic faith" in their own man-made system has led them to distort the true faith once delivered to the saints. While the authors warn about distorted views of God and false religious systems, their own book is contaminated with distortions and false reasoning similar to what we have just noted. They have taken theological misunderstandings and errors and turned them into components of an addictive disease. By taking theological and spiritual problems and putting them into the addiction realm, they have taken the role and authority which rightfully belong to pastors, theologians, and even lay Christians and given that role and authority to psychologically trained professionals and lay leaders of Twelve-Step programs.

Even their use of the word *toxic* pulls the behavior or thinking away from the idea of sinfulness and puts it into an addictive disease category, thereby ripping thinking and behaving which might otherwise be called "sin" away from an exclusively biblical evaluation and answer. In mixing psychology and the Bible they have wrested the spiritual life right out of the church and put it into psychological therapy, treatment centers, and Twelve-Step psycho-religious programs and self-help groups.

Another Christian clinical psychologist who writes about religious addictions and codependency is Dr. Margaret Rinck. She uses some of the same misleading arguments as Arterburn and Felton. She thinks that people who oppose psychology oppose science and research. She says that "when the facts come from psychological research, they are afraid to accept them."[30] In actuality, those of us who oppose the incorporation of psychological counseling theories into the church use and quote research.

The psychology Rinck and others want to give Christians is that part of psychology which attempts to understand the human condition—why we are the way we are and how to change. Psychological research that maintains strict scientific guidelines does **not** support the kinds of psychology she promotes. Rinck depends on the personal opinions of men and women for her authoritative-sounding statements. Instead of giving scientific research support she simply repackages the unbiblical psychological opinions of Robin Norwood, Melody Beattie, Anne Wilson Schaef, John Bradshaw, and other worldly codependency/recovery gurus.

Like all other promoters of the psychological opinions of men, Rinck uses the "all truth is God's truth" cliché. What she fails to tell us is that most of what she teaches comes from opinions of men rather than what may be discovered from "general revelation." Even strict scientific investigation falls short of truth and can at best reveal information about the natural laws of God's created universe. Psychological theories and therapies are a far cry from the truth Jesus talks about concerning the human condition and the promises of God.

It is difficult to determine what psychological notions about the condition of man, his motivations, and his behavior might hope to find a place in the "all truth is God's truth" basket. There are over 250 different (competing and often conflicting) systems of psychological counseling and over 10,000 often contradictory techniques. The confusion of psychology was demonstrated in 1985 at a large convention of over 7000 psychiatrists, psychologists, and social workers. Such psycho-celebrities as Carl Rogers, Albert Ellis, R. D. Laing, Bruno Bettleheim, and Joseph Wolpe attended. Criticism from the speakers themselves included reports that most of the present distinct schools of psychotherapy are doomed to fizzle, that psychiatry is not a science, and that nothing new in human relations has surfaced from a century of psychotherapy.[31]

The various debates and differences of opinion led behavior therapist Dr. Joseph Wolpe to confess that "an outside observer would be surprised to learn that this is what the evolution of psychotherapy has come to—a Babel of conflicting voices."[32] So when people use the convenient cliché "all truth is God's truth," remember that the psychological opinions of unsaved men more resemble a "Babel of conflicting voices" than "God's truth."

Rinck also belittles the spiritual aspect of man and magnifies the psychological. She calls such statements as "If they'd just find Jesus," and "If they'd just make Christ Lord of their life" "Christian clichés."[33] Those happen to be statements that incorporate the essence of salvation and sanctification. Calling them "Christian clichés" reveals her low view of Scripture and her high view of man-made psychological systems. She fails to realize that her own book is filled with addiction and codependency/recovery clichés. Rinck says:

> While a "spiritual experience" with Christ is essential to recovery from any sin-based problem, it is not the *only* thing necessary."[34] (Emphasis hers.)

Her problem is that she reduces "spiritual" to "experience." Thus, instead of help found in the whole counsel of God, the Bible, she brings forth help outside Scripture.

Rinck accuses those who believe that the Bible does what it says concerning all matters of life and conduct as holding a

Greek-Dualistic view, which comes down to saying that the material world is evil and the spiritual world is good. What she misunderstands is that human activities originate from the spiritual dimension of man and that one cannot separate man into "spiritual" and "psychological."

Rinck is the one who believes in a false dualism when she limits the "spiritual world" without realizing that "nonphysical realities" include everything that her kind of psychology seeks to rip away from the word "spiritual." The nonphysical, spiritual aspect of the human condition includes motivation, thoughts, emotions, attitudes, beliefs, actions, and reactions. Neither can one rip "human activities" from the spiritual realm. The Bible clearly reveals that outward actions originate from the inner (nonphysical, spiritual) man (Matthew 15:18-19).

Arterburn, Felton, and Rinck are not alone. Numerous others discuss religious addictions and fail to realize that they are promoting the most popular "toxic faith" systems of the day: Twelve-Step programs and psychotherapy with its underlying psychologies. God's Word is the only standard by which to evaluate behavior and belief. To evaluate religious belief with the wisdom of men is preposterous. The Bible is the only standard by which to evaluate faith and practice.

9

SINFUL
SUBSTITUTES

Alcoholics Anonymous Steps Six and Seven are continuations of Step Five and have to do with change. Step Five has to do with admitting "wrongs," Step Six with being ready for God to remove "defects of character," and Step Seven with asking God to remove those "shortcomings." All three steps involve "God," alter the significance of sin, and present a Christless sanctification.

Step Six: "**Were entirely ready to have God remove all these defects of character.**"[1]
The object of Step Six is to get rid of "defects of character" and "shortcomings." The underlying goal is to overcome the addiction by perfecting the character. The power for the endeavor is a deity defined by subjective knowledge and experience. At face value this sounds like a worthy decision—to be "ready to have God remove these defects of character." Nevertheless, in spite of the religious and moralistic nature of this step, it is not dependent upon the One and Only Creator of the universe.

Step Six comes with a promise: success! In his essay about Step Six, Bill Wilson includes this as a typical AA member's testimony:

Sure, I was beaten, absolutely licked. My own will-

> power just wouldn't work on alcohol. Change of
> scene, the best efforts of family, friends, doctors, and
> clergymen got no place with my alcoholism. I simply
> couldn't stop drinking and no human being could
> seem to do the job for me. But when I became will-
> ing to clean house and then asked a Higher Power,
> God as I understood Him, to give me release, my
> obsession to drink vanished. It was lifted right out
> of me.[2]

Notice here that "no clergyman" could help. Is that because
pastors failed to preach the Gospel? When a person is truly
saved, he is released from the domination of sin and has the
opportunity to replace old habits with godly habits and the
fruit of the Spirit. Paul gave the antidote to drunkenness:

> And be not drunk with wine, wherein is excess; but
> be filled with the Spirit; Speaking to yourselves in
> psalms and hymns and spiritual songs, singing and
> making melody in your heart to the Lord; Giving
> thanks always for all things unto God and the
> Father in the name of our Lord Jesus Christ; Sub-
> mitting yourselves one to another in the fear of God
> (Ephesians 5:18-21).

Or could it be that the person whom Wilson quotes refused to hear the true Gospel? Jesus describes this condition:

> For this people's heart is waxed gross, and their
> ears are dull of hearing, and their eyes they have
> closed; lest at any time they should see with their
> eyes and hear with their ears, and should under-
> stand with their heart, and should be converted,
> and I should heal them (Matthew 13: 15).

Pride refuses to hear the gospel because the gospel must be
preceded by the law of God by which all are condemned.

The law of God, clarified by Jesus throughout His ministry, together with the good news of God's mercy and salvation, will motivate people to open their hearts to Him or to
harden their hearts. When a person exercises saving faith,
given to him by the grace of God, he believes both the law
which would condemn him and the gospel which saves him

from that condemnation and gives him new life. When a person hardens his heart, he may believe enough of the law to feel threatened, but instead of accepting the death blow to self and the offer of new life in Jesus, he defends himself with self-justification (excuses), self-righteousness (developing his own moral character), and self-deception (avoidance of the truth through rationalizing or anesthetizing the mind with distractions or drugs).

On the other hand, if the person who gave the above testimony (quoted by Wilson) had ever eagerly received the good news of Jesus Christ, he may never have became rooted and grounded in Him. Perhaps he was like the man in the parable of the seed that fell into stony places, who "heareth the word, and anon with joy receiveth it; yet hath he not root in himself, but dureth for a while; for when tribulation or persecution ariseth because of the word, by and by he is offended" (Matthew 13:20-21).

It is also important to notice the continual reference to willpower not being enough. This is natural since those involved in promoting AA evidently demonstrated insufficient will power before their conversion to the Twelve Steps. The authors of *Dying for a Drink* insist that will power is not enough and yet they state emphatically that cultures in which drunkenness is not condoned have almost no alcoholics. They say, "Moslems and Mormons, who forbid the drinking of alcoholic beverages, have almost no alcoholism in their communities."[3] Obviously the will, influenced by peer pressure, keeps them abstinent. Nevertheless, the same authors seem critical of Christians for having moralistic, judgmental attitudes toward drunkenness.[4] Furthermore, the entire Twelve-Step program is limited to will power unless it is energized by occultic forces that would respond to any conceptualized deity.

Research has not ruled out the strength of the will when it comes to habits:

> Most people who quit their bad habits . . . do so on their own in a five-stage process: 1) accumulated unhappiness; 2) the moment of truth, or last straw; 3) changing daily patterns (throwing away ash

trays, for example); 4) a growing sense of control; 5)
support from family and friends.[5]

The Effectiveness of AA.

In spite of numerous testimonies claiming success in AA,
we know of no studies that support its effectiveness. If there
are any, we would like to know about them. The so-called
effectiveness of AA comes through personal testimonies and
anecdotal stories. And of course such testimonies leave out
the many failures of the movement.

In a book about treatment of addictive behaviors, William Miller and Reid Hester present a chapter titled "The
Effectiveness of Alcoholism Treatment: What Research Reveals." They say:

> In spite of the fact that it inspires nearly universal
> acclaim and enthusiasm among alcoholism treat-
> ment personnel in the United States, Alcoholics
> Anonymous (A.A.) wholly lacks experimental sup-
> port for its efficacy.[6]

They first refer to some studies on AA that "yield results that
are virtually uninterpretable." Then they say:

> Only two studies have employed random assignment
> and adequate controls to compare the efficacy of A.A.
> versus no intervention or alternative interventions.
> Brandsma *et al* (1980) found no differences at 12-
> month follow-up between A.A. and no treatment,
> and at 3-month follow-up those assigned to A.A.
> were found to be significantly *more* likely to be binge
> drinking, relative to controls or those assigned to
> other interventions (based on unverified self-re-
> ports). Ditman and Crawford (1966) assigned court
> mandated "alcohol addicts" to A.A., clinic treatment,
> or no treatment (probation only). Based on records of
> rearrest, 31% of A.A. clients and 32% of clinic-treat-
> ed clients were judged successful, as compared with
> 44% success in the untreated group (Ditman, Craw-
> ford, Forgy, Moskowitz, & MacAndrew, 1967).[7] (Em-
> phasis theirs.)

They also refer to other studies evaluating multidimensional programs that reveal no advantage for AA. They mention one study comparing a "complex treatment program (including A.A., medication, outpatient, and inpatient care)" with "a single session of counseling consisting of feedback and advice." A twelve-month follow-up revealed that the complex program with AA "was no more effective in modifying alcohol consumption and problems" than the single counseling session with advice.[8]

This is their concluding statement concerning AA:

> To be sure, these studies (like most any research) can be criticized for methodological weaknesses, and as always "further research is needed." Given the absence of a single controlled evaluation supporting the effectiveness of A.A. and the presence of these negative findings, however, we must conclude that at the present time **the alleged effectiveness of A.A. remains unproved**.[9] (Emphasis added.)

Dr. Stanton Peele, who is a senior health researcher at Mathematica Policy Research and author of *Diseasing of America: Addiction Treatment Out of Control*, says, **"Several studies have shown that those who quit drinking via A.A. actually have higher relapse rates than those who quit on their own."**[10] (Emphasis added.)

Nevertheless AA claims great success. The Foreword of the Second Edition of *Alcoholics Anonymous* says:

> Of alcoholics who came to A.A. and really tried, 50% got sober at once and remained that way; 25% sobered up after some relapses, and among the reminder, those who stayed on with A. A. showed improvement. Other thousands came to a few A.A. meetings and at first decided they didn't want the program. But great numbers of these—about two out of three—began to return as time passed.[11]

Since they indicate no controlled research studies and since no corroborating evidence has been supplied by researchers in the field of alcoholism, these percentages are guesses and opinions. Numbers like 50% are meaningless unless there is research support. Chapter 5 of *Alcoholics Anonymous* (Third

Edition) says:

> Rarely have we seen a person fail who has thor-
> oughly followed our path. Those who do not recover
> are people who cannot or will not completely give
> themselves to this simple program, usually men and
> women who are constitutionally incapable of being
> honest with themselves. There are such unfortu-
> nates. They are not at fault; they seem to have been
> born that way.[12]

Thus the program is touted as a great success even though
many have failed to benefit from being involved. Unfortunately, in spite of the research, most people still believe the claims
of AA.

Ineffective Addiction Treatment Programs.

Besides the efficacy of AA being questioned by the research, there is also evidence that both individual psychotherapy and other addiction treatment programs are usually ineffective. *Newsweek* magazine reports, "Individual psychotherapy, the rehab experts agree, is notoriously ineffective in treating addiction."[13]

In contrast to the advertisements for secular and Christian treatment centers, the testimony to the United States
Senate Committee on Governmental Affairs states:

> Residential treatment settings yield no higher over-
> all rates of successful outcome than less expensive
> nonresidential treatment alternatives. Longer resi-
> dential programs likewise have not been shown to be
> more effective than shorter programs. . . .
>
> There is no single superior treatment approach for
> alcohol problems. . . .
>
> Specific and relatively brief (1-3 session) interven-
> tions have been shown to reduce long-term alcohol
> consumption and related problems.[14]

Dr. Herbert Fingarette says that "both independent and
government research show expensive disease-oriented treatment programs to be largely a waste of money and human
resources."[15] He says that "medical treatment for alcoholism

is ineffective." He continues:

> Medical authority has been abused for the purpose
> of enlisting public faith in a useless treatment for
> which Americans have paid more than a billion
> dollars. To understand why the treatment does no
> good, we should recall that many different kinds of
> studies of alcoholics have shown substantial rates of
> so-called "natural" improvement. As a 1986 report
> concludes, "the vast majority of [addicted] persons
> who change do so on their own." This natural rate of
> improvement, which varies according to class, age,
> socioeconomic status, and certain other psychologi-
> cal and social variables, lends credibility to the
> claims of success made by programs that "treat" the
> "disease" of alcoholism.[16]

Thus people in treatment may actually be benefiting from the
natural rate of improvement rather than the treatment itself.
As we mentioned earlier, Peele thinks people have a better
chance to quit and stay sober if they do it on their own. We
cited research in Chapter Four which revealed that "Most recovery from alcoholism is **not** the result of treatment."[17]

The following statistic indicates that not all alcoholics are
doomed without AA or other treatment:

> The average problem drinker is 25 to 35, married,
> and working, and has never been treated for alco-
> holism. Fewer alcohol abusers are over 40; "matur-
> ing out" is common, as in heroin addiction.[18]

Treatment only seems to be helpful because "patients usually
come into treatment at a low point and therefore almost always improve for a while."[19] However, the recidivism rate is
extremely high. The same is true for heroin addicts. *The Harvard Medical School Mental Health Letter* says:

> The relapse rate among treated heroin addicts is
> very high, but there is much evidence that addicts
> in the community often eventually cure themselves
> without formal treatment.[20]

AA and treatment programs operate on the basis of faith and
hope rather than on the basis of research and results, just

like all other religions.

Moralistic Character Development or Jesus?

In his essay on Step Six, Wilson emphasizes that it is not enough to be willing to have God remove only those character defects that stand in the way of personal happiness. However, Wilson does not go far enough. He does not realize that man is born with original sin, is totally depraved, and needs to crucify the flesh (Galatians 5:24). More has to go than "defects of character." The entire old life must go.

Until he met the Lord Jesus Christ on the road to Damascus, the Apostle Paul spent his entire life being willing to have God remove all the defects of his character. He describes his own righteousness this way:

> Though I might also have confidence in the flesh. If any other man thinketh that he hath whereof he might trust in the flesh, I more: Circumcised the eighth day, of the stock of Israel, of the tribe of Benjamin, an Hebrew of the Hebrews; as touching the law, a Pharisee; Concerning zeal, persecuting the church; touching the righteousness which is in the law, blameless (Philippians 3:4-6).

If anyone had reached the pinnacle of moral perfection by personal diligence, Paul had. Nevertheless, Paul declares:

> But what things were gain to me, those I counted loss for Christ. Yea doubtless, and I count all things but loss for the excellency of the knowledge of Christ Jesus my Lord: for whom I have suffered the loss of all things, and do count them but dung, that I may win Christ (Philippians 3:7-8).

There is a vast difference between true Christianity and efforts to remove character defects with the help of any "God as we understood Him."

Codependency/Recovery Step Six.

The expression "defects of character" takes on a whole new perspective in Melody Beattie's book *Codependents' Guide to the Twelve Steps*. Just as God may be subjectively defined in the Twelve Steps, Beattie thinks it's okay to redefine "defects of character" into what we are "ready to ask God to heal us from." She quotes a woman by the name of Beth to help her readers accept the idea that something needs to be "let go of."

> "I hate the language of 'defects of character,' " said Beth. "I chose to look at this Step this way: became entirely ready to have God heal us. I don't believe that we act out because we're defective or bad. I **believe we act codependently because we're wounded. And telling someone who's wounded that he or she is defective or that they've sinned or that they fall short of the mark is abusive.**"[21] (Emphasis added.)

From the tone of the chapter, this expresses Beattie's sentiments exactly. The statement undercuts the entire Bible and Jesus Christ in one blow. "Beth" is actually accusing Jesus Himself of being abusive. Jesus came to save people from their **sinful reactions** as well as from their sinful actions and their sinful natures. No one can escape this description.

Beattie doesn't think it matters, "Whether we call them defects of character or our protective devices."[22] This is an amazing transition. First *sin* is changed to *defects of character* in AA and then *defects of character* become *wounds* or *protective devices* in codependency/recovery. Notice the move from a biblical description to a psychological diagnosis.

And what must be "let go of"? Besides listing a number of attitudes and activities that would be labeled "sin" in the Bible, she lists the common psychological self-jargon of "Low self-esteem," "Our self-neglect," "Self-rejection," "Self-hatred," "Lack of self-trust," and "Our abuse from childhood."[23] She says:

> We become ready to be healed from our pasts, from unresolved feelings of guilt, anger, hurt, and grief over the many losses we've endured. We become ready to let go of the negative beliefs that we latched onto as a result of our pasts: that we're unlovable, a disappointment, a burden, not good enough, stupid, unworthy, a problem, and a bother.[24]

Jesus does heal us from our past, but not through some kind of psychological means of dredging up the past and blaming our own attitudes and actions on what happened to us. Rather than simply telling us to let go of "negative beliefs," Jesus enables us to know the truth which sets us free from the bondage of self and sin. That truth includes both the law of God and the gospel of Christ. Jesus takes the focus off ourselves, whereas codependency/recovery programs keep the focus on self but add rose-colored glasses.

Beattie is not alone in turning "defects of character" into "wounds" and "self-protective devices." The Christian authors of *Love is a Choice* list all kinds of behaviors under "denial" and "repression," both of which are called "protective devices." Their explanations for codependent behavior focus on the hurts of the past, denial of those hurts, and internalized anger, which they contend leads to both addiction and codependent behavior. Rather than only confessing one's own sins and following the biblical process of change, these authors encourage their readers to "probe your own feelings and memories" and "seek professional counsel" because there are "deep wounds" that must be "exposed and healed" (through psychological techniques). They say, "The first and continuing step is introspection."[25] They are among those who recommend regressive therapy, which was discussed earlier.

The idea is that one must probe the past, confess the sins of others, feel the pain, and express the anger from the past before one can be "healed" from codependency and other addictions. The reason given for today's sin is what happened to the person in the past. In contrast, the Bible reveals two reasons for sin: the nature of man (sinful) and temptation. "But every man is tempted, when he is drawn away of his own lust, and enticed" (James 1:14).

Along with psychologizing "defects of character" comes the notion that these are simply expressions of unmet needs. In *Serenity: A Companion for Twelve Step Recovery*, the Christian authors say:

> As a rule, most defects of character involve some imbalance in the expression of and the experience of our most basic human needs.[26]

Again, these defects of character are rooted in not having "our most basic human needs" met, rather than in our own sinfulness. These authors treat codependents and other "addicts" as passive victims in their discussion of Step Six. They say:

> As we work Step 6 of our recovery program, we are much like emotional cripples requiring "surgery" in order to restore us as whole, functioning individuals.[27]

"Self-protective devices" and unmet psychological "needs" are at the heart of many popular psychological theories. They begin with Sigmund Freud's ego defense mechanisms and continue with Alfred Adler's inferiority/superiority theories and Abraham Maslow's hierarchy of needs. These theories supply explanations for behavior that both contradict and compete with biblical doctrines of man. While folks would like to find a lot of reasons for sinful behavior, responses, and habits, the fundamental reason is the sinful nature yielding to temptation.

The popular codependency/recovery movement places the reason for a whole host of behaviors on other people and on relationships. Since behaviors which would be identified as sin in the Bible are relabeled "codependent behavior," the answer given by the codependency/recovery gurus is to change yourself by taking care of yourself and putting your own needs first. Self is to reign supreme through recovery. Only those aspects of self that don't feel right are to be "let go of." Not only does self reign; self deserves the very best. Beattie boldly declares: "We become ready to let go of all of our 'don't deserves': don't deserve love, happiness, success."[28] The notion that people deserve love, happiness, and success comes from believing that all people are good underneath it all.

In contrast to the self-love, I-deserve mind-set, the Bible presents humanity as sinful and therefore at the mercy of the goodness of God. All that is good comes from Him and in mercy He gives good to the just and the unjust. The crucial difference is between the humanistic psychological self-love talk about deserving and the biblical revelation of the goodness of God and His grace. Even Christians who have received the very life of God do not deserve anything. They have privileges and they have promises related to their birthright relationship with God. Even the word *birthright* implies grace and privilege in this context, rather than inherent deserving. While we may have the privilege to be happy, for instance, we do not have the right to be happy. God may grant the privilege to be happy, the government may establish a civil right to pursue happiness, but where is the basis for an inherent right to be happy? It is implied in the serpent's temptation and intrinsic in the fruit from the tree of the knowledge of good and evil.

Beattie advises her readers not to limit Step Six to defects, since this works on feelings, which she contends are not defects.[29] She evidently does not connect feelings with attitudes and actions. Indeed, a feeling in itself may not be wrong, but feelings are not isolated. On the other hand, Beattie does talk about certain behaviors that need to be "let go of." She says that when people are really sick of their behavior they are ready to change.[30] And when they despair of all hope of changing they can follow her example and say:

> Thank you, God, for who You are. Thank you for this program that says I don't have to do it alone. Thank you that I am right where I am supposed to be.[31]

It is interesting that Beattie thanks "God for who You are," especially because there is no biblical doctrine of God in her books. Who He has revealed Himself to be, the One and Only God of the Bible, is absent from her books. In God's place is a nebulous higher power, who is there for anyone on anyone's terms. Beattie also asserts that she is "right where I am supposed to be." How does she know that she is "right where [she is] supposed to be"? She knows, because she feels that way, not because she has any revealed Word of God to confirm it.

Beattie continues:

> Thank you for this defect. Thank you that I can't change it. Thank you that you can.[32]

First sins become defects. And now, Beattie says they come from God. Where in the Bible does it say that we are to thank God for our sinfulness, our sins, or our habitual sins? God does not even tempt us to sin (James 1:13). With that kind of theology, one wonders why Beattie's books are so popular among Christians. It is a sad indictment on the discernment of professing Christians.

Step Seven: "Humbly asked Him to remove our shortcomings."[33]

Steps Six and Seven are closely connected. Six emphasizes being ready and Seven is the activity. It is entirely possible that a person could remain passively in Step Six just waiting for a magical transformation. Therefore, Step Seven invites some form of deity to do the work. The object is to get rid of "defects of character" and "shortcomings." Once again, euphemisms are used to discount sin and therefore eliminate the need for the saving work of Jesus Christ Alone.

Humility, the opposite of pride, is presented as the necessary attitude for Step Seven. In his essay about this step Bill Wilson says:

> Indeed, the attainment of greater humility is the foundation principle of each of A.A.'s Twelve Steps. For without some degree of humility, no alcoholic can stay sober.[34]

He connects lack of humility to the very process of alcoholism saying that "our crippling handicap had been our lack of humility."[35] And what is that lack? It is pride! Indeed, rather than having a "disease" that drove them to drink, Wilson here identifies lack of humility and lust for pleasing self to be the problem. He says:

> For thousands of years we have been demanding more than our share of security, prestige, and romance. When we seemed to be succeeding, we drank to dream still greater dreams. When we were frustrated, even in part, we drank for oblivion. **Never was there enough of what we thought we wanted.**[36] (Emphasis added.)

Wilson is right in this analysis. Pride and lust are the roots of life-dominating sins!

But how does he propose to move from pride and self-sufficiency to humility and reliance on God? He says:

> It was only by repeated humiliations that we were forced to learn something about humility. It was only at the end of a long road, marked by successive defeats and humiliations, and the final crushing of our self-sufficiency, that we began to feel humility as something more than a condition of groveling despair.[37]

He then declares that the "humble admission of powerlessness over alcohol" is the "first step toward liberation from its paralyzing grip."[38] Thus, through great humiliation and failure a person comes to admit his powerlessness over "disease." While this may bring a degree of humility, it does not get to the core problem: total depravity, the sinful condition of the self. Neither does it root out pride. Nor does it reveal that this life-dominating sin has been against God Himself.

Christianity does not demand humiliation to develop humility. But it does require a person to recognize his own sinfulness. True humility does not come about through humiliation, but through hearing and responding to the Word of God. When a person then compares his own life with the requirements of a holy God, he discovers that he has fallen so short of the goal there is no way he could ever reach it on his own. He discovers that he is absolutely lost and without hope apart from the mercy of God. Then, and only then, is he truly ready to hear the Gospel: that Jesus Christ died in his place to pay the debt of every sin he ever committed. The person's own recognition of total depravity and his huge debt of sin puts him in a place of humility. Then the glorious offer of God's grace through Jesus Christ is so wonderful that even deeper humility with gratitude is the response.

Christian humility comes from remembering that we cannot and we did not save ourselves. Paul explains the process this way:

> And you hath he quickened, who were dead in

> trespasses and sins. . . . God, who is rich in mercy, for his great love wherewith he loved us, even when we were dead in sins, hath quickened us together with Christ. . . . For by grace are ye saved through faith; and that not of yourselves: it is the gift of God: Not of works, lest any man should boast. For we are his workmanship, created in Christ Jesus unto good works, which God hath before ordained that we should walk in them. (Ephesians 2:1, 5, 9-10.)

There is no room for boasting in the Christian life, except for boasting in Christ. Nevertheless pride remains strong in the flesh. That is why Christians are called to walk by the indwelling power of the Spirit.

Christian humility also comes from looking at Jesus and thereby becoming like Him:

> But we all, with open face beholding as in a glass the glory of the Lord, are changed into the same image from glory to glory, even as by the Spirit of the Lord (2 Corinthians 3:18).

It is truly the life of Jesus in a believer that brings humility. Jesus said:

> Come unto me, all ye that labour and are heavy laden, and I will give you rest. Take my yoke upon you, and learn of me; for I am meek and lowly in heart: and ye shall find rest unto your souls. For my yoke is easy, and my burden is light. (Matthew 11:28-30.)

Here is both a demonstration of humility and a call to meekness (humility).

True humility comes only from Jesus Christ. If Christians have been poor examples of humility, it is not because of the insufficiency of Christ, but rather because those Christians are walking after the flesh and have failed to put on Christ. They may even have reason to question their salvation. Was it easy believism for them? Or did they truly recognize their lostness in the light of God's law, and did they truly believe in Jesus Christ, that He died in their place the death they rightly deserved?

Codependency/Recovery Step Seven.

Whereas Wilson's essay is challenging from a moralistic perspective, codependency/recovery books stress "healing." After all, they don't believe any of those behaviors would have occurred if there had not been "wounds." Whereas Wilson saw humiliation as a means to attaining humility, authors of codependency/recovery books want to be sure that "we do not confuse *humility* with *humiliation*." Two Christian authors, Hemfelt and Fowler, are also quite concerned about equating humility with low self-esteem. Their faith in Maslow's hierarchy of needs can be seen in their declaration: "When our self-esteem has been restored to a proper state of balance, we are able to comfortably humble ourselves before Him."[39]

Because of the tremendous emphasis on the need for self-worth in humanistic psychology and throughout recovery literature, no one wants to diminish self-worth. However, is it possible that through faith in psychological theories and therapies Christians have limited pride to haughtiness and have forgotten that pride was the motivating drive in the Garden of Eden and continues today as a driving force to please self in one way or another? Humanistic psychology simply turned the motivating sin of pride into a motivating need for self-worth, thus stripping it of sinfulness and making it a seemingly natural, legitimate, and even worthy motivation. What a subtle but complete shift. Thus what God regards as the sinful motivation of pride, psychologists have changed to a natural (not sinful) motivation of the "need" for self-worth. And while pride always leads to sin, only "unhealthy" attempts to meet the "need" for self-worth are considered sin among those Christians who have bought into the need psychology of self-worth.

Besides a humility that incorporates self-esteem and self-worth, recovery books present a limited form of "shortcomings" that need to be "let go of." Melody Beattie says:

> Yes, there are some things about us—about you and me—that we need to get rid of. But we need to keep who we are, ourselves, our inherent personalities, and the traits and qualities and idiosyncrasies that make us special and unique.[40]

Obviously Beattie, who uses God-talk all the way through her books, has no conception of Romans 6 and the fact that salvation includes death to the old self and newness of life in Jesus.

> Know ye not, that so many of us as were baptized into Jesus Christ were baptized into his death? Therefore we are buried with him by baptism into death: that like as Christ was raised up from the dead by the glory of the Father, even so we also should walk in newness of life. (Romans 6:3-4.)

While one does not lose his basic personality when one is born again, all of self must go to the cross. Pride is at the root of deciding what God can and cannot change. For Beattie, the self does not die. The self enlarges. She declares emphatically that "God doesn't remove me." Thus she rejects Romans 6:6.

> Knowing this, that our old man is crucified with him, that the body of sin might be destroyed, that henceforth we should not serve sin.

For Beattie, self can remain, because self is god. At the beginning of her chapter on Step Seven she quotes from *The Tao of Pooh*:

> There are things about ourselves that we need to get rid of; there are things we need to change. . . . The first thing we need to do is recognize and trust our own Inner Nature, and not lose sight of it. For within the Ugly Duckling is the Swan, inside the Bouncy Tigger is the Rescuer who knows the Way, and in each of us is something Special, and that we need to keep.[41]

Thus for Beattie and the preponderance of recovery writers, the natural self is wise, beautiful, and special. The inner person is perfect and good. This belief contradicts Scripture and declares that Christ's death was not necessary. Such a view of the person has more to do with Hinduism than with Christianity, and with the wisdom of men (psychology) than the wisdom of God (the Bible).

Christians need to be wary of the recovery movement because it is a seductive temptation to turn to self even when it is talking about turning to God and asking "God to remove our shortcomings." Paul warned the Colossians to beware of philosophies of men, and that is exactly what this movement offers. He said:

> As ye have therefore received Christ Jesus the Lord, so walk ye in him: Rooted and built up in him, and stablished in the faith, as ye have been taught, abounding therein with thanksgiving. Beware lest any man spoil you through philosophy and vain deceit, after the tradition of men, after the rudiments of the world, and not after Christ. For in him dwelleth all the fulness of the Godhead bodily. And ye are complete in him, which is the head of all principality and power. (Colossians 2:6-10.)

Psychological theories and therapies, AA steps and traditions, and codependency/recovery programs excel in "philosophy and vain deceit, after the tradition of men, after the rudiments of the world, and not after Christ." **Christians who use and promote such systems of help are leaving the fountain of Living Water and hewing for themselves and others "broken cisterns, that can hold no water"** (Jeremiah 2:13).

10

COMMITMENT TO RECOVERY

Steps Eight and Nine go together the same way as Six and Seven. One is a decision and preparation for action and the other is the action itself. But, without the Bible as the sole standard and without Jesus as the only God and Savior, these two steps are no different from any other moralistic or religious plan for self-improvement. Any attempt to biblicize them only creates an unequal yoking. Step Ten is simply a reminder to repeat the earlier steps as a continuous program for life.

Step Eight: "Made a list of all persons we had harmed, and became willing to make amends to them all."
Step Nine: "Made direct amends to such people wherever possible, except when to do so would injure them or others."[1]

Steps Eight and Nine have some merit on a purely human level if they are taken at face value. In contrast to a number of psychological therapies and recovery books that emphasize the wrongs of others, Bill Wilson had the courage and forthrightness to emphasize "where **we** have been at fault" and to make "a vigorous attempt to repair the damage **we** have done."[2] (Emphasis added.) He even warns about the temptation to shift the focus onto the other person's faults:

> The moment we ponder a twisted or broken rela-
> tionship with another person, our emotions go on
> the defensive. To escape looking at the wrongs we
> have done another, we resentfully focus on the
> wrong he has done us. This is especially true if he
> has, in fact, behaved badly at all. Triumphantly we
> seize upon his misbehavior as the perfect excuse for
> minimizing or forgetting our own.[3]

Wilson ends his essay on Step Eight by saying:

> We shall want to hold ourselves to the course of
> admitting the things *we* have done, meanwhile for-
> giving the wrongs done us, real or fancied.[4] (Empha-
> sis his.)

Wilson remains fairly moralistic throughout his essay and
does not slip into some of the blatant errors of promoting self-
centeredness that codependency/recovery writers express.

Codependency/Recovery Reversals.

Although Co-dependents Anonymous uses the identical
AA wording for Steps Eight and Nine, codependency/recovery
programs do not follow the original intent of the Steps. That's
because these people feel more like victims than perpetrators
of harm. Melody Beattie experienced it from both positions,
having been an alcoholic and later diagnosing herself as a
codependent. From this position of "authority," Beattie says:

> When I began recovery from addictions and got to
> this Step in my recovery, my inappropriate behavior
> toward others was clear. The list of people I had
> harmed and the behaviors with which I had harmed
> them were glaring. There was no justifying, ra-
> tionalizing, or explaining them away. I had done
> wrong.
>
> When I began recovery from codependency and got
> to this same place—this place of taking responsi-
> bility for myself and my behavior in my relation-
> ships—my list was foggy, vague, and littered with
> my own sense of victimization.[5]

And no wonder! Without the standard of the Bible and without the work of the Holy Spirit, all of us can see the mote in our brother's eye and ignore the beam in our own. That is why David prayed, "Search me, O God, and know my heart: try me, and know my thoughts: And see if there be any wicked way in me, and lead me in the way everlasting" (Psalms 139:23-24).

Beattie does not mention that the Bible could be helpful in making the distinction. However, she puts forth a plan for sorting these things out. For both Steps Eight and Nine she proposes "three lists: people who have harmed you, people you have harmed, and the person you may have harmed the most—yourself."[6] Step Eight consists of going into the past and writing out the lists. Step Nine consists of what is to be done with the lists.

Confessing the Sins of Others.

On the first list goes the name of anyone and every one who has hurt, rejected, or even disappointed the so-called codependent. Beattie says: "This is an important list, and it is your chance to get it all out. Get every name on that list you can think of—everyone who owes *you* an amend."[7] (Emphasis hers.) Then comes the action, making "amends to people who have harmed us."[8] The purpose of the action is not for the benefit of the other person, but rather for the codependent, so that she can be free to take care of herself, own her own power, trust her own feelings, and meet her own needs.[9] This is done through the process of experiencing the feelings of all those past abuses, reexperiencing the pain of it all, going through the so-called five stages of grief, and finally forgiving the other person.

The five stages of grief initially came from observations nurses made as they worked with terminally ill patients and their families. Not everyone experienced all stages, but each stage was something that had been observed. Then various people got hold of the idea, wrote about it, and made it into a rather rigid system with stage one being denial; two, anger; three, feelings of guilt; four, sadness; and five, resolution. Other psychologists may reword and renumber them. For instance, in *Love Is a Choice*, the Christian authors present six stages of grief:

1.   Shock and Denial.
2.   Anger.
3.   Depression.
4.   Bargaining and Magic.
5.   Sadness.
6.   Forgiveness, Resolution, and Acceptance.[10]

For them, depression comes from "anger turned inward." They contend that anger which should have been felt and expressed gets buried.

Pat Springle plays the same message. He says:

> We feel hurt when we are condemned, manipulated, or neglected, and become angry with the one who hurt us. We repress these painful emotions, only to have them emerge in displaced anger, disproportionate anger, or depression.[11]

Therapists often emphasize and exaggerate the second stage, anger, because many of them believe that unless anger is expressed it will be repressed and result in depression or illness. Of course this reveals their Freudian psychodynamics, especially the hydraulic model of energy. As mentioned earlier, this theory has largely been discredited in the research.

Unfortunately, psychologists and other helping professionals can easily fall into the error of encouraging grief to be expressed in every one of those stages and of suspecting that if anyone misses one of the stages, he is in denial or he has not properly grieved. Two Christian psychiatrists, Paul Meier and Frank Minirth, who have simply carried over their Freudian orientation into their work with codependency/recovery, say in one of their earlier books:

> The second stage that **all** of us experience whenever we suffer a significant loss is an angry reaction toward someone other than ourselves. We even feel anger toward the person who died, even though he had no choice in the matter. This ***always*** happens when a young child loses one of his parents due to

> death or divorce.[12] (Bold emphasis added; italics
> theirs.)

Notice how they insist that "all of us experience" this stage of
grief "whenever we suffer a significant loss." In fact, those
authors go on to say, "**Every** normal human being, after suffering a significant loss or reversal, goes through **all** five
stages of grief."[13] (Emphasis added.)

These five stages were meant to describe what happens
when people mourn the death of a loved one. However, therapists and other recovery workers now apply those stages to
any loss, such as the loss of a childhood dream or the loss of a
relationship. In fact, those stages are applied to almost any
kind of disappointment. Thus, if a person says that things
weren't too bad during childhood, that is denial. The person
must enter into anger before the grief can be thoroughly dealt
with. Therefore, therapists and recovery groups empasize the
expression of anger.

On a national television broadcast, John Bradshaw encouraged women to express their anger and told them that
anger was their power.[14] He was trying to help them separate
themselves from circumstances and people in their past. This
is typical of codependency/recovery programs. If a person only
expresses sadness, that is not enough, because anger must
supposedly precede sadness. And if anger has not yet been
expressed, it is supposedly being covered up by sadness and
must be brought out.

In their book on codependency/recovery, *Love Is a Choice*,
the Christian authors accuse Christians who forgive before
expressing anger and intensely feeling the pain, of bypassing
"the painful parts of the grieving process." They say:

> Although it sounds scriptural and is certainly
> spiritually well-intended, it won't work. The pain
> has not been dealt with. . . .
>
> The grief process is built into us. . . . When we abort
> that process, we end up forgiving (and no doubt
> quite sincerely) in an atmosphere of emotional
> dishonesty.[15]

What these authors are saying, in essence, is that forgiveness is dependent on expressing anger rather than on the forgiveness of Christ. Is the cross of Christ made void?

Paul would not have agreed with such psychological nonsense. He said that we are to forgive one another "even as God for Christ's sake hath forgiven you" (Ephesians 4:32). "Even as" means "in the same way." Does God have to get His anger out before He can forgive us? Or, did Jesus pay the price for that forgiveness? Are we not to follow His example by His enabling, rather than some system invented by twentieth-century western psychiatrists? Jesus had much to say about forgiving one another. Doesn't it seem strange that He did not talk about how much we are to feel and express our anger before we can forgive anyone?

What kind of forgiveness follows reexperiencing the pain of the past through going through this contrived grief process? Is it biblical? Clearly, the forgiveness here is primarily for the benefit of the forgiving party. And it may deceitfully place the forgiver in a position of superiority over the forgiven, at least in the mind of the forgiver. At best this is human forgiveness based on emotions. Biblical forgiveness, on the other hand, is based upon Christ's death. He enables believers to forgive because He first forgave them, not because they have reexperienced the pain of the past and gone through five (or six) stages of grief.

Making Amends in Codependency/Recovery.

Next comes the list of "making amends to those we have harmed."[16] Again there is a self-serving emphasis. Beattie says, "We are on our way to freeing ourselves from guilt, taking responsibility for ourselves, removing ourselves as victims, and restoring these relationships." She emphasizes the importance of "taking care of ourselves with people in an attitude of self-respect" while making amends.[17] She says:

> . . . we are not responsible for feelings the other person may have about the incident. . . . Our part is to make a direct amend, then do whatever work we need to do on ourselves to be done with our shame and guilt.[18]

And in the course of all of this we are to "forgive ourselves" and be "gentle to ourselves."[19]

Making Amends to Me, Myself, and I.

The third list (me, myself, and I) focuses on how poorly we've treated ourselves. Beattie says: "We also need to be willing to make amends to ourselves for not treating ourselves with the respect we deserve."[20] She further moralizes: "We owe ourselves an apology and changed behavior for not allowing ourselves to receive the love and nurturing we need, especially from ourselves."[21] She says, "I needed to forgive myself and develop a better relationship with myself."[22]

The Bible teaches us about God's forgiveness and about forgiving one another. It is silent when it comes to forgiving self. And there are some fundamental principles in Scripture that would mitigate against forgiving self. While we may harm ourselves by wrong attitudes and actions when sinning against others, confession and forgiveness are between persons. Often what we may consider to be sins against ourselves are actually sins against God. For instance, when we condemn ourselves we are playing god. When we worry and fret we are not trusting Him—and that is sinning against God, not against ourselves. Therefore, those are sins against God for Him to forgive.

When we forgive ourselves we are playing God as much as when we condemn ourselves. We can go through the paces of forgiving ourselves, but we are left in our sin, because only God can cleanse us from sin. When God forgives, the sin and the condemnation are ⌐⌐ hen we forgive ourselves, we are denying the sufficie ⌐y of God's forgiveness and playing god with ourselves. Furthermore, some of the so-called wrongs we have committed against ourselves according to Beattie, such as not loving ourselves enough, are not wrong to begin with (and not even true). Therefore, forgiving ourselves for those things merely intensifies self-centered activities supported by humanistic psychology, but not encouraged by Scripture.

Steps Eight and Nine may be used for purposes of making amends to other people, but they may also be used to enhance the self. Unfortunately, most of the recovery programs of self-help use the Steps to enhance, strengthen, esteem, and love the self. Melody Beattie's dedication at the beginning of *Codependent No More* says it all: "This book is dedicated to me." In spite of some benefits to forgiving others and making amends, the original intent of Steps Eight and Nine are overshadowed by ways to serve the self.

A Biblical Alternative.

Christians do not need the help of Steps Eight or Nine or any of the others for that matter. All that is needed is in the Bible. The Bible gives wisdom and direction for behaving, confessing sins, making amends, and living in loving relationships with one another. The Bible clearly identifies what is sin and what is not sin, and it gives directions for what to do if sinned against by another person. Rather than turning to umpteen recovery books, Christians need to study their Bibles. The Word of God will do all that it says it does according to 2 Timothy 3:16-17, Hebrews 4:12-13, 2 Peter 1:1-10, and numerous other passages. Jesus Christ has given new life by which Christians can walk in agape love and righteousness, please God, and benefit those around them.

When churches adopt and adapt Twelve-Step Programs they are telling the world that the Bible is not sufficient to deal with problems of sin. They are telling the world that any old higher power will do and that it is fine to be unequally yoked to unbelievers or nonChristian belief systems. But more than that, they are revealing their ignorance of the Word of God and the power of God. Indeed they have become reduced to "having a form of godliness, but denying the power thereof" (2 Timothy 3:5).

Step Ten: "Continued to take a personal inventory and when we were wrong promptly admitted it."[23]

Step Ten is actually a reminder to repeat Steps Four through Nine. Therefore, Twelve-Step recovery programs never end. They are a way a life—a religion. In his essay on Step Ten, Bill Wilson says:

> As we work the first nine Steps, we prepare
> ourselves for the adventure of a new life. But when
> we approach Step Ten we commence to put our A.A.
> way of living into practical use, day by day, in fair
> weather or foul.[24]

He then talks about learning and growing through taking a daily inventory.

Besides the daily inventory, such as at the end of the day, Wilson speaks of on-the-spot checks in the midst of disturbing situations. He urges:

> In all these situations we need self-restraint, honest
> analysis of what is involved, a willingness to admit
> when the fault is ours, and an equal willingness to
> forgive when the fault is elsewhere.[25]

This sounds terrific. However, by what standard is this "honest analysis" to be made? What is the basis for an accurate self-appraisal?

Because the Bible is not the standard for judgment, personal inventory depends upon subjective values to determine what is right or wrong. Subjective values or morals may be pronounced by various members of recovery groups or one's therapist or "sponsor," or found in any number of recovery books. Subjectivity reigns and whatever subjective opinions seem to have the most authority will become the shaky standard.

What are some of the subjective standards of morality that "recovering codependents" use for Step Ten? Besides some of the usual common-sense morals of our culture, Beattie gives guidance from popular humanistic psychology. From her faith in need psychology, she believes that one of the most important goals of recovery is to love and nurture the self. Therefore all activities that focus on loving self, pleasing self, nurturing self, trusting self, empowering self, and feeling good about self are automatically good. Any activities that focus outward rather than inward are suspect. And because she firmly believes in the purity and innocence of "the child within" she declares, "Not nurturing and taking care of the child within is a wrong-doing."[26]

So-called experts on codependency/recovery claim that codependents lack boundaries between themselves and other people. Anne Wilson Schaef blames "the family, the school, and the church" for actively "training people not to form boundaries." She is also opposed to any biblical standard by which to evaluate behavior because she is opposed to **all** external reference points for evaluating "thinking, feeling, seeing, and knowing." She says:

> In order to have and experience boundaries, a person must start with an internal referent (knowing what one feels and thinks from the inside) and then relate with the world from that perspective.[27]

Therefore the answer for recovery is an inward focus and an emphasis on the self.

Even so-called Christian recovery books put the needs of the self at top priority. For instance, in his book *The Pleasers*, Kevin Leman advises women to work on pleasing themselves. He says that he's not suggesting that his readers "follow Robert Ringer down his self-centered path to looking out for Number One." Instead, he says, "Your primary goal in trying to please yourself is to even things up a bit." Then he suggests:

> *Make yourself the "primary Project" for the year.* That is, spend some time and money on yourself. Buy some new clothes or something else you've been wanting for a long time, like a new wall hanging for the study. Then wear those clothes and use whatever you buy.[28] (Emphasis his.)

He further advises women to "work out a schedule that gives you regular opportunities to be good to yourself."[29]

In their list of "five components of this ongoing inventory" of Step Ten, two Christian authors put "the need for love, acceptance, and security" right at the top. This is the first question they instruct "recovering codependents" to ask:

> What are our needs? These include basic needs, such as the need for love, acceptance, and security. . . .[30]

Besides faith in need psychology, these authors believe in

Freudian defense mechanisms covering up fear, hurt and anger. Therefore they encourage examining feelings:

> What are our feelings? Especially we need to allow grief feelings to surface and be expressed. We also need to watch out for deep feelings of resentment, because resentment covers anger, anger covers hurt, hurt usually covers fear, and again, the deepest fear is that our basic human needs are not going to be met. In relationships we fear being rejected or abandoned.[31]

These authors have these unbiblical psychological opinions laced throughout the *Serenity* edition of the New Testament. Nevertheless, there is nothing in the Bible that teaches that resentment comes from unmet needs.

Again, there is a mistaken assumption that psychological needs justify the desires of the self and even turn those desires of the self into motives from the purest part of our being, the inner child or the inner self. The Bible connects resentment (bitterness) with the flesh which must be put off, not a self to be nurtured. The Bible does not associate resentment with unmet legitimate needs. Furthermore, if a person's deepest fear is that of rejection or that his psychological, emotional needs will not be met, he is in clear violation of the principles of Scripture.

Beattie says she used to be afraid of Step Ten, because she thought it was "fearlessly searching out and focusing on my bad points, my defects, and what I was doing wrong." She was relieved with her "different vision of this Step." She has conveniently transformed it into "a tool that allows me to continue to be aware of myself, instead of focusing on others" and "a tool that helps me treat myself in a nurturing, accepting way."[32] Thus, Step Ten convolutes upon itself to serve self. Self is more important than any relationship in recovery programs. Codependency/recovery therapies, programs, and books appeal to the flesh and strengthen the flesh. The Bible gives one answer for the flesh: crucifixion and replacement with new life in Jesus.

11

RELIGIONS
OF RECOVERY

Steps Eleven and Twelve once again emphasize the spiritual nature of the Twelve-Step programs. Indeed these are religions of recovery with prayer, meditation, and proselytization. These religions are **not** Christianity. Nor do they truly mix with Christianity any more than Jesus would be willing to be one of many gods. Nevertheless, unsuspecting Christians may mistake such religious sounding words as being compatible with what they hear in church. And churches that should know better blissfully house Twelve-Step programs. In doing so they demonstrate more faith in AA and psychology than in Jesus Christ and the Word of God.

Step Eleven: "Sought through prayer and meditation to improve our conscious contact with God *as we understood Him,* praying only for knowledge of His will for us and the power to carry that out."[1] (Emphasis in original.)

Bill Wilson's moralizing throughout his essays on the Twelve Steps may further confuse people. Some of his talk about prayer even sounds Christian. He picked up the language of prayer with the Thee's and Thou's during his early contact with the Oxford Group, and he made prayer a daily practice. Nevertheless, it is abundantly clear that "God *as we*

217

understood Him" is not the Triune God of the Bible, who has revealed Himself and who has declared that He is the Only God and there are no others. Thus when Wilson talks about praying to God, it is not at all clear that he is referring to Almighty God. Likewise, when he talks about prayer and meditation and conscious contact with God, he does not limit himself exclusively to Christian prayer, Christian meditation, and relationship with Jesus Christ. Many people pray to other gods and practice meditation. Many believe they are contacting God when in fact they are contacting other spirits.

Wilson placed great confidence in matters of spirituality that are forbidden by Scripture. As mentioned earlier, he was involved in necromancy (contacting the dead), using the Ouija board, and channeling messages. He was not alone in his involvement with psychic phenomena. Other AA members were similarly interested and involved. In a letter written to Sam Shoemaker in 1958, Wilson wrote the following:

> Throughout A.A., we find a large amount of psychic phenomena, nearly all of it spontaneous. Alcoholic after alcoholic tells me of such experiences and asks if these denote lunacy—or do they have real meaning? These psychic experiences have run nearly the full gamut of everything we see in the books. In addition to my original mystic experience, **I've had a lot of such phenomenalism myself.**[2] (Emphasis added.)

Could his occult and mystical experiences be related to his "conscious contact" with "God *as we understood Him*"?

In the same letter, Wilson also told about his experimentation with LSD (lysergic acid diethylamide) in hopes of understanding psychic phenomena and proving an afterlife. He also thought that it might be possible to attain a mystical state through LSD. He said:

> [There is] the probability that prayer, fasting, meditation, despair, and other conditions that predispose one to classic mystical experiences do have their chemical components. [3]

In fact he did not think it really mattered if mystical states were brought on through fasting, LSD, or any other means. However, in spite of believing LSD to be "about as harmless as aspirin," he discontinued experimentation in 1959 because of his responsibility as a founder of AA.[4]

Step Eleven for Codependency/Recovery.

Again Co-dependents Anonymous takes out the gender pronouns *Him* and *His,* thus avoiding the Father and the Son. Otherwise Step Eleven is the same for codependency/recovery as for AA. Melody Beattie's discussion of Step Eleven also starts out with the usual kind of talk about prayer. An unsuspecting reader might even think she prays to the God of the Bible.

Beattie declares that Step Eleven is her "favorite Step." For her this step is equivalent to the expression "go with the flow." She says:

> I am slowly learning that not only can I go with the flow, I can trust it. I am part of it. If I am plugged into my Higher Power and God's will for me, I will know what I'm supposed to do and when I'm supposed to do it. Taking care of myself, owning my power, will be—and is—a natural part of the flow.[5]

According to Beattie, there is no need to read the Bible to discern God's will. All one has to do is "go with the flow," take care of oneself, and own one's own power. And without the help of the Bible she declares, "God's will meant learning to trust God, **and me.**"[6] (Emphasis added.)

Beattie says, "Prayer is how we talk to God. Meditating is how God talks to us." Yet, not once does she suggest that God might talk to us through His Word, the Bible. Instead, she suggests meditation books, subliminal tapes, and "alternative forms of meditation."[7] It is interesting to see the variety of meditation books that are written especially for codependency/recovery. They are the devotionals for the religion of recovery and can be found in any bookstore, including Christian bookstores.

Besides using meditation books, Beattie suggests listening to tapes and then says:

Some people like subliminal tapes. These are tapes with messages audible only to the subconscious mind. . . . The messages are subject-oriented, such as serenity, letting go of fear, accepting ourselves, and the like.[8]

It is not surprising that Beattie advocates subliminal tapes since she has bought into all kinds of other unproven psychological theories.

The theory behind the use of subliminals is that the messages which are below the audio level or visual level will be received directly by the unconscious mind, thus by-passing conscious evaluation. At the audible level, subliminal tapes contain music or sounds from nature, such as ocean waves. Below these audible sounds are verbal messages that are inaudible as far as conscious perception. According to this theory, the subconscious mind can distinguish the inaudible verbal messages from the audible sound messages, respond to them, and act upon them.

The notion of the unconscious receiving messages directly through finer perceptive mechanisms than available to the conscious mind is based upon a theory of the unconscious proposed by Sigmund Freud. As mentioned earlier, Freud taught that the driving force behind human behavior is the unconscious mind. He described the mind as being like an iceberg with most of the mass (the unconscious) below the surface. According to Freud, it is out of this internal (subterranean) unconscious abyss, of which we are unaware, that our external behavior arises. The promoters of subliminals are basically Freudian, most without even knowing it. Most are unaware that Freud's ideas about the unconscious and other matters have been discredited because they have not been supported either neurologically or scientifically. Moreover, the Freudian unconscious is contrary to the Word of God. No Scripture passage supports such an idea. The Bible is consciously and volitionally oriented.

The University of California, Berkeley, *Wellness Letter* refers to "the complete lack of any scientific evidence that such messages can alter human behavior. Nevertheless, one survey shows that 68 percent of the public believes in subliminal tapes." The article goes on to say that "double blind tests have consistently shown that these products [subliminal tapes] fail to produce their claimed effects."[9] Our file on subliminals is filled with other studies which fail to support the promises made by subliminal promoters.

Through the use of subliminal tapes and the supposed power of the Freudian-invented unconscious, individuals are told that they can stop smoking, improve their sex life, lose weight, improve sleep, overcome fears, relieve stress, and be headache-free, along with hundreds of other promises and possibilities. Unfortunately, some subliminal promoters even suggest cancer cures, as well as deliverance from other physical problems. Such promises have been referred to as "one of the biggest rip-offs going" and "another form of health fraud."[10]

Think about the claim for subliminals. The claim is that the unconscious mind can understand messages that are below the level of perception, repeated as many as 100,000 times an hour, at the same time the person is consciously hearing musical or other pleasant sounds. The conscious mind processes speech significantly below the level of the subliminal messages. Therefore it would be necessary for the unconscious mind to hear more words per hour than the conscious mind and at a level below what the conscious mind is able to perceive. If anyone is helped by such tapes, attribute it to the placebo effect and not to the tapes, since the human mind (conscious or unconscious) is neither capable of perceiving such messages nor acting upon them.

Besides being a waste of time, subliminals encourage faith in Freud and his unconscious motivation notions instead of faith in God and His Word. They encourage mindlessness rather than diligent study of God's Word. They encourage magical passivity rather than obedience. Instead of equipping the saints, they disarm them and make them vulnerable for the next gimmick—the next trick to bypass the mind and the will and to opt for the 60-second, effortless transformation. The Word of God is clear about the relationship between faith in God, diligent study of His Word, and obedience. As Paul instructs and warns Timothy:

> Study to shew thyself approved unto God, a
> workman that needeth not to be ashamed, rightly
> dividing the word of truth. But shun profane and
> vain babblings: for they will increase unto more
> ungodliness (2 Timothy 2:15-16).

Remember that Beattie defines "meditating" as "how God talks to us." Therefore she is saying that God talks to people through subliminal tapes. She also suggests "therapeutic massage as a way to relax, meditate, and become centered." Then to encourage her readers she says:

> Some people use alternative forms of meditation. "I
> was rageful at traditional religion," said Jake, "but I
> discovered that my anger at religion pushed me
> away from all forms of spiritual expression. Now I
> have found a spiritual path through some Native
> American practices, Zen meditation, and shamanis-
> tic practices. I am discovering, in the process, a
> strong sense of my spirituality."[11]

It's a wonder that so many Christians continue to buy and sell Beattie's books. Evidently no one seems to mind that she approvingly opens the door to shamanism. After all, the goal of prayer and meditation for Beattie is not to know Jesus Christ, but rather "to quiet our selves and our thoughts, relax, become centered and peaceful, and tune into God and ourselves."[12] Transcendental Meditation would probably do just fine.

Nor does anyone seem to notice that she disapprovingly closes the door to biblical doctrine in her discussion on prayer, meditation and knowing God's will. She says:

> I used to think that following God's will for my life
> meant following a rigid set of rules, instructions,
> and prohibitions . . . . Now I've learned that's
> codependency.

> Often in my life, God's will is that still small voice
> we call instinct or intuition. It is within us, **not in a
> book of rules**.[13] (Emphasis added.)

While she does not reject the Bible entirely (even the devil quoted it), she definitely says that God's will is "not in a book of rules." But, among other things, the Bible **is** a book of rules. It is the Law of God. But for Beattie, everything she needs to know from God is right inside her. She has equated His "still small voice" with human instinct and human intuition. And Christians follow this?!

Yes, Christians follow this. And Christian churches support the Twelve Steps which allow this kind of spirituality and this kind of erroneous understanding of God. Indeed, many hope that the Twelve Steps will lead right into the Kingdom of God. Hemfelt and Fowler express this faith. In their discussion on Step Eleven they say:

> As recovering persons, we may use our support groups and recovery literature as springboards toward spiritual and emotional growth. We will probably reach a level, though, at which we hunger for an even deeper contact and communication with God. This is where the organized church, the Bible, other Christian literature, and prayer and meditation become indispensable tools for lasting spiritual growth.[14]

Then these men use Bill Wilson as an example of that statement. They say that he "found great encouragement through Christian literature and the Bible" and that he "came back again and again" to Oswald Chamber's book *My Utmost for His Highest*.[15] They fail to mention that Wilson never joined a church and never testified that Jesus was the only way to the Father. They fail to note that Wilson was highly critical of all organized religion and that he declared, "The thing that still irks me about all organized religions is their claim how confoundedly right all of them are."[16] And they fail to mention Wilson's heavy involvement in the occult.[17]

Step Twelve: "Having had a spiritual awakening as the result of these steps, we tried to carry this message to alcoholics, and to practice these principles in all our affairs."[18]

Bill Wilson formulated the Twelve Steps out of his own experience and out of the experience of other drunks. For him, the "spiritual awakening" preceded any Twelve Steps.

Steps One and Two capsulize his own experience of a "spiritual awakening." Therefore it was not "the result of these steps," but rather the initial impetus. The same was true of Melodie Beattie. Her "spiritual awakening" preceded her working through the Twelve Steps.

"Spiritual Awakening."

While she was in treatment for drug abuse at Willmar State Hospital, Beattie managed to obtain a marijuana cigarette from another patient. She took it out to the grounds of the facility and sat down on the lawn. She said:

> It wasn't the drug of my choice. But it was a drug. And I was hoping it would do something to change the way I felt—keep me high and not feeling.

> I inhaled, exhaled, then stared up at the sky. In a moment, the clouds seemed to open up. **I felt the power of the universe speaking to me. I felt, for the first time in my life, the clear presence of God.**[19] (Emphasis added.)

She describes how this "Presence" permeated her so that she knew that she had "no right to continue doing to myself what I was doing." She says, "Whether I liked it or not, God was real. The heavens seemed to open up and turn purple. My consciousness was transformed."[20]

Beattie attributes that experience to be the reason why, except for one incident, she has been "chemically free ever since—by the grace of God and with the help of the Twelve Steps." She declares:

> That was my spiritual awakening. It transformed me. It transformed my life. It didn't happen as a result of working the Twelve Steps: It enabled me to work these Steps and enabled the Steps to work in my life.[21]

Beattie's "spiritual awakening" and Wilson's "spiritual awakening" have more in common with New Age mysticism than with conversion to Christianity. And Beattie's religion and Wilson's religion have more to do with New Age syncretism than with Christianity. The Twelve-Step recovery religions are quite similar to the varieties of New Age religions that say, "Whatever is truth to you is your truth and whatever is god to you is your god." In fact, the essence of the varieties of Twelve-Step recovery religions is the very essence of a one world religion that would embrace all faiths (including humanism and atheism) as long as no one criticizes anyone else's faith. The aim of the Oxford Group that inadvertently spawned AA was world conversion.[22] Perhaps that aim will be fulfilled by the vast Twelve Step recovery movement, now that it has embraced almost everyone through the expansion of the definitions of *addiction, codependency,* and *spirituality.*

The Twelve-Step religions of recovery may transform present circumstances by rearranging the works of the flesh, but that transformation is vastly different from being delivered from "the power of darkness" and being "translated. . . into the kingdom of His dear Son," Jesus Christ (Colossians 1:13). The seeming "good news" of the religions of recovery is a far cry from the gospel of Jesus Christ, which brings eternal life—new life that begins at conversion and continues throughout eternity in the very presence of God. While many religions may appear to go in the same direction, there is only one way that leads to eternal life and that is through saving faith in the death and resurrection of Christ Jesus. Thus everyone needs to be suspicious of any "spiritual awakening" which does not conform to Scripture and any steps or doctrines that have not originated from Scripture.

The Bible warns about religious transformations that may appear good and therefore deceive many:

> For Satan himself is transformed into an angel of light. Therefore it is no great thing if his ministers also be transformed as the ministers of righteousness; whose end shall be according to their works. (2 Corinthians 11:13-14.)

Not all spiritual transformations are of God. There are seducing spirits and doctrines of devils. Any spiritual path that is not Jesus Christ Himself ultimately leads to eternal separation from God, for Jesus explicitly said: "I am the way, the truth, and the life: no man cometh unto the Father, but by me" (John 14:6).

Carried the Message.

Very shortly after Wilson's own sobriety, he envisioned a movement that would bring recovery to other alcoholics. Since he had been helped by another alcoholic, he believed the essence of the movement would be "recovered alcoholics who would help others."[23] His biographer says of Wilson's early attempts at helping other drunks:

> And he was hardly humble about the crusade he was on; while he did realize that working with other alcoholics gave him a tremendous lift, he did not realize that he actually needed the sick alcoholic.[24]

In spite of his drive to help other alcoholics, Wilson met with frustration. His emphasis on his own mystical experience turned some people off. Therefore Dr. Silkworth, who had first convinced him that alcoholism was an illness like an allergy, told him that he needed to talk more about alcoholism being an illness. Silkworth suggested that Wilson needed to convince alcoholics that this "illness" would either drive them mad or kill them. Silkworth said, "Coming from another alcoholic, one alcoholic talking to another, maybe that will crack those tough egos deep down. . . . Only then can you begin to try out your other medicine, the ethical principles you have picked up from the Oxford Group."[25]

At the same time Wilson was trying to rebuild his career. An opportunity opened up for him in Akron, Ohio, and while there he began to feel the urge to drink again. As Wilson later recalled, "I thought, 'You need another alcoholic to talk to. You need another alcoholic as much as he needs you.' "[26] This was the beginning of his relationship with Dr. Robert Smith, who was the other drunk Wilson helped to help himself, and who later became the cofounder of Alcoholics Anonymous.

Even the zeal of helping others ends up for personal benefit in the Twelve Step Program. This is also the appeal to stay with the group and continue to bring in new members. AA teaches that if a recovering alcoholic (or any other recovering addict of anything) wants to keep on recovering, he

must be actively spreading the message. Thus, he must prose-
lytize others, and he must keep on bringing others into the
fold. He is warned that if he does not continue to attend meetings and help out in some way he is doomed to return to his
former addiction. That is one of the reasons the program has
continued to grow and expand. And that is why people who
have been involved in AA are great promoters of codepen-
dence/recovery. Their hope for sobriety depends on bringing
more people into their way of life.

And how does Beattie propose that the message be
carried to others? Again it is putting self first. She says:

> We carry the message in subtle, but powerful, ways:
> by doing our own recovery work and becoming a
> living demonstration of hope, self-love, self-nurtur-
> ing, and health. Learning to remove ourselves as
> victims, take care of ourselves, and walk our own
> path is a powerful message.[27]

Once again the whole point of carrying the message is doing
what is best for self, whether to maintain sobriety or to nurture and empower self. And this message is for everyone.

The Babel of Psychological Messages.

The Twelve-Step message is a mixed psycho-religious
message. It consists of varieties of religious experience, varieties of values and ethical principles, and varieties of psychological theories all wrapped together in a disease package.
Wilson read psychologist William James book *Varieties of
Religious Experience* to understand his own spiritual experience and then he continued to attempt to understand himself
through varieties of psychological theories.

After a speaking tour from October 1943 to January
1944, Wilson experienced deep depression. In fact, he battled
depression for the next eleven years. In 1944 he began to see
a psychiatrist. His biographer says, "Psychiatric treatment
was just one of the many routes that Bill would investigate in
an attempt to understand and heal himself of the negativity
that was making his life such an intolerable burden."[28]

In a letter to a friend, Wilson wrote:

> I had some psychiatric attention years ago. That
> helped a good deal in my understanding, but I didn't
> find it especially curative. It took down my fear of
> these conditions, but the effect was not positive
> enough to fully overcome them.[29]

In spite of not finding any real help for his depression
through psychological therapy, Wilson nevertheless picked up
psychological jargon and notions and incorporated them into
some of his writing. In his essay about Step Twelve, Wilson
identifies the problem with alcoholics as being "deep-lying
inferiorities."

Whether he realized it or not, he was promoting Alfred
Adler's theory of inferiority-superiority. Wilson says:

> We have seen that we were prodded by unreason-
> able fears or anxieties into making a life business of
> winning fame, money, and what we thought was
> leadership. So false pride became the reverse side of
> that ruinous coin marked "Fear." We simply had to
> be number one people to cover up our deep-lying
> inferiorities.[30]

Was it "false pride"? Or was it the sin of pride that God
hates? Is having to be better than others ("number one
people") over-compensation or egotistical pride? The answer
depends on whether one evaluates behavior according to a pet
psychological theory or according to the Bible. It all depends
on whether one has a psychological mind-set or a biblical
mind-set.

Now that psychological therapists with great varieties of
psychological theories are cashing in on the ever-growing
popularity of the recovery movement, the literature is strewn
with contradictory theories and techniques. However, in her
book *Co-Dependence Misunderstood-Mistreated*, Dr. Anne
Wilson Schaef declares that "traditional mental health
techniques and theories have been singularly unsuccessful in
the treatment of addictions." She continues:

> Even so, many mental health professionals continue
> to receive exorbitant fees and schedule endless
> hours with persons who are making little or no

> progress. Through this process, the mental health professional exhibits one of the major characteristics of co-dependence itself—denial.[31]

Not only are the old stand-by theories and techniques being adjusted and misapplied, but new ones are being created. Schaef says:

> But because the treatment of addictions now involves money and prestige, traditional professionals believe that it should be within their domain, and so they are generating theories and techniques consistent with a mental health perspective.[32]

Nevertheless, what we have seen is the same old theories simply applied to addictions and codependence in both the secular and Christian market. But, in addition, "Christian psychologists" are dispensing the AA religion.

And the market continues to expand. Everybody seems to have an addiction/codependence "illness," including the therapists. Even though Schaef is a therapist herself she contends that "most mental health professionals are untreated co-dependents who are actively practicing their disease in their work in a way that helps neither them nor their clients."[33] In fact she refers to herself as "a recovering therapist."[34] Therefore the message, whatever Twelve-Step mixture one comes up with, is for all.

The Message of Self.

The Co-dependents Anonymous Step Twelve reads: "Having had a spiritual awakening as the result of these steps, we tried to carry this message to other co-dependents, and to practice these principles in all our affairs."[35] And what is the message to the so-called codependents of the world? It is the message of self. Beattie says:

> It is a message of self-love, self-nurturing, paying attention to our own issues, and taking responsibility for ourselves, whether that means addressing our own behaviors or owning our power to take care of ourselves. . . .
>
> **Our message is that we are lovable and de-**

serving people, and we need to begin loving ourselves.[36] (Emphasis added.)

This is not only Beattie's theme. It is a major theme of all of the codependency/recovery literature and it comes from humanistic psychology. It is a gospel of self-love, self-acceptance, and self-nurturing that was formulated by such humanistic psychologists as Alfred Adler, Abraham Maslow, and Carl Rogers. It follows the lie that I must first love myself before I can love others. It assumes that people (and particularly codependents) do not love themselves. By now it should be clear that people do, in fact, love themselves. The answer does not come from more self-love, self-worth, or self-esteem. The answer to the problems of sinful habits, sinful "addictions" and sinful relationships is Jesus Christ and Him crucified. The answer lies in God's love, not divorced from His truth.

Truly we are living in the days spoken of by Paul:

> For the time will come when they will not endure sound doctrine, but after their own lusts, shall they heap to themselves teachers, having itching ears; And they shall turn away their ears from the truth, and shall be turned unto fables (2 Timothy 4:3-4).

Indeed, many have turned away from sound doctrine and rejected the God of the Bible. By creating gods of their own understanding, they have followed the fables of Freud (unconscious drives, denial, and repression), Adler (innate goodness, early childhood recollection, striving for self-worth, inferiority-superiority), Fromm (unconditional love), Maslow (hierarchy of needs, such as self-esteem and self-actualization), Rogers (unconditional acceptance) and other psychological theorists. They have believed in the religions of recovery whereby original sin is recast into "disease" and habitual sins are "shortcomings", "character defects," or "addictions."

The religion of recovery is truly a model of transpersonal psychology which seeks to combine the psychological with the spiritual. And, it is the most popular among other New Age religions. A follower of the religion of recovery is free to believe in any god of his own understanding, making, and choosing, as long as he does not impose the doctrines of his god on others. And, just as sobriety is the goal of AA, personal happiness is the goal of the codependents. The road to "recovery" is the "self-salvation" of the "inner child," who has suffered as a "victim" of the abusive life-style of another person, and the way is through the "self-care" of "feeling your own feelings" and "having a love affair with yourself."

Twelve-Step Communities.

Perhaps one of the strongest features of Alcoholics Anonymous, Al-Anon, Co-Dependents Anonymous, Adult Children of Alcoholics, and the myriad of other Twelve-Step groups is their atmosphere of community. In fact, a number of writers suggest that such groups meet a profound desire for acceptance and community. An article in *Alcoholism* about the founders of AA says:

> When two or three alcoholics came together as a group to help one another, the group itself became a higher power than the individual. For those who could not accept religious dogma, as such, the group served as their "higher power." They were able to stay sober by virtue of belonging to the group and believing in the power of community with other alcoholics to maintain their sobriety.[37]

Members of such a group are not isolated in their problems but are joined together in community with others with like problems.

Many segments of our population have lost a sense of community. Certain strains of habitual sin isolate individuals, but here those very sins become the basis for fellowship. In fact, the only requirement for full acceptance into the community of recovery is to say, "I am John. I'm an alcoholic" (or "recovering alcoholic"), or "I am Jane. I'm a recovering codependent" (or recovering whatever). Fellowship, unity, and community are based on common "addictions."

There are so many meetings that a person can attend a meeting nearly every day of the week. And, the more addictive "diseases" one has, the greater the opportunities for belonging. For instance, Melodie Beattie can belong to at least two communities, as a recovering alcoholic and a recovering codependent. Anne Wilson Schaef calls herself a "recovering therapist," but she now has joined the ranks of recovery from "romance addictions."[38] Even rape is a ticket to belonging to groups for "recovering sex addicts."

Not only do recovering addicts belong to a community; they feel totally accepted. There are two bases for this acceptance: 1) The others in the group are afflicted with the same "disease." They can honestly say those "essential five words": "I know how you feel." 2) They are accepting of any person or behavior (unless, of course, it is criticism of the group or anyone in the group). They attempt to express what Carl Rogers called "unconditional positive regard." As in the old Oxford Group "house parties," people can tell their sordid stories without the group responding with lifted eyebrows or criticism. They find their relief from telling their own stories and being accepted and understood and they find their strength from hearing the stories from one another. People never seemed to weary of hearing Bill Wilson's story, which became affectionately known as his "bedtime story."

The sense of community and belonging is so appealing that great numbers of people will remain in recovery for a long time just to continue to be part of the group. In fact, some observers are concerned with the groups becoming replacement addictions—that people shift their dependency to the group. Rather than being "codependent" in family relationships, a person becomes dependent on the group. Indeed, many become extremely dependent upon the group for their sobriety, for their sense of belonging, and for their continued recovery. For some, the Twelve-Step group is more important than family, friends, or church. In fact, it is the new family for Adult Children and other codependents who are "reparenting" themselves.

Members of Twelve-Step groups have expressed criticism against churches for not providing the same kind of accepting and supportive atmosphere. The error is probably on both sides. People may expect a church to accept them without reservation and without confronting their sin. And members of churches may forget that we would all stand guilty before

God if He had not provided a propitiation for our sins. There is no excuse for haughtiness or pride. However, there is a place for believers to confront one another in love and to speak the truth in love.

> Brethren, if a man be overtaken in a fault, ye which are spiritual, restore such an one in the spirit of meekness; considering thyself, lest thou also be tempted. Bear ye one another's burdens, and so fulfil the law of Christ. (Galatians 6:1-2.)

Such confrontation is motivated by love and is for the purpose of restoration.

Jesus calls us into community based upon our relationship with Him. It is not a community based upon habitual sins, but upon love for God and for each other. And it is fellowship based upon truth. John says:

> But if we walk in the light, as He is in the light, we have fellowship one with another, and the blood of Jesus Christ His Son cleanseth from all sin. (1 John 1:7.)

Notice the importance of the light and the blood of Jesus. In fact, the fellowship is so closely related to Jesus that it is referred to as the Body of Christ. When local churches lose sight of the centrality of Christ and the essence of the fellowship of believers, they will fail to be life-giving in their evangelism and life-sustaining in their discipleship. Furthermore, they may fall prey to other programs and become enveloped by Twelve-Step religions and communities.

Recovery or Revival?

Copying Twelve Step programs is not a biblical way to renew or revitalize a local congregation. Nevertheless there are churches that are actively adopting Twelve-Step programs for their entire congregations. Call them whatever you will: Twelve Steps to Wholeness; Twelve Steps to Spiritual Growth; Twelve-Step Christianity. These programs constitute just one more way the church tries to attract the world by becoming just like the world. Christians are thus further enticed into thinking like the world and becoming like the world.

One example of taking what is popular in the world and creating a Christian brand is a Twelve-Step version adapted for Christians and promoted by the Institute for Christian Living (ICL). By changing a few words, the Twelve Steps of Alcoholics Anonymous have been transformed into Twelve Steps for Christian Living. Numerous churches have been using this program for their people. *Christianity Today* reports that ICL is a "nonprofit organization" with "14 therapists on staff who provide counseling services at over 30 satellite sites in area churches."[39] It's the perfect combination for the worldly church of the 90s: psychology, Twelve-Steps and Jesus!

Churches also use Twelve-Step programs for outreach to their communities. It's a new tool of evangelism. They attempt to attract people so that they can gently slip in the idea that Jesus is their Higher Power. And, indeed, such programs are evangelistic, but to a Twelve-Step gospel focused on "examining the past" and thereby "freeing them from dysfunctional patterns of living."[40] Not only are prospective proselytes and lay people involved in recovery programs; so are church staff members. One leader says:

> The more into recovery they are from their own codependency, the less likely they will relate to people in a care-taking rather than a care-giving manner.[41]

What better way than a combination of the best of the world and the best of the Bible?

A number of projects, classes and seminars are psychologizing the church along with the Twelve-Step programs. For example, LIFE Seminars equip pastors and lay people to minister ideas of the anti-Christian Albert Ellis, repackaged to look like renewing the mind according to Romans 12:1-2. Rather than being renewed by the Lord and His Word, however, people learn how to do it themselves by examining beliefs that go back as far as the womb. The goal of the seminars is to make the church a "therapeutic growth community" with a heavy focus on psychological theories and techniques, group encounter, visualization, personality types and tests, and an emphasis on loving self.[42] Thus all can be therapized, including the codependents.

Dr. Margaret Rinck, in her book *Can Christians Love Too Much*, says:

> LIFE Seminars/Christian Information Committee, Inc. is one of the few organizations of which I am aware that **fundamentally integrates the Christian worldview with psychology** and educational resources to provide a systematic training program to church leaders for renewal in the local church.[43] (Emphasis added.)

She also says, "Renewal in the local church is a key issue for the Christian community as we attempt to address institutional issues of codependency in our midst."[44] And, of course from the perspective of her writing, psychology must play a major role in that church renewal. Psychological opinions and practices, combined with hymn singing, Bible study, and prayer, are the new wave of the future—**a perfect picture of an apostate church**. Perhaps the Oxford Group Movement is still with us, only under a different name and a different shape, to fulfill the dream of its founder, Frank Buchman, for *Remaking the World*.[45]

In his book *The Frog in the Kettle*, George Barna predicts what America's religious faith will be like in the year 2000:

> Americans, never quite satisfied with their options, and rarely pleased with old traditions and old rules, will create their own religions. They will mix and match the best of each faith to which they are exposed and emerge with a synthetic faith.[46]

We contend that this is already happening through Twelve-Step religions. Barna continues his prediction:

> In all likelihood, they will seek a blend of elements that will give them a sense of control over life, personal comfort and acceptance and a laissez-faire life-style philosophy. It is likely that from Christianity they will borrow Jesus' philosophy of love and acceptance. From Eastern religions they will borrow

ideas related to each person being his or her own
god, the center of the universe, capable of creating
and resolving issues through his or her own power
and intelligence. From Mormonism they will extract
the emphasis upon relationships and family, toward
establishing a greater sense of community.[47]

Barna notes that some New Age groups are already doing
this, but he evidently has not noticed that his description particularly fits Twelve-Step codependency/recovery psychoreli-
gions. But they don't have to borrow community from Mormonism. They already have embraced it from AA, which bor-
rowed it from the Oxford Group.

Barbara Goodin sent us the following hymn for this new
religion. It can be sung to the tune of "The Church's One
Foundation."

1. The church's one foundation
   Is co-dependency;
   Relationships are in
   As is psychotherapy.
   We do not read our Bibles
   For God is out of date;
   Our self-help books and magazines
   Will keep us feeling great.

2. We each have our addictions,
   Like infidelity;
   We use our twelve-step programs
   To help us feel so free.
   We do not follow Jesus,
   For narrow is His way;
   His rules are much too negative
   For Christians to obey.

3. Our families were dysfunctional
   There's so much help we need;
   Like years and years of counseling
   Our self-esteem to feed.
   We've heard the blood of Jesus
   Our sins will wash away;
   This doesn't feel right to us.
   The world doesn't talk this way.

4.   The church is getting better,
     More social and more fun;
     There's lots and lots of seminars
     To keep us on the run.
     The radicals are leaving
     And we think that's just swell;
     There's no more boring preaching
     On heaven and on hell.

5.   Oh, yes, it's getting better
     Our image is so nice;
     No talk now of a Savior
     Or God's Own Sacrifice.
     With warm and fuzzy feelings,
     We strive for unity;
     And Jesus, our good buddy,
     Brings peace and harmony.[48]

At the bottom of the page she wrote, "Now please revive your spirit and renew your commitment by singing the *true* words of this glorious hymn, 'The Church's One Foundation,' written by Samuel S. Wesley and Samuel J. Stone." Indeed! Let us do more than that. Let us return to the faith once delivered to the saints and to the Word of God and our Lord Jesus Christ. **Jesus has not called us to work the Twelve Steps. He calls us to live in Him and walk in the Spirit.**

NOTES

Chapter 1: And Codependency for All. . .
1. Elizabeth Taylor, "Taking Care of Herself." *Time*, 10 December 1990, p. 106.
2. David Treadway, "Codependency: Disease, Metaphor, or Fad?" *Networker*, January, February 1990, p. 40.
3. Sharon Wegscheider-Cruse, "Co-dependency: The Therapeutic Void." *Codependency: An Emerging Issue*. Hollywood, FL: Health Communications, 1984, p. 3.
4. Elizabeth Kristol, "Declarations of Codependence." *The American Spectator*, June 1990, p. 21.
5. Melinda Blau, "No Life to Live." *American Health*, May 1990, p. 58.
6. Robert Hemfelt, Frank Minirth, and Paul Meier. *Love Is a Choice*. Nashville: Thomas Nelson Publishers, 1989, p. 11.
7. Lynette Lamb, "Is Everyone Codependent?" *Utne Reader*, May/June 1990, p. 26.
8. John Bradshaw quoted by Lynette Lamb, "Is Everyone Codependent?" *Utne Reader*, May/June 1990, p. 26.
9. E. Brooks Holifield. *A History of Pastoral Care in America: From Salvation to Self-Realization*. Nashville: Abingdon Press,1983, pp. 231ff.
10. Robert Coles quoted by Wendy Kaminer, "Chances Are You're Codependent Too." *New York Times Book Review*, 11 February 1990, p. 1.
11. John MacArthur. *Our Sufficiency In Christ*. Dallas: Word Publishing, 1991, p. 67.
12. *Ibid.*, p. 30.
13. *Ibid.*, p. 60.

Chapter 2: And Her Name Is Codependence.
1. Melody Beattie. *Codependent No More*. San Francisco: Harper & Row, Publishers, 1987, p. 27.
2. *Ibid.*, p. 30.
3. Robert Subby and John Friel, "Codependency: A Paradoxical Dependency." *Codependency: An Emerging Issue*. Hollywood, FL: Health Communications, 1984, p. 31.
4. Elizabeth Kristol, "Declarations of Codependence." *The American Spectator*, June 1990, p. 21.
5. Anne Wilson Schaef. *Co-Dependence Misunderstood-Mistreated*. San Francisco: Harper & Row, Publishers, 1986, p. 29.
6. Robert Subby, "Inside the Chemically Dependent Marriage: Denial and Manipulation." *Co-Dependency, An Emerging Issue, op. cit.*, p. 26.
7. David Treadway, "Codependency: Disease, Metaphor, or Fad?" *Networker*, January/February, 1990, pp. 40-41.
8. Andrew Meacham, "Thomas Szasz: The Politics of Addiction." *Focus*, August/September, 1989, p. 20.
9. Dann Denny, "Intensive Program Breaks down Co-dependent Patterns." *Herald Times* (Bloomington/Bedford, IN), 5 November 1989, p. F-1.
10. Beattie, *op. cit.*, p. 31.
11. Robert Hemfelt, Frank Minirth, and Paul Meier. *Love Is a Choice*. Nashville: Thomas Nelson Publishers, 1989, p. 11.
12. Treadway, *op. cit.*, pp. 40-41.
13. Pat Springle. *Codependency: Emerging from the Eclipse*. Houston: Rapha Publishing, 1989, p. 3.
14. J. P. Chaplin. *Dictionary of Psychology*, New Revised Edition. New York: Dell Publishing Co., Inc., 1968. p. 105.
15. *Webster's New World Dictionary*, Second College Edition. New York: Simon and Schuster, 1984.
16. Beattie, *op. cit.*, p. 32.
17. Hemfelt, Minirth, Meier, *op. cit.*, p. 73.
18. Wendy Kaminer, "Chances Are You're Codependent Too." *New York Times Book Review*, 11 February 1990, p. 1.
19. Marianne Walters, "The Codependent Cinderella Who Loves Too Much. . . Fights Back." *The Family Networker*, July/August 1990, p. 53.
20. *Ibid.*, p. 54.
21. *Ibid.*, p. 55.
22. Schaef, *op. cit.*, p. 5.
23. "Codependency." University of California Berkeley *Wellness Letter*, October 1990, p. 7.
24. *Ibid.*
25. *Ibid.*
26. *Ibid.*
27. Beattie, *op. cit.*, p. 22.
28. *Ibid.*, p. 33.
29. Thomas Wright quoted by Beattie, *op. cit.*, p. 33.
30. Beattie, *ibid.*, p. 22.

31. Quoted by Kate Sherrod, "It's a Dangerous World for Women in America." *Santa Barbara News-Press*, 16 December 1990, p. A-17.
32. Beattie, *op. cit.*, p. 27.
33. Sharon Wegscheider-Cruse, "Co-Dependency: The Therapeutic Void." *Co-Dependency: An Emerging Issue.* Pompano Beach, FL: Health Communications, 1984, p. 1.
34. Schaef, *op. cit.*, dedication page.
35. *Ibid.*, p. 21.
36. *Ibid.*, p. 29.
37. "Codependency," *Wellness Letter, op. cit.*, p. 7.
38. Thomas Szasz. *The Myth of Psychotherapy.* Garden City: Anchor/Doubleday, 1978, pp. 182-183.
39. E. Fuller Torrey. *The Death of Psychiatry.* Radnor: Chilton Book Company, 1974, p. 40.
40. Szasz, *op. cit.*, p. 7.
41. Thomas Szasz. *The Myth of Mental Illness*, Revised Edition. Harper & Row, Publishers, 1974, p. 262.
42. Harriet Lerner quoted by Carol Tavris, "The Politics of Codependency." *Networker*, January/February, 1990, p. 43.
43. Kristol, *op. cit.*, p. 23.
44. Melinda Blau, "Adult Children Tied to the Past." *American Health*, July/August 1990, p. 61.
45. Kaminer, *op. cit.*, p. 26.
46. John H. Taylor, "Tranquilizers, Anyone?" *Forbes*, 10 December 1990, pp. 214, 216.
47. Schaef quoted by Beth Ann Krier, "Everyday Addicts." *Los Angeles Times*, 29 July 1990, p. E-1.
48. Anne Wilson Schaef, "Escape from Intimacy." Santa Barbara City College Mind/Supermind Lecture, 11 February 1991.
49. Schaef, *Co-Dependence, op. cit.*, p. 35.
50. Kristol, *op. cit.*, p. 23.
51. *Ibid.*, p. 22.
52. Richard W. Seefeldt and Mark A. Lyon quoted in "Adult Children of Drinkers Don't Fit ACOA Pattern." *Brain/Mind Bulletin*, February 1991, pp. 1-2.
53. *Ibid.*, p. 2.
54. Richard W. Seefeldt and Mark A. Lyon, "Personality Characteristics of Adult Children of Alcoholics: Fact or Fiction?" p. 19. University of Wisconsin. A version of this paper was presented at the annual convention of the American Association for Counseling and Development, Cincinnati, March 1990.
55. Friends in Recovery. *The Twelve Steps for Christians.* San Diego: Recovery Publications, 1988, p. 1.
56. *Ibid.*, p. 18.
57. Melinda Blau, "No Life to Live." *American Health*, May 1990, p. 58.
58. Melody Beattie quoted by Kristol, *op. cit.*, p. 21.
59. "Codependency," *Wellness Letter, op. cit.*, p. 7.
60. David L. Rosenhan, "On Being Sane in Insane Places." *Science*, Vol. 179, January 1973, p. 252.
61. *Ibid.*, pp. 252-253.
62. Martin and Deidre Bobgan. *Prophets of PsychoHeresy I.* Santa Barbara, CA: EastGate Publishers, 1989, Chapters 9, 16, 17.
63. Robin Norwood. *Letters from Women Who Love Too Much.* New York: Simon and Schuster Pocket Books, 1988.
64. Hemfelt, Minirth, Meier, *op. cit.*, pp. 70-71.
65. *Ibid.*, p. 71.
66. "Is There an Addictive Personality?" University of California, Berkeley, *Wellness Letter*, Vol. 6, Issue 9, June 1990, p. 1.
67. Hemfelt, Minirth, Meier, *op. cit.*, p. 70.
68. Martin and Deidre Bobgan. *PsychoHeresy: The Psychological Seduction of Christianity.* Santa Barbara, CA: EastGate Publishers, 1987, Chapter 3.
69. John Bradshaw. *Healing the Shame that Binds You.* Deerfield Beach, FL: Health Communications, Inc., 1988, p. 14.
70. *Ibid.*, p. 16.
71. *Ibid.*, p. 64.
72. *Ibid.*, pp. 127-128.
73. *Ibid.*, p. 128.
74. *Ibid.*, p. 129.
75. *Ibid.*, p. 126.
76. *Ibid.*
77. Diane Clough, "Victims or Volunteers." *Aglow*, September/October, p. 16.
78. John Bradshaw quoted in *Psychotherapy Book News*, Vol. 25, 28 March 1991, p. 57.
79. Letter to Ann Landers, "Breaking an Addiction to 'Love.' " *Santa Barbara News-Press*, 5 February 1990, p. B-5.
80. Karl Popper, "Scientific Theory and Falsifiability." *Perspectives in Philosophy.* Robert N. Beck, ed. New York: Holt, Rinehart, Winston, 1975, p. 343.
81. *Ibid.*, pp. 344-345.
82. *Ibid.*, p. 344.
83. *Ibid.*, p. 343.
84. Hemfelt, Minirth, Meier, *op. cit.*, pp. 46-48.
85. John MacArthur. *Our Sufficiency In Christ.* Dallas: Word Publishing, 1991, p. 70.

Chapter 3: Love Misunderstood and Misapplied.
1. Robin Norwood. *Women Who Love Too Much.* Los Angeles: Jeremy P. Tarcher, Inc., 1985.
2. Melody Beattie. *Codependent No More.* San Francisco: Harper & Row, Publishers, 1987, p. 109.
3. *Ibid.*, p. 6.
4. *Ibid.*, p. 38.
5. *Ibid.*, p. 115.

6. Nathaniel Brandon quoted by Beattie, *ibid.*, p. 116.
7. Beattie, *ibid.*, p. 116.
8. Robert Hemfelt, Frank Minirth, and Paul Meier. *Love Is a Choice*. Nashville: Thomas Nelson Publishers, 1989, p. 239.
9. Pat Springle. *Codependency: Emerging from the Eclipse*. Houston: Rapha Publishing, 1989, p. 11.
10. Brochure entitled "Road to Recovery." Rapha Hospital Treatment Centers, Houston, TX.
11. Springle, *op. cit.*, p. 13.
12. *Ibid.*
13. *Ibid.*, p. 87.
14. *Ibid.*
15. *Ibid.*, p. 89.
16. *Ibid.*, p. 134.
17. *Ibid.*, pp. 96-97.
18. Martin and Deidre Bobgan. *PsychoHeresy: The Psychological Seduction of Christianity*. Santa Barbara, CA: EastGate Publishers, 1987, Chapters 2 and 3.
19. Andrew M. Mecca, Neil J. Smelser, and John Vasconcellos, eds. *The Social Importance of Self-Esteem*. Berkeley: University of California Press, 1989.
20. *Ibid.*, p. 15.
21. *Ibid.*, p. 21.
22. David L. Kirk, "Lack of Self Esteem is Not the Root of All Ills." *Santa Barbara News-Press*, 15 January 1990.
23. Neil Smelser quoted in "Vindication Claimed for Self-Esteem Idea." *Santa Barbara News-Press*, 30 September 1989, p. A-18.
24. Thomas Scheff quoted in "UCSB Professor Gets $6,000 for a Chapter in State Book." *Santa Barbara News-Press*, 8 January 1988, p. B-3.
25. David Shannahoff-Khalsa. *Toward a State of Esteem*. Sacramento: California State Department of Education, 1990, p. 142.
26. John D. McCarthy and Dean R. Hoge, "The Dynamics of Self-Esteem and Delinquency." *American Journal of Sociology*, Vol. 90, No. 2, p. 407.
27. Harry H., L. Kitano, "Alcohol and Drug Use: A Sociocultural Perspective." *The Social Importance of Self-Esteem*, *op. cit.*, p. 320.
28. *Ibid.*
29. "Firm Control May Benefit Kids." *Brain/Mind Bulletin*, September 1989, p. 2.
30. William Coulson, "Maslow, too, was Misunderstood." *La Jolla Program*, Vol. XX., No. 8, April, 1988, p. 2.
31. David Myers. *The Inflated Self*. New York: The Seabury Press, 1980, pp. 20-21.
32. *Ibid.*, p. 24.
33. David G. Myers and Malcolm A. Jeeves. *Psychology Through the Eyes of Faith*. San Francisco: Harper & Row, Publishers, 1987, p. 133.
34. *Brain/Mind Bulletin*, May 1990, p. 3.
35. Erich Fromm. *Man for Himself: An Inquiry into the Psychology of Ethics*. New York: Holt, Rinehart and Winston, 1947, pp. 128-130.
36. *Ibid.*, p. 130.
37. "Firm Control May Benefit Kids," *op. cit.*, p. 2.
38. Richard Baxter. *Saints' Everlasting Rest*, abridged by Benjamin Fawcett. Welwyn, England: Evangelical Press, 1978, p. 315.
39. Charles H. Spurgeon. *Spurgeon's Expository Encyclopedia*, 1834-1892, Vol. 1. Grand Rapids, MI: Baker Book House, 1985, p. 458.
40. Matthew Henry. *Matthew Henry's Commentary in One Volume*. Grand Rapids, MI: Zondervan Publishing House, 1960, p. 1220.
41. A. W. Tozer. *The Pursuit of God*. Harrisburg, PA: Christian Publications, Inc., 1948, pp. 45-46.
42. Margaret J. Rinck. *Can Christians Love Too Much?* Grand Rapids, MI: Zondervan Publishing House, 1989, p. 16.
43. *Ibid.*, pp. 16-17.
44. *Ibid.*, p. 17.
45. Jay E. Adams. *Handbook of Church Discipline*. Grand Rapids, MI: Zondervan Publishing House, 1986.
46. John Vasconcellos, "Preface." *The Social Importance of Self-Esteem*., *op. cit.*, p. xv.
47. Carl Rogers quoted in *The Social Importance of Self-Esteem*, *op. cit.*, p. xii.
48. Vasconcellos, *op. cit.*, p. xii.

Chapter 4: Twelve-Step Programs: Sin or Sickness?

1. *Twelve Steps and Twelve Traditions*. New York: Alcoholics Anonymous World Services, Inc., 1952, 1953, 1981.
2. *Pass It On: The story of Bill Wilson and how the A.A. message reached the world*. New York: Alcoholics Anonymous World Services, Inc., 1984, p. 102.
3. *Alcoholics Anonymous*, Third Edition. New York: Alcoholics Anonymous World Services, Inc., 1976, p. 92.
4. *Beginner's Manual*. Milwaukee: Greater Milwaukee Central Office, Alcoholics Anonymous, ND, p. 31.
5. *Twelve Steps and Twelve Traditions*, *op. cit.* According to *Pass It On: The story of Bill Wilson and how the A.A. message reached the world* (*op. cit.*, p. 354), Wilson wrote *Alcoholics Anonymous* and *Twelve Steps and Twelve Traditions*, even though the books do not indicate his authorship.
6. *Twelve Steps and Twelve Traditions*, *op. cit.*, p. 23.
7. *Ibid.*
8. *Ibid.*
9. *Pass It On*, *op. cit.*, p. 304.
10. Herbert Fingarette. *Heavy Drinking: The Myth of Alcoholism as a Disease*. Berkeley: University of California Press, 1988.

11. Herbert Fingarette, "Alcoholism: The Mythical Disease," *Utne Reader*, November/December 1988, p. 64.
12. *Ibid.*
13. *Ibid.*, p. 65.
14. Stanton Peele. *Diseasing of America: Addiction Treatment Out of Control.* Lexington, MA: D. C. Heath and Company, 1989, p. 25.
15. Fingarette, "Alcoholism: The Mythical Disease," *op. cit.*, p. 68.
16. *Ibid.*
17. Peele, *op. cit.*, p. 27.
18. "Alcohol Abuse and Dependence." *Harvard Medical School Mental Health Review*, Number Two Revised, p. 10.
19. *Twelve Steps and Twelve Traditions*, *op. cit.*, p. 22.
20. Stanton Peele, "Control Yourself." *Reason*, February 1990, p. 25.
21. Herbert Fingarette, "We should Reject the Disease Concept of Alcoholism." *The Harvard Medical School Mental Health Letter*, Vol. 6, No. 8, February, 1990, p. 4.
22. Fingarette, "Alcoholism: The Mythical Disease," *op. cit.*, p. 64.
23. Peele, "Control Yourself," *op. cit.*, p. 25.
24. Anderson Spickard and Barbara Thompson. *Dying for a Drink.* Dallas: Word Publishing, 1985, p. 41.
25. Bob and Pauline Bartosch. *Alcoholism. . . Sin or Sickness?* La Habra, CA: Overcomers Outreach, 1987, p. 1.
26. *Ibid.*, pp. 1-2.
27. Fingarette, "We should Reject the Disease Concept of Alcoholism," *op. cit.*, p. 6.
28. *Ibid.*
29. Deborah Franklin, "Is There an Addictive Personality?" *In Health*, November/December 1990, p. 44.
30. "Alcohol Abuse and Dependence," *op. cit.*, p. 1.
31. *Ibid.*, pp. 1-2.
32. "Children at Risk for Alcoholism." *The Harvard Medical School Mental Health Letter*, Vol. 6, No. 2, August 1989, p. 5.
33. Peele, "Control Yourself," *op. cit.*, p. 23.
34. Margaret J. Rinck. *Can Christians Love Too Much?* Grand Rapids, MI: Zondervan Publishing House, 1989.
35. "Genetic Link to Alcoholism Refuted," *Psychiatric News*, Vol. 26, No. 2, 18 January 1991, p. 1.
36. Annabel M. Bolos *et al*, "Population and Pedigree Studies Reveal a Lack of Association Between the Dopamine D2 Receptor Gene and Alcoholism." *Journal of the American Medical Association*, Vol. 264, No. 24, December 26, 1990, p. 3156.
37. "Genetic Link to Alcoholism Refuted," *op. cit.*, p. 18.
38. Peele, *Diseasing of America*, *op. cit.*, pp. 27-28.
39. Fingarette, "Alcoholism: The Mythical Disease," *op. cit.*, p. 69.
40. Thomas Szasz. *The Myth of Psychotherapy.* Garden City: Anchor/Doubleday, 1978, p. xxiv.
41. Peele, *Diseasing of America*, *op. cit.*, pp. 26-27.
42. Robert Hemfelt, Frank Minirth, and Paul Meier. *Love Is a Choice.* Nashville: Thomas Nelson Publishers, 1989, p. 281.
43. P. Zimbardo, "Mind Control."*On Nineteen Eighty-Four.* Palo Alto: Stanford Alumni Association, 1983, p. 210.
44. Dr. Robert Maddox, "Defining the Christian Doctor."*The Journal of Biblical Ethics in Medicine*, Vol. 5, No. 1, Winter 1991, p. 15.
45. Ronald Taffel quoted by Melinda Blau, "Adult Children Tied to the Past." *American Health*, July/August 1990, p. 60.
46. Herbert Fingarette quoted by Jim and Phyllis Alsdurf, "The 'Generic Disease.' " *Christianity Today*, 9 December 1988, pp. 36-37.
47. John MacArthur. *Our Sufficiency In Christ.* Dallas: Word Publishing, 1991, p. 71.
48. *Ibid.*
49. *Ibid.*, pp. 71-72.
50. *Ibid.*, p. 72.
51. Hemfelt, Minirth, Meier, *op. cit.*, p. 28.
52. Marianne Walters, "The Codependent Cinderella Who Loves Too Much . . . Fights Back." *The Family Therapy Networker*, July/August 1990, p. 55.
53. Hemfelt, Minirth, Meier, *op. cit.*, p. 20.
54. Melody Beattie. *Codependents' Guide to the Twelve Steps.* New York: Prentice Hall Press, 1990, p. 6.
55. Robert Hemfelt and Richard Fowler. *Serenity: A Companion for Twelve Step Recovery.* Nashville: Thomas Nelson, Inc., 1990, p. 13.
56. Robin Norwood. *Letters from Women Who Love Too Much.* New York: Pocket Books, 1988, p. 111.
57. Beattie, *op. cit.*, p. 12.

Chapter 5: Twelve-Step Religions.
1. *Twelve Steps and Twelve Traditions.* New York: Alcoholics Anonymous World Services, Inc., 1952, 1953, 1981.
2. *Pass It On: The story of Bill Wilson and how the A.A. message reached the world.* New York: Alcoholics Anonymous World Services, Inc., 1984, p. 105.
3. *Ibid.*, p. 108.
4. *Ibid.*, p. 109.
5. *Ibid.*, p. 111.
6. *Ibid.*
7. *Ibid.*, p. 115.
8. *Ibid.*
9. *Ibid.*, p. 114.

10. *Ibid.*, p. 118.
11. *Ibid.*, p. 119.
12. Ernest Kurtz. *Not-God: A History of Alcoholics Anonymous.* Center City, MN: Hazelden Educational Services, 1979, p. 19.
13. *Pass It On, op. cit.*, p. 121.
14. *Ibid.*
15. *Ibid.*
16. *Ibid.*, p. 124.
17. William James. *The Varieties of Religious Experience* (1902). New York: Viking Penguin, Inc., 1982, p. xxiv.
18. *Ibid.*, p. 419.
19. *Pass It On, op. cit.*, p. 124.
20. *Ibid.*, p. 125.
21. Robert Hemfelt, Frank Minirth, and Paul Meier. *Love Is a Choice.* Nashville: Thomas Nelson Publishers, 1989, p. 12.
22. Wilson quoted in *Pass It On, op. cit.*, pp. 127-128.
23. Wm. C. Irvine. *Heresies Exposed.* New York: Loizeaux Brothers, Inc., 1921, p. 54.
24. R. Wright Hay quoted by Irvine, *ibid.*, p. 53.
25. *Ibid.*, p. 46.
26. Irvine, *ibid.*, p. 44.
27. Lewis Sperry Chafer quoted by Irvine, *ibid.*, p. 46.
28. *Pass It On, op. cit.*, p. 170.
29. Irvine, *op. cit.*, p. 47.
30. *Ibid.*, p. 48.
31. J. Gordon Melton. *The Encyclopedia of American Religions*, Vol. 2. Wilmington, NC: McGrath Publishing Company, 1978, p. 476.
32. Wilson quoted in *Pass It On, op. cit.*, pp. 127-128.
33. Irvine, *op. cit.*, p. 57.
34. *Ibid.*, p. 47.
35. *Ibid.*, pp. 58-59.
36. *Pass It On, op. cit.*, p. 128.
37. A. J. Russell, ed. *God Calling.* New York: Jove Publications, 1978.
38. Irvine, *op. cit.*, pp. 58-59.
39. J. C. Brown quoted by Irvine, *ibid.*, p. 49.
40. Rowland V. Bingham quoted by Irvine, *ibid.*, p. 50.
41. Irvine, *ibid.*, p. 54.
42. Harold T. Commons quoted by Irvine, *ibid.*, pp. 55-56.
43. Irvine, *ibid.*, p. 60.
44. "Spiritus contra Spiritum: The Bill Wilson/C.G. Jung Letters: The roots of the Society of Alcoholics Anonymous." *Parabola*, Vol. XII, No. 2, May 1987, p. 68.
45. *Ibid.*, p. 69.
46. Carl Jung. *Memories, Dreams, Reflections.* Edited by Aniela Jaffe; translated by Richard and Clara Winston. New York: Pantheon, 1963, p. 183. (See also pp. 170-199.)
47. "Spiritus contra Spiritum," *op. cit.*, p. 70.
48. *Ibid.*, p. 71.
49. *Pass It On, op. cit.*, pp. 156, 275.
50. *Ibid.*, p. 276.
51. *Ibid.*, p. 275
52. *Ibid.*, p. 278.
53. *Ibid.*, pp. 278-279.
54. *Ibid.*, p. 198.
55. *Ibid.*, p. 280.
56. *Ibid.*, p. 281.
57. *Ibid.*, p. 283.
58. *Ibid.*
59. Melody Beattie. *Codependents' Guide to the Twelve Steps.* New York: Prentice Hall Press, 1990, p. 39.
60. *Ibid.*
61. *Ibid.*, p. 40.
62. *Ibid.*
63. Wendy Kaminer, "Chances Are You . . . God." *New York Times Book Review*, 11 February 1990, p. 27.
64. Pat Springle. *Codependency: Emerging from the Eclipse.* Houston: Rapha Publishing, 1989, p. 141.
65. *Ibid.*, pp. 141-142.
66. *Ibid.*, p. 145.
67. Robert Hemfelt and Richard Fowler. *Serenity: A Companion for Twelve Step Recovery.* Nashville: Thomas Nelson, Inc., 1990, p. 151.
68. *Ibid.*, p. 139.
69. *Pass It On, op. cit.*, p. 198.
70. *Ibid.*, p. 199.
71. *Ibid.*
72. Elizabeth Kristol, "Hole in the Soul." *The American Spectator*, June 1990, p. 22.
73. Richard Rohr, "Breathing Under Water: A Spirituality of the 12 Steps." *Catholic Update*, September 1990.
74. Aldous Huxley quoted in *Pass It On, op. cit.*, p. 368.

Chapter 6: Twelve-Step Idolatry.
1. *Twelve Steps and Twelve Traditions.* New York: Alcoholics Anonymous World Services, Inc., 1952, 1953, 1981.

2. *Alcoholics Anonymous*, Third Edition. New York: Alcoholics Anonymous World Services, Inc., 1976, p. xx.
3. *Beginner's Manual*. Greater Milwaukee Central Office, Alcoholics Anonymous, ND, p. 35.
4. David Berenson, "Alcoholics Anonymous: From Surrender to Transformation." *Utne Reader*, November/December 1988, p. 70.
5. *Spiritual Milestones in Alcoholics Anonymous*. A.A. of Akron, Ohio, ND, pp. 4, 13, 14.
6. *Alcoholics Anonymous, op. cit.*, p. 59.
7. *Twelve Steps and Twelve Traditions, op. cit.*, pp. 34-35.
8. *Alcoholics Anonymous, op. cit.*, p. 93.
9. *Twelve Steps and Twelve Traditions, op. cit.*, pp. 39-40.
10. Robert Hemfelt and Richard Fowler. *Serenity: A Companion for Twelve Step Recovery*. Nashville: Thomas Nelson, Inc., 1990, p. 34.
11. *Spiritual Milestones in Alcoholics Anonymous, op. cit.*, p. 13.
12. *Ibid.*
13. *Ibid.*, pp. 13-14.
14. *Ibid.*, p. 14.
15. Robin Norwood. *Letters from Women Who Love Too Much*. New York: Pocket Books, 1988, p. 239.
16. Veronica Ray. *Design for Growth: A Twelve-Step Program for Adult Children*. San Francisco: Harper & Row, Publishers, 1989. (Quoted by Elizabeth Kristol, "Hole in the Soul." *The American Spectator*, June 1990, p. 22.)
17. Melody Beattie. *Codependent No More*. San Francisco: Harper & Row, Publishers, 1987, p. 87.
18. Elizabeth Kristol, "Hole in the Soul." *The American Spectator*, June 1990, p. 22.
19. Melody Beattie. *Codependents' Guide to the Twelve Steps*. New York: Prentice Hall Press, 1990, p. 50.
20. *Ibid.*
21. *Ibid.*, p. 51.
22. Hemfelt and Fowler, *op. cit.*, p. 35.
23. Beattie, *Codependents' Guide to the Twelve Steps, op. cit.*, p. 51.
24. *Ibid.*, p. 50.
25. Jay E. Adams. *The Biblical View of Self-Esteem, Self-Love, Self-Image*. Eugene, OR: Harvest House Publishers, 1986, p. 106.

Chapter 7: Here's Looking at Me.

1. *Twelve Steps and Twelve Traditions*. New York: Alcoholics Anonymous World Services, Inc., 1952, 1953, 1981.
2. *Ibid.*, p. 42.
3. *Ibid.*, p. 43.
4. *Ibid.*, p. 44.
5. *Ibid.*, p. 45.
6. *Ibid.*, p. 46.
7. *Ibid.*, p. 45.
8. *Ibid.*, p. 47.
9. *Ibid.*
10. *Ibid.*, p. 48.
11. *Ibid.*
12. *Ibid.*, p. 50.
13. Melody Beattie. *Codependents' Guide to the Twelve Steps*. New York: Prentice Hall Press, 1990, p. 64.
14. *Ibid.*, p. 65.
15. *Ibid.*
16. *Ibid.*, p. 63.
17. Bernie Zilbergeld. *The Shrinking of America*. Boston: Little, Brown and Company, 1983, p. 210.
18. Beattie, *op. cit.*, p. 63.
19. Melody Beattie. *Codependent No More*. San Francisco: Harper & Row, Publishers, 1987, back cover.
20. Shelley E. Taylor. *Positive Illusions: Creative Self-Deception and the Healthy Mind*. New York: Basic Books, Inc., 1989.
21. Beattie, *Codependents' Guide to the Twelve Steps, op. cit.*, p. 70.
22. Ernest R. Hilgard, Rita L. Atkinson, Richard C. Atkinson. *Introduction to Psychology*, Seventh Edition. New York: Harcourt Brace Janovich, Inc., 1953, pp. 389-390.
23. *Ibid.*, p. 390.
24. *Ibid.*, pp. 390-391.
25. *Ibid.*, p. 426.
26. Adolf Grunbaum. *Foundations of Psychoanalysis*. Berkeley: University of California Press, 1984, back cover flap.
27. David Holmes, "Investigations of Repression." *Psychological Bulletin*, No. 81, 1974, p. 649.
28. *Ibid.*, p. 650.
29. Martin and Deidre Bobgan. *Prophets of PsychoHeresy I*. Santa Barbara, CA: EastGate Publishers, 1989, Chapters 9, 16, 17.
30. Robert Hemfelt and Richard Fowler. *Serenity: A Companion for Twelve Step Recovery*. Nashville: Thomas Nelson, Inc., 1990, p. 14.
31. Lester Grinspoon and James B. Bakalar, "Alcohol Abuse and Dependence." *Harvard Medical School Mental Health Review*, No. 2, Revised, 1990, p. 5.
32. Alice Miller. *The Drama of the Gifted Child*. New York: Basic Books, Inc., 1983.
33. Melinda Blau, "Adult Children: Tied to the Past." *American Health*, July/August 1990, p. 57.
34. *Ibid.*, p. 58.
35. *Ibid.*
36. Elizabeth Kristol, "Declarations of Codependence." *The American Spectator*, June 1990, p. 22.
37. Sigmund Freud. *The Ego and the Id*. Translated by Joan Riviere; revised and edited by James

Strachey. New York: W. W. Norton and Company, Inc., 1960, p. 13.
38.   Robert Hemfelt, Frank Minirth, and Paul Meier. *Love Is a Choice*. Nashville: Thomas Nelson Publishers, 1989, p. 194.
39.   John Searle. *Minds, Brains and Science*. The 1984 Reith Lectures. London: British Broadcasting Corporation, 1984, pp. 44, 55-56.
40.   Nancy Andreasen. *The Broken Brain*. New York: Harper & Row, Publishers, 1984, p. 90.
41.   Edmund Bolles. *Remembering and Forgetting*. New York: Walker and Company, 1988, p. 139.
42.   *Ibid.*, p. xi.
43.   Carol Tavris, "The Freedom to Change." *Prime Time*, October 1980, p. 28.
44.   Bernard L. Diamond, "Inherent Problems in the Use of Pretrial Hypnosis on a Prospective Witness." *California Law Review*, March 1980, p. 314.
45.   *Ibid.*
46.   *Ibid.*, p. 348.
47.   Hemfelt, Minirth, Meier, *op. cit.*, p. 65.
48.   *Ibid.*, p. 63.
49.   *Ibid.*

Chapter 8: Judging by What Standard?
1.   *Twelve Steps and Twelve Traditions*. New York: Alcoholics Anonymous World Services, Inc., 1952, 1953, 1981.
2.   *Ibid.*, p. 56.
3.   Shelley E. Taylor and Jonathon D. Brown, "Illusion and Well-Being: A Social Psychological Perspective on Mental Health." *Psychological Bulletin*, Vol. 103, No. 2, 1988, p. 197.
4.   *Ibid.*, p. 193.
5.   Shelley E. Taylor. *Positive Illusions: Creative Self-Deception and the Healthy Mind*. New York: Basic Books, Inc., 1989.
6.   Taylor and Brown, *op. cit.*, p. 194.
7.   *Ibid.*
8.   *Ibid.*, p. 197.
9.   *Ibid.*, p. 204.
10.   Taylor, *op. cit.*, pp. 244-245.
11.   *Ibid.*, p. 245.
12.   Taylor and Brown, *op. cit.*, p. 205.
13.   Charles M. Sheldon. *In His Steps* (1896). New York: G. P. Putnam's Sons, reprint 1984.
14.   Sigmund Freud. *The Future of an Illusion*. Translated by James Strachey. New York: W. W. Norton and Company, Inc., 1961, p. 43.
15.   Leslie Phillips and Joseph Smith. *Rorschach Interpretation: Advanced Technique*. New York: Grune and Stratton, 1953, p. 149.
16.   David N. Elkins, "On Being Spiritual Without Necessarily Being Religious." *Association for Humanistic Psychology Perspective*, June 1990, p. 5.
17.   Stephen Arterburn and Jack Felton. *Toxic Faith*. Nashville: Thomas Nelson, Inc., 1991, pp. 76-77.
18.   Thomas Ice and Robert Dean, Jr. *A Holy Rebellion*. Eugene, OR: Harvest House Publishers, 1990, pp. 21-22.
19.   *Ibid.*, p. 23.
20.   Ray Stedman. *Folk Psalms of Faith*. Glendale, CA: Regal Books, 1973, p. 41.
21.   Arterburn and Felton, *op. cit.*, p. 77.
22.   Franklin D. Chu and Sharland Trotter. *The Madness Establishment*. New York: Grossman Publishers, 1974, p. 4.
23.   Arterburn and Felton, *op. cit.*, p. 77.
24.   I. S. Cooper. *The Victim Is Always the Same*. New York: Harper & Row, Publishers, 1973.
25.   Ann Brooks. *"If I Die, Will You Love Me?"* Basehor, KS: Whitestone Publishers,1987.
26.   Richard B. Stuart. *Trick or Treatment: How and When Psychotherapy Fails*. Champaign: Research Press, 1970, p. i.
27.   *Ibid.*, p. 197.
28.   Hans H. Strupp, Suzanne W. Hadley, Beverly Gomes-Schwartz. *Psychotherapy for Better or Worse*. New York: Jason Aronson, Inc. 1977, pp. 51, 83.
29.   Quoted by Nicole Brodeur, "Center Aids Christian Sex Addicts," *Orange County Register*, 13 February 1989, p. B5.
30.   Margaret J. Rinck. *Can Christians Love Too Much?* Grand Rapids, MI: Zondervan, 1989, p. 68.
31.   Ann Japenga, "Great Minds on the Mind Assemble for Conference." *Los Angeles Times*, 18 December 1985, Part V, p. 1.
32.   *Ibid.*
33.   Rinck, *op. cit.*, p. 64.
34.   *Ibid.*, p. 69.

Chapter 9: Sinful Substitutes.
1.   *Twelve Steps and Twelve Traditions*. New York: Alcoholics Anonymous World Services, Inc., 1952, 1953, 1981.
2.   *Ibid.*, p. 63.
3.   Anderson Spickard and Barbara Thompson. *Dying for a Drink*. Dallas: Word Publishing, 1985, p. 26.
4.   *Ibid.*, p. 61.
5.   "Self-Care Roundup." *Omni Longevity*, November 1988, p. 14.
6.   William Miller and Reid Hester, "The Effectiveness of Alcoholism Treatment: What Research Reveals." *Treating Addictive Behaviors: Processes of Change*. W. R. Miller and N. Heather, Eds. New York: Plenum Press, 1986, p. 135.
7.   *Ibid.*, p. 136.
8.   *Ibid.*
9.   *Ibid.*

10. Stanton Peele, "Mr. Peele Responds." *Reason*, May 1990, p. 12.
11. *Alcoholics Anonymous*, Third Edition. New York: Alcoholics Anonymous World Services, Inc., 1976, p. xx.
12. *Ibid.*, p. 58.
13. Jean Selignan et al, "Getting Straight." *Newsweek*, 4 June 1984, p. 65.
14. William R. Miller, "The Effectiveness of Alcoholism Treatment Modalities." Testimony to the U. S. Senate Committee on Governmental Affairs, 16 June 1988, pp. 13-14.
15. Herbert Fingarette, "We should Reject the Disease Concept of Alcoholism." *The Harvard Medical School Mental Health Letter*, Vol. 6, No. 8, February, 1990, p. 6.
16. Herbert Fingarettte, "Alcoholism: The Mythical Disease." *Utne Reader*, November/December 1988, pp. 67-68.
17. "Alcohol Abuse and Dependence."*The Harvard Medical School Mental Health Review*, Number Two Revised, 1990, p. 10.
18. "Treatment of Alcoholism—Part II." *The Harvard Medical School Mental Health Letter*, Vol. 4, No. 1, July 1987, p. 2.
19. *Ibid.*, p. 3.
20. "Are Untreated Addicts Different?" *The Harvard Medical School Mental Health Letter*, Vol. 3, No. 3, September 1986, p. 7.
21. Melody Beattie. *Codependents' Guide to the Twelve Steps*. New York: Prentice Hall Press, 1990, p. 101.
22. *Ibid.*
23. *Ibid.*, pp. 102-103.
24. *Ibid.*, pp. 103-104.
25. Robert Hemfelt, Frank Minirth, and Paul Meier. *Love Is a Choice*. Nashville: Thomas Nelson Publishers, 1989, p. 92.
26. Robert Hemfelt and Richard Fowler. *Serenity: A Companion for Twelve Step Recovery*. Nashville: Thomas Nelson, Inc., 1990, p. 51.
27. *Ibid.*, p. 147.
28. Beattie, *op. cit.*, pp. 103-104.
29. *Ibid.*, p. 104.
30. *Ibid.*, p. 105.
31. *Ibid.*, p. 106.
32. *Ibid.*
33. *Twelve Steps and Twelve Traditions*, *op. cit.*
34. *Ibid.*, p. 70.
35. *Ibid.*, p. 71.
36. *Ibid.*, p. 70.
37. *Ibid.*, p. 72.
38. *Ibid.*, p. 73.
39. Hemfelt and Fowler, *op. cit.*, p. 55.
40. Beattie, *op. cit.*, p. 111.
41. *Ibid.*

Chapter 10: Commitment to Recovery.
 1. *Twelve Steps and Twelve Traditions*. New York: Alcoholics Anonymous World Services, Inc., 1952, 1953, 1981.
 2. *Ibid.*, p. 77.
 3. *Ibid.*, p. 78.
 4. *Ibid.*, pp. 81-82.
 5. Melody Beattie. *Codependents' Guide to the Twelve Steps*. New York: Prentice Hall Press, 1990, p. 119.
 6. *Ibid.*, p. 137.
 7. *Ibid.*, p. 120.
 8. *Ibid.*, p. 138.
 9. *Ibid.*, pp. 138-139.
10. Robert Hemfelt, Frank Minirth, and Paul Meier. *Love Is a Choice*. Nashville: Thomas Nelson Publishers, 1989, pp. 217-232.
11. Pat Springle. *Codependency: Emerging from the Eclipse*. Houston: Rapha Publishing, 1989, p. 128.
12. Frank B. Minirth and Paul D. Meier. *Happiness Is a Choice*. Grand Rapids: Baker Book House, 1978, p. 36.
13. *Ibid.*, p. 39.
14. John Bradshaw on the Oprah Winfrey Show, February 1991.
15. Hemfelt, Minirth, and Meier, *op. cit.*, p. 232.
16. Beattie, *op. cit.*, p. 140.
17. *Ibid.*, p. 146.
18. *Ibid.*
19. *Ibid.*, p. 149.
20. *Ibid.*, p. 124.
21. *Ibid.*, p. 147.
22. *Ibid.*, p. 151.
23. *Twelve Steps and Twelve Traditions*, *op. cit.*
24. *Ibid.*, p. 88.
25. *Ibid.*, p. 91.
26. Beattie, *op. cit.*, p. 163.
27. Anne Wilson Schaef. *Co-Dependence Misunderstood-Mistreated*. San Francisco: Harper & Row, Publishers, 1986, p. 46.
28. Kevin Leman. *The Pleasers*. Old Tappan, NJ: Fleming H. Revell Company, 1987, p. 296.
29. *Ibid.*, p. 297.
30. Robert Hemfelt and Richard Fowler. *Serenity: A Companion for Twelve Step Recovery*. Nashville:

Thomas Nelson, Inc., 1990, p. 67.
31. *Ibid.*
32. Beattie, *op. cit.*, p. 158.

Chapter 11: Religions of Recovery.
1. *Twelve Steps and Twelve Traditions.* New York: Alcoholics Anonymous World Services, Inc., 1952, 1953, 1981.
2. *Pass It On: The story of Bill Wilson and how the A.A. message reached the world.* New York: Alcoholics Anonymous World Services, Inc., 1984, p. 374.
3. *Ibid.*, p. 375.
4. *Ibid.*, pp. 375-376.
5. Melody Beattie. *Codependents' Guide to the Twelve Steps.* New York: Prentice Hall Press, 1990, p. 172.
6. *Ibid.*, p. 177.
7. *Ibid.*
8. *Ibid.*, pp. 178-179.
9. University of California, Berkeley, *Wellness Letter*, January 1991, p. 1.
10. Gene Emery, "Subliminal Tapes Called a 'Rip-off' Therapy." *Chicago Sun-Times*, January 16, 1990, p. 4.
11. Beattie, *op. cit.*, p. 179.
12. *Ibid.*
13. *Ibid.*, pp. 183-184.
14. Robert Hemfelt and Richard Fowler. *Serenity: A Companion for Twelve Step Recovery.* Nashville: Thomas Nelson, Inc., 1990, p. 72.
15. *Ibid.*
16. *Pass It On, op. cit.*, p. 283.
17. *Ibid.*, pp. 275, 280, 374.
18. *Twelve Steps and Twelve Traditions, op. cit.*
19. Beattie, *op. cit.*, p. 187.
20. *Ibid.*, p. 188.
21. *Ibid.*
22. *Pass It On, op. cit.*, p. 128.
23. *Ibid.*, p. 126.
24. *Ibid.*, p. 133.
25. *Ibid.*
26. *Ibid.*, p. 136.
27. Beattie, *op. cit.*, p. 189.
28. *Pass It On, op. cit.*, p. 295.
29. *Ibid.*, p. 296.
30. *Twelve Steps and Twelve Traditions, op. cit.*, p. 123.
31. Anne Wilson Schaef. *Co-Dependence Misunderstood-Mistreated.* San Francisco: Harper & Row, Publishers, 1986, p. 7.
32. *Ibid.*, p. 10.
33. *Ibid.*, p. 4.
34. Anne Wilson Schaef, "Escape from Intimacy." Santa Barbara City College Mind/Supermind Lecture, 11 February 1991.
35. Beattie, *op. cit.*, p. 270.
36. *Ibid.*, p. 189.
37. "The Fellowship: The First Fifty Years." *Alcoholism*, February/January 1985, p. 53.
38. Schaef, "Escape from Intimacy," *op. cit.*
39. "Taking the Twelve Steps to Church." *Christianity Today*, 9 December 1988, p. 31.
40. Jim and Phyllis Alsdurf, "In Colorado Springs: A Church Reaches Out." *Christianity Today*, 9 December 1988, p. 33.
41. *Ibid.*
42. LIFE Seminars, P. O. Box 24080, Cincinnati, OH 45224.
43. Margaret Rinck. *Can Christians Love Too Much?* Grand Rapids, MI: Zondervan, 1989, p. 199.
44. *Ibid.*
45. Frank Buchman. *Remaking the World.* London: Blandford Press, 1961.
46. George Barna. *The Frog in the Kettle.* Ventura, CA: Regal Books, 1990, p. 141.
47. *Ibid.*
48. Barbara Goodin, "Challenge to a Dying Church." Used by permission.

For Further Reading

Four Temperaments, Astrology & Personality Testing, by Martin and Deidre Bobgan, reveals the link between the four temperaments, which are being embraced by numerous Christians, and astrology. The Bobgans evaluate present teachings promoted by popular Christians and explore reasons why people might believe and follow this unbiblical and unscientific theory of individual differences. They also describe various other systems of categorizing people according to personality traits. In addition, they provide a short course on what standards must be met for a personality test to be considered valid, and they demonstrate that such tests as the Myers-Briggs Type Indicator, the Taylor-Johnson Temperament Analysis, and the Personal Profile System do not meet that criteria. The Bobgans encourage Christians to leave the speculations of the world and return to the Word of God for wisdom and understanding.

The Grand Demonstration: A Biblical Study of the So-Called Problem of Evil by Dr. Jay E. Adams explores the seeming paradox between a good God and the existence of evil. Adams does not hesitate to look at the horror of evil. Nor does he lose confidence in the goodness of God as he penetrates deeply into the scriptural teaching about the nature of God and the existence of evil. If you have ever wondered how a good God could allow such evils as sin, rape, disease, war, pain and death, you will find a definitive, well-reasoned, biblically-based answer in this book.

Lord of the Dance: The Beauty of the Disciplined Life by Deidre Bobgan is an inspirational book for women who desire a deeper, more intimate walk with their Lord. The beauty, intensity, grace and discipline of classical ballet form a backdrop for exploring the greater beauty and glory of a disciplined walk with the Lord. Deidre draws parallels between the training of a ballet dancer and living the Christian life. Descriptions of the daily instruction, deep devotion, personal discipline, and performance of the ballerina, in response to her teacher and choreographer, bring fresh insights into the relationship between a woman and her Lord.

For Further Reading

PsychoHeresy: The Psychological Seduction of Christianity exposes the fallacies and failures of psychological counseling theories and therapies for one purpose: to call the church back to curing souls by means of the Word of God and the work of the Holy Spirit rather than by man-made means and opinions. Besides revealing the anti-Christian biases, internal contradictions, and documented failures of secular psychotherapy, *PsychoHeresy* examines various amalgamations of secular psychologies with Christianity and explodes firmly entrenched myths that undergird those unholy unions. *PsychoHeresy* includes critiques of Dr. Richard Dobbins, Dr. James Dobson, Dr. H. Newton Malony, Dr. Cecil Osborne, Dr. M. Scott Peck, Dr. Charles Solomon, Dr. Paul Tournier, and H. Norman Wright. (EastGate Publishers, 1987.)

Prophets of PsychoHeresy I is a sequel to *PsychoHeresy* in that it is a more detailed critique of the writings of four individuals who attempt to integrate psychological counseling theories and therapies with the Bible: Dr. Gary Collins, Dr. Lawrence Crabb, Jr., Dr. Paul Meier, and Dr. Frank Minirth. The book deals with issues, **not** personalities. For some readers, this book will be a confirmation of their suspicions. For others it will be an encouragement to be steadfast in the faith. For still others it will be a difficult challenge. Yet others will simply take a stronger stand for integration and all it implies. (EastGate Publishers, 1989.)

Prophets of PsychoHeresy II is a critique of Dr. James C. Dobson's teachings on psychology and self-esteem. In addition, several chapters are devoted to a discussion on self-esteem, from the perspective of the Bible, research, and historical development. The book evaluates teachings rather than personalities. The purpose of the book is to alert readers to the inherent spiritual dangers of psychological theories and therapies and to uphold the sufficiency of God's provisions through Jesus Christ, the Holy Spirit, and the Word of God for all matters of life and conduct. (EastGate Publishers, 1989.)

BOOKS BY MARTIN AND DEIDRE BOBGAN

PsychoHeresy:
The Psychological Seduction of Christianity
(EastGate Publishers)

Prophets of PsychoHeresy I
Critiquing Dr. Gary Collins, Dr. Lawrence Crabb, Jr.
Dr. Paul Meier and Dr. Frank Minirth
(EastGate Publishers)

Prophets of PsychoHeresy II
Critiquing Dr. James Dobson
(EastGate Publishers)

12 Steps to Destruction
Codependency/Recovery Heresies
(EastGate Publishers)

Four Temperaments, Astrology & Personality Testing
(EastGate Publishers)

Hypnosis and the Christian
(Bethany House Publishers)

How To Counsel from Scripture
(Moody Press)

Lord of the Dance
(EastGate Publishers)

If you would like to be on a mailing list
to receive additional information
about psychoheresy, please write:

EastGate Publishers
4137 Primavera Road
Santa Barbara, CA 93110